CHEATING JUSTICE

CHEATING JUSTICE

How Bush and Cheney Attacked the Rule of Law
and Plotted to Avoid Prosecution—
and What We Can Do about It

Elizabeth Holtzman
WITH
Cynthia L. Cooper

BEACON PRESS
BOSTON

Beacon Press
25 Beacon Street
Boston, Massachusetts 02108-2892
www.beacon.org

Beacon Press books
are published under the auspices of
the Unitarian Universalist Association of Congregations.

16 15 14 13 12   8 7 6 5 4 3 2 1

This book is printed on acid-free paper that meets the uncoated paper
ANSI/NISO specifications for permanence as revised in 1992.

Text design by Wilsted & Taylor Publishing Services

Library of Congress Cataloging-in-Publication Data

Holtzman, Elizabeth.
Cheating justice : how Bush and Cheney attacked the rule of law and plotted to avoid
prosecution—and what we can do about it / Elizabeth Holtzman, Cynthia Cooper.
p. cm.
Includes bibliographical references and index.
ISBN 978-0-8070-0321-3 (hardback)
1. Terrorism—Prevention—Law and legislation—United States. 2. Administrative
responsibility—United States. 3. Misconduct in office—United States. 4. United States—
Politics and government—2001–2009. 5. War on Terror, 2001–2009. I. Cooper, Cynthia.
II. Title.
KF9430.H65 2012
973.931—dc23   2011038208

We would like to dedicate this book to those in the U.S. government who, regardless of personal risk, stood up against the Bush administration's assault on the rule of law, on peace, and on human rights.

CONTENTS

Why We Shouldn't Simply Move On

Before President George W. Bush left office, many people speculated that he would pardon himself as protection against possible future prosecution for crimes. People assumed he would do the same for Vice President Richard B. Cheney and his top cabinet officials, advisors, and aides. There was a good deal of discussion on cable TV news, blogs, opinion columns, and political talk shows: How extensive is the pardon power? Had self-pardons been tried before? When would it happen?

"In Bush Final Days, Are Pardons in the Works?" asked NPR's *All Things Considered* on November 23, 2008.[1] "Will Bush Pardon Himself?" wrote Human Rights Watch director Kenneth Roth in the *Daily Beast*.[2] "Get ready for mass pardons," headlined a pundit in the *Hill*'s blog.[3]

The president did nothing of the sort. Instead, he retired without a seeming ruffle of tension, helicoptering out of Washington, D.C., and heading to a new home in a Dallas suburb and his ranch in Crawford, Texas. When he publicly emerged, two years later, he was touting a newly published memoir, and proudly proclaiming that he had approved a form of torture, waterboarding—"Damn right," he said in his memoir, *Decision Points*.[4] The former president had no apologies for starting a war in Iraq that had taken the lives of thousands and ruined many more: he thought the world was better off for it, even though no weapons of mass destruction, his ostensible reason for the war, were found in Iraq.

The vice president didn't even wait for his term of office to end before he started burnishing his role in waterboarding, war, and warrantless surveillance. "Those who allege that we've been involved in torture, or that somehow we violated the Constitution or laws with the terrorist surveillance program simply don't know what they're talking about," he said in an ABC News interview on December 15, 2008.[5]

Neither seemed perturbed by the prospect of prosecution. Now we know why.

While in office, they had already created walls of protection to prevent the sting of the law from reaching them. Behind the scenes, President Bush and Vice President Cheney worked—tirelessly, it seems—to inoculate themselves against every manner and form of accountability for misdeeds.

They passed provisions changing the laws that they had violated, then giving the changes retroactive application. They made existing laws so convoluted and confusing that probably no prosecutor could enforce them. E-mails in their computers conveniently disappeared, and the retention systems failed. They stamped "state secrets" on legal actions that might open their misdeeds to scrutiny. They set up straw facades and fake justifications, and even slipped them in the law as pop-up defenses.

In short, in an unprecedented way in American history, they engineered and fixed the system from the inside, building buffers of protection for themselves—behind a moat, on a hill, locked and gated, seemingly above the law. This book explores how the Bush administration used its power to manipulate the system, cheat justice, and get away with crimes.

Except . . . they had a lot of ground to cover. Their transgressions were so vast that they left open some small keyholes where the law can still reach them. This book is also about how to hold them accountable for the crimes they committed.

In the years since they departed, more information has emerged about their actions—documents have been declassified, investigative reporters and authors have probed, nonprofit groups have filed Freedom of Information actions; in some areas, Congress has conducted inquiries. Former White House personnel have stepped forward; whistleblowers have revealed secrets and leaked documents; lawsuits have pried open hidden truths. Bit by bit, the record is unfolding. The president and vice president have even incriminated themselves.

This book describes the multifarious ways in which President Bush and his team violated America's criminal laws and the sophisticated countermeasures they took to avoid being held liable for these violations. Showing a breathtaking contempt for the rule of law, they disregarded laws that got in their way and, when exposed, rushed to Congress to push through a rewritten version of those laws to their specifications to get off the hook. They did this while much of the nation was still absorbing and rebounding from the attacks of 9/11.

Understanding the depth of their crimes highlights one thing—it is even more important for our democracy that we refuse to let them get away with it.

A president and vice president who have committed serious misdeeds in office must be held accountable. Fortunately, this is a situation that the framers of the Constitution anticipated. The founders were wise enough to know that presidents would be fallible and, as such, might commit a variety of crimes. The presidency, the founders knew, was not always going to be held by people who did the right thing or acted honorably; they explicitly provided for impeachment while presidents held office, and prosecution of presidents after they left office, too.

Thus far, President Bush, Vice President Cheney, and their team seem to have gotten away with their misdeeds. Their motto seems to be "Catch me if you can," and they remain unindicted, unprosecuted, and unaccountable.

Why do we need accountability at all? To ignore the misdeeds of the president and vice president is to signal to the American people that their crimes are of no importance. To give them a free pass for their illegal activities and violations is to send a message to future presidents—do what you will, break any law, don't worry. To turn our backs and look away is to say that we, the people, are oblivious, blinded, unaware of their deceits and destruction—or, worse yet, that we are nodding in agreement and giving our consent. Without strong action holding them responsible, the precedent of a runaway lawless administration will continue to haunt us. Have we celebrated 220 years of our Constitution to reach a point where, like a banana republic, our highest elected leaders can engage in crimes of illegal surveillance, lying to take the nation into war, torture, disappearance and degradation with impunity? Let's hope not. Failing to hold the most powerful among us accountable is the sign of a democracy that is losing its way.

In order for a movement for accountability to rise and for the sake of generations to follow, it's important to say that some of us were not blind, that some of us were willing to act.

It may be a difficult path to follow, but the alternative is more difficult to imagine—an America without accountability and justice.

THE BUSH-CHENEY ADMINISTRATION:
A DISASTER FOR DEMOCRACY

As someone who witnessed Watergate up close—I was on the House Judiciary Committee that voted for the articles of impeachment against President Richard Nixon in 1973—I became increasingly concerned about long-lasting ramifications of the illegal acts and injurious decisions of the Bush administration.

While President Bush and Vice President Cheney were in office, I advocated for their impeachment. For me, the model was what happened when President Nixon committed grave offenses against the Constitution and laws of the United States. In response, the country came together and refused to allow a president to take the law into his own hands. The American people were outraged by his systemic abuses of power and his lies. The House Judiciary Committee reviewed dozens of volumes of evidence about illegal behavior by President Nixon extending over several years—including the covert bombing of Cambodia, illegal wiretapping, the Watergate break-in, and the conspiracy to obstruct justice, that is, the cover-up—and came to the conclusion that impeachment was necessary. The vote reached across party lines, and the country accepted the verdict.

All these years later, I still remember that it was hard to vote for President Nixon's impeachment, even though I was no fan of his policies and particularly disagreed with his pursuit of war in Vietnam. While few were eager to find our president engaged in criminality, it strengthened the country to know that, in the end, most Americans valued the rule of law more than the fate of any one person. The process in Watergate had worked well to protect the nation from a criminal president.

The Nixon impeachment process, because it was done so fairly, has withstood the test of time, and remains a high-water mark in the nation's efforts to make sure its officials respect the law.

I also believed that more than enough evidence existed to conclude that President Bush and Vice President Cheney had violated their oaths of office and committed "high crimes and misdemeanors"—and in ways especially damaging to our democracy.[6] But unlike Nixon, President Bush and Vice President Cheney did not face impeachment proceedings, nor did any significant legal review of their actions take place.

In contrast to the situation with President Nixon, there has been no official reckoning of the actions of President Bush. A grand jury named President Nixon an unindicted co-conspirator. A House Judiciary Committee impeachment report set forth his "high crimes and misdemeanors." An official record was made of his misconduct, so that history could not mistake it and it could not be whitewashed with propaganda, memoirs, or an attempt to rewrite the facts.

Even without a Bush-Cheney impeachment, I knew that accountability could come after they left office. That was another lesson from Watergate. President Gerald Ford, who took office when Nixon resigned, recognized that a former president could be prosecuted for his crimes in office. President Ford took the extraordinary step of issuing a pardon to former president Nixon, insisting that he had "suffered enough" by having to resign in order to avoid impeachment. President Ford's pardon of Nixon to prevent a possible prosecution was roundly denounced at the time because it created a dual sense of justice. The American people did not want one set of criminal standards for a president and another for the rest of us. This may well have been the most important factor in Ford's defeat in the next election.

When I started thinking about paths to accountability for the criminal misdeeds of President Bush and Vice President Cheney, I intended to make the case for prosecution. Based on what I already knew and had researched and written about, I expected to find a range of illegality—and I did. What I hadn't expected to find were the mounting pieces of information and evidence that showed a pattern and practice by which President Bush and Vice President Cheney, after undertaking illegal actions and keeping them secret, went on to set up fake justifications for their behavior, blamed others, inserted hidden defenses in the law, and schemed to protect themselves from the consequences of their criminal conduct by every means possible. As I examined the facts more closely, I saw that they had even succeeded in changing laws in an attempt—possibly successful—to exonerate themselves.

This could happen only in a country still traumatized by the World

Trade Center and Pentagon attacks and willing to believe a president, no matter what. Taking advantage of this post-9/11 atmosphere, President Bush conducted illegal wiretapping, lied about it, and when exposed, asserted that he could flout the law. Surveillance of Americans—secret and unnoticed—can do permanent damage by chilling diversity and depth of opinion and speech. President Bush, no doubt, knew how sensitive Americans are to invasions of their privacy. Before he left office, he pushed through changes in the law that might protect him from prosecution.

President Bush secretly authorized and unleashed systemic torture and cruel and inhuman treatment in the interrogation and handling of detainees. While in the White House, he denied that he had authorized torture. "We do not torture," the president said on many occasions, even issuing a statement to the United Nations on June 26, 2004, reaffirming the commitment to the elimination of torture worldwide.[7] But he must have realized that torture and cruel and inhuman treatment could not be hidden forever. While still in office, the president secured legal opinions purporting to allow torture and pushed through provisions to undermine the War Crimes Act and render it largely useless in affixing criminally responsibility against him.

Torture and cruel and inhuman treatment violate solemn treaties, as well as our own laws. The horrid pictures of prisoner abuse at Abu Ghraib, according to various testimonies, encouraged jihad against U.S. soldiers, endangering their lives. As a former district attorney, I know that highly trained, experienced investigators can frequently obtain vital information without ever lifting a finger against the person being questioned.

As for starting a war by lies and deception, no more serious legal violations can be envisioned—thousands of lives lost, expenditures of a trillion dollars, and the violation of our treaty obligations against fighting an unprovoked war.

The devastation caused by the Bush administration is so vast that, in some ways, we have been numbed to its extent and corrosiveness. Now that they are out of office, reasserting the rule of law and holding President Bush and Vice President Cheney answerable, where possible, is a necessary task.

Active steps are needed to investigate the misconduct of the Bush-Cheney administration: a special prosecutor to investigate possible illegal actions and bring charges where appropriate; a truth commission to make sure that all of the facts and actions are established for a historical record; new legislation by Congress to patch holes in the law to prevent repetition of the same behavior; citizen action to demand that our constitutional standards be upheld.

Prosecution is by no means a minor matter. Prosecutors must analyze the evidence and the law, persuade a grand jury to return an indictment, try the case before a jury. The evidence must meet each element of the crime in the statute and overcome defenses that those charged may assert. Prosecution isn't something to be approached lightly—but it is critical to serious accountability.

The argument that conducting investigations would tear the country apart is not true, but in any case is no reason to desist from requiring accountability. America is certainly strong enough to weather a fair and professional investigation of presidential criminality. During the Watergate inquiry, the same argument that the country would somehow suffer harm turned out to be untrue.

Our nation prohibits titles of nobility precisely in order to guard against the formation of a legal hierarchy in our society. Presidents are not kings; they are ordinary human beings, subject to ordinary temptations, who must be treated like any other persons if they have broken the law. We do not have an aristocracy of former government officials with immunity.

The danger to our democracy is seen most starkly when former Bush administration officials trumpet their crimes, proudly and publicly, without any fear that they will be held to account. As with any crime that goes unprosecuted, the failure to take action against a former president who has committed crimes stands as an indictment of the society that permits the impunity. The failure to prosecute trivializes the acts constituting the crime, suggesting, in the case of President Bush, that torture, disappearance, cruel and inhuman treatment, abrogation of our treaties, violation of our laws on privacy, deception of the Congress, and subversion of the constitutional checks on war making are minor matters, easily overlooked. It means rejecting what used to be regarded as core American values, and even worse, sends a clear signal to future presidents that they may act with similar disregard for the law.

ONE

Lies That Embroiled Us in War and Occupation in Iraq

President Bush walks confidently, a slight bounce in his step, as he heads to the podium in the House of Representatives for his 2003 State of the Union address to Congress. An American flag pin prominently placed on his left lapel is set off by a blue-on-blue tie. At the podium, he picks up two manila folders and presents them to the two men on a raised dais behind him—Vice President Cheney on one side, Speaker of the House Dennis Hastert, a Republican from Illinois, on the other. They accept the folders, shake his hand.

Turning back to the audience, the president stands and smiles lightly while the members of Congress rise and clap—both sides of the aisle, applauding for fifty-four seconds before the Speaker introduces him. The president begins his address, his voice modulated with a mixture of calm and certitude. He has a written text in front of him, and he refers to it from time to time. But he is practiced, and it shows: he delivers the speech well.

Nearly one-third of the speech is devoted to Iraq, and most of what it says marches toward a future war. The president is laying out the case for why the United States should attack Iraq years after it was defeated in the first Gulf War led by his father.[1] But there is one problem: several of the "facts" that the president includes about Iraq are not true. They are not merely exaggerated claims, but complete falsehoods, propaganda designed to push the Congress to war. Several months later—but after the war has started—the White House concedes that a few false words had worked their way into what, by all appearances, was a highly rehearsed moment.

President Bush and his Oval Office insiders gave a new twist to the concepts of deceit and fraud in embroiling the nation in war and occupation in Iraq. Without a flutter, they deliberately rolled out a months-long "marketing" strategy beforehand, purposely deceiving both the public and Congress about the reasons and need to attack Iraq. What's more, along the way they seem to have plotted personal escape routes from the consequences of their deceptions.

No one likes being duped, but it takes more than a mere lie to meet the standards for criminal prosecution. A prosecutable fraud has several elements, each of which must be met. Among other things, the falsehoods must be intentional and they must be central to the misrepresentation. Falsehoods designed to deceive Congress may constitute a crime in some cases, but under federal law, these situations are narrowly defined. When the fraud is used to drive the nation into an aggressive war and seemingly limitless occupation, resulting in thousands of deaths, vast property destruction, and the expenditure of billions of taxpayer dollars, the ethical stakes are high.

The reality is that President Bush, Vice President Cheney, and key players in the Bush administration wanted to start a war in Iraq, which, they knew, also meant occupying the country and reshaping it thereafter. The facts did not support their military adventurism, so they concealed some facts and invented others in order to advance their objectives. Because public awareness of the lies could have short-circuited their endeavors, or led to impeachment or prosecution, Bush officials soon began a cover-up— no cost to democracy was too great to protect their hides.

President Bush, Vice President Cheney, their political guru Karl Rove, and others still continue the pattern of lying and concealment. Although it is now clear from all available evidence that the Bush administration engaged in a deceitful campaign to launch a war and the occupation of Iraq, and that enormous suffering and loss have resulted, accountability is nowhere in sight. In his book *Decision Points*, released in November 2010, President Bush defended the war in Iraq, even though weapons of mass destruction, his main argument for the war, did not exist.

President Bush and his advisors engaged in an extensive false information campaign to ensnare the nation into war and its aftermath. By carefully choosing what was said, by whom, and in what context, the president and White House operatives managed to slip around the laws that protect Congress from deceit. They were determined to insulate themselves from prosecution, and as a result, many of the most blatant lies delivered by the Bush officials may not be prosecutable. Despite this, the president and his team left open one possibility: prosecution of their conspiracy to defraud the Congress. Given the egregious nature of their acts and their tragic and ongoing consequences, this should be pursued—with vigor.

Staggering personal and financial costs have been incurred in the Iraq War begun by President Bush on March 19, 2003. As documented in "Faces of the Fallen" in the *Washington Post*, by early 2011, eight years after the invasion of Iraq, more than 4,400 American soldiers had been killed.[2] Hundreds of soldiers from Britain, Australia, Denmark, Spain, and other nations also died, reports iCasualties.org,[3] while tens of thousands of Iraqi civilians lost their lives and millions were displaced, according to analysis by the Brookings Institution.[4] At least 2 million U.S. service members were deployed to Iraq by May 6, 2010, and more than thirty thousand were injured, according to "The Iraq War Ledger." A 2008 study by the RAND think tank found that as many as 500,000 military personnel suffered post-traumatic stress or brain injuries.[5] War spending cost U.S. taxpayers more than $740 billion (fifteen times the initial Bush estimates), notes the Iraq War Ledger,[6] and the war in Iraq lasted longer than the Revolutionary War, the Civil War, or the U.S. engagement in World War II. Even after combat troops were finally withdrawn at the end of August 2010, more than fifty thousand U.S. military personnel were left operating in Iraq, along with tens of thousands of private military contractors; thousands of troops can be expected to stay for years to come, reported the *Christian Science Monitor* in February 2011.[7]

President Bush, Vice President Cheney, and others in the top echelons of the administration lied to the American people hundreds of times about the need, the reasons, and the evidence for engaging in a war in Iraq, according to documentation by the Center for Public Integrity, an investigative journalism organization.[8] The real reason that the United States entered into a war in and occupation of Iraq is still unknown. Speculation abounds. Was it for oil contracts? Was it to build military bases in the Middle East? Was it to avenge an attempted assassination of President Bush's father? Or to show up his father for deciding not to invade Iraq during the first Gulf War? Was it to power up the military, play down Vietnam? Was it to brand President Bush as a "war president" and win reelection?

What is known is that the war was initiated by a planned and plotted campaign of deceit that preceded it by many months, even years. The founders of our democracy understood that presidents, like kings, would be prone to seek unnecessary wars, draining the treasury dry and putting citizens' lives at risk. They created a system of checks and balances in the U.S. Constitution to restrain the executive's war-making power—or so they thought. Article I, Section 8 gives Congress the power to declare war, as well as an array of other war powers, such as the power to raise armies and navies, and the power to control military appropriations. In Article II, Section 2, the president is given power as the commander in chief of the army and navy "when called into actual Service of the United States."[9]

The founders believed that so long as a president alone could not start a war and had to seek congressional support for funding a war and calling up troops, presidential war-making ambitions might be reined in. Congress, they hoped, would be more attentive to popular concerns and would be able to check a president's unjustified war intentions. But they may not have fully anticipated the danger posed by a president who would lie and deceive Congress to maneuver around the checks and balances carefully put in place by the Constitution.

UNMASKING CRIMINAL DECEIT

False statements and fraud are central to claims against the president. Fraud in people's daily experience ranges from a Bernard Madoff–type investment scheme to a used-car dealer who rolls back the odometer. Although fraud laws vary in their details, in general, a criminal prosecution for fraud involves certain common elements, each of which must be proven. A criminal fraud, as described in a basic legal dictionary, is comprised of "an intentional misrepresentation of material existing fact made by one person to another with knowledge of its falsity and for the purpose of inducing the other person to act, and upon which that person relies with resulting injury or damage."[10]

Two federal laws, in particular, should concern President Bush and his colleagues. One may provide enough wiggle room for them to avoid prosecution. The other may offer a firm basis, even an imperative, for arrest and trial.

False Statements

The False Statements Accountability Act of 1996 (18 USC § 1001) makes it a crime to submit false information to Congress in particular situations. Under Section 1001 the statement submitted to Congress must be false, the falsehood must be "material" or central to the misrepresentation, and the person making it must act "knowingly and willfully."

There are exceptions within the law: not all statements to Congress, even if false, are prosecutable. The law applies to Congressional communications only in "administrative matters" (including "a document required by law") or to "any investigation or review, conducted pursuant to the authority of any committee, subcommittee, commission or office of the Congress." The punishment for violation of Section 1001 is imprisonment for up to five years and a fine.[11]

Recent application of the law illustrates both how it functions in contemporary cases and crucial obstacles presented by the case of President Bush and his Iraq War lies. One publicized use of the "false statements" law emerged in criminal charges against Major League Baseball players. In August 2010, former Yankees pitcher Roger Clemens was indicted for allegedly making false statements to Congress in testimony that he gave to a House Committee, in which he denied using any steroids or human growth hormones, despite contradictory testimony of a trainer.[12] "When a witness, such as Roger Clemens, lies, as I think he did, he should be held accountable," then committee chair Representative Henry Waxman of California told ESPN on August 20, 2010.[13] In the case of ballplayer Miguel Tejada, the prosecutor spoke movingly at a sentencing hearing about the need for accountability, words that should ring in the ears of President Bush. Tejada pleaded guilty in March 2009 to making a false statement to Congress about the use of banned substances. Assistant U.S. attorney Steven Durham said, "People have to know that when Congress asks questions, it's serious business. And if you don't tell the truth—and we can prove you haven't told the truth—then there will be accountability," reported the Associated Press. Durham continued, "What people are not entitled to do . . . is to provide untruthful or dishonest answers. No one has that right. Not the people who are well-known—and not the people who are unknown."[14]

But a rigorous review of Section 1001 in the more serious matter of the president's false statements to Congress about the need for war and occupation may not find the same applicability.

Conspiracy to Defraud the United States

The second law that should concern the Bush team is U.S. Code Title 18, Section 371, a provision of the federal criminal code that makes it a federal crime to *conspire* to defraud the United States government through "deceit, craft, trickery or dishonest means." In order to be prosecuted, two or more persons must conspire together and the people charged must take steps to implement the conspiracy through an overt act, as described by the *U.S. Attorneys Criminal Resource Manual*.[15] The U.S. Supreme Court interpreted the statute in 1910 as covering: "any conspiracy for the purpose of impairing, obstructing or defeating the lawful functions of any department of Government."[16] The acts of "impairing, obstructing or defeating" extend beyond cheating the government out of money,[17] and include activities intended to "frustrate the functions of an entity of the United States," that is, interfering with or obstructing legitimate government authority, according to a 2010 overview by the Congressional Research Service.[18] This law was used in Watergate-related cases to prosecute H. R. Haldeman, a top aide to President Nixon, and others, and was also central to the prosecutions of top officials in the Iran-Contra scandal in the Reagan administration.[19]

In addition to obstacles to prosecution presented by the specific requirements in both Section 1001 and Section 371, there are, as with any criminal charge, possible defenses that President Bush, Vice President Cheney, and others might raise. They apparently knew this, too. In a pattern seen in other areas, they appear to have carefully studied the law to seek ways to avoid prosecution and to set up as many barriers as possible to charges that might be brought against them. Some of their manipulations succeed; others can be pierced.

———————

The facts will show that the president and his team made numerous provably false statements about the necessity for embroiling the United States in a war in Iraq. In the face of clear deceptions, the question then becomes: How do the federal laws apply—or, as the case may be, *fail* to apply—to statements, documents, and actions of President Bush, Vice President Cheney, and other Bush administration officials?

Three specific areas merit consideration by a prosecutor, two falling under Section 1001 on false statements to Congress, and another under Section 371 on a conspiracy to defraud the government.

1. Did President Bush and others working with him commit the crime of making false statements to Congress under Section 1001 when the president, in his State of the Union Address of 2003, stated that Iraq was a threat to the United States and was amassing the materials for nuclear weapons, when the record showed that these statements were not true?

2. Did President Bush and others working with him commit the crime of making false statements to Congress under Section 1001 when the president delivered a "letter of determination" to Congress in March 2003, required by Congress before any military engagement in Iraq could be commenced, and in which he certified that specific conditions set by Congress had been met, when, in fact, they had not been met and the truth was otherwise?

3. Did President Bush and others working with him commit the crime of Conspiracy to Defraud Congress under Section 371 when they presented false statements to the Congress, as well as to the public, about the necessity for war and occupation in Iraq?

THE ROAD TO WAR

Prosecution for a fraud first requires showing the facts and how they were misrepresented. President Bush, Vice President Cheney, and their team made a raft of statements and representations about the need and objectives for launching a war in Iraq. A prosecutor will want to ask what specific false statements were made either directly to Congress or as part of a conspiracy to defraud Congress. Unlike a prosecutor, who has the power to investigate, subpoena documents, and interview witnesses, independent analyses are, of course, limited to publicly available facts. But they are plentiful. Investigative reporters, researchers, activists, congressional reports, and inquiries in other nations have brought a substantial amount of information to light.

Here is a snapshot of some of the findings of these investigators. Five general categories of material are especially relevant to fraud charges: evidence that the Bush administration had a preexisting determination to enter a war in Iraq, dating to its earliest days in office; active engagement by President Bush and his team in a "marketing" campaign that willingly falsified information about the need for war and occupation; deceptions making false links between 9/11 perpetrators and Iraq; false claims to make it seem that Iraq had weapons of mass destruction when the evidence indicated that it did not; and lies and distortions about the available intelligence reports, the work of weapons inspectors, and the efforts to exhaust peaceful solutions.

Understanding how falsehoods about Iraq may become a prosecutorial concern involves looking at the earliest days of the Bush administration.

The path to the war and occupation in Iraq began almost from the moment that President George W. Bush and his team entered the White House—two years and two months before his administration sent tanks rolling into Baghdad. "Overthrow of the regime" in Iraq was on the agenda at the first National Security Council meeting in winter 2001, nine months *before* the September 11 attacks, Treasury Secretary Paul O'Neill told author Ron Suskind in *The Price of Loyalty*.[20]

Iraq was not believed to be a threat to the United States at that time. Intelligence agencies in 1999 and 2000 felt that Iraq's nuclear, chemical, biological, and long-range missile arsenals and capability had been destroyed in the first Gulf War. No direct evidence showed any renewal of production, according to a comprehensive analysis of prewar intelligence published by the Carnegie Endowment for International Peace in 2004.[21]

What is true is that nearly a dozen top Bush officials had been part of a group that had previously called for Saddam Hussein's overthrow. In 1998, Donald Rumsfeld, who would become defense secretary in the Bush cabinet, and Paul Wolfowitz, who would become his deputy, were among those who signed a report by the neoconservative Project for the New American Century in Washington, D.C., and a letter with recommendations on Iraq to then president Bill Clinton.[22] They said, among other things, that Saddam Hussein could put the world's oil supply at risk and that new military bases were needed in the Middle East to support "global leadership" in this "energy production region."[23]

After the 9/11 attacks nine months into President Bush's term, discussion immediately arose about taking military action against Iraq, although the evidence definitely showed that the attacks were carried out by nineteen men from Osama bin Laden's al Qaeda, which was based in Afghanistan. Like bin Laden, fifteen of the terrorists were from Saudi Arabia, with others from Egypt, Lebanon, and the United Arab Emirates. None was from Iraq; none lived in Iraq—and Iraq had nothing to do with 9/11. The 9/11 Commission later confirmed that there was "no credible evidence that

Iraq and al Qaeda cooperated on attacks against the United States," said Walter Pincus and Dana Milbank in the *Washington Post* on June 17, 2004.[24]

This was also known at the time of the attacks. In fact, the al Qaeda network and its associations were already familiar to the United States. President Bush was briefed on the al Qaeda threats in his first week in office. A mere three weeks before the 9/11 attacks, President Bush had been warned in a personal briefing by the CIA of a possible imminent al Qaeda strike inside the United States, according to the 9/11 Commission Report—those warnings are described further in chapter 2.[25] Then, on the day after the attacks, Richard Clarke, a highly regarded White House expert on terrorism, spoke with President Bush personally and told him that there was no connection between Saddam and the 9/11 events, Clarke said in his 2004 book *Against All Enemies*.[26] But the president pressured him. Clarke recalled on *60 Minutes*: "The president . . . said, 'I want you to find out whether Iraq did this.' Now he never said, 'Make it up.' But the entire conversation left no doubt that George Bush wanted me to come back with a report that said Iraq did this." At the president's insistence, Clarke filed an additional report days later with the findings of top CIA and FBI experts, again concluding that Iraq was not involved in the 9/11 attacks. He explained that the religious fundamentalists of al Qaeda actively rejected Saddam Hussein for his secular attitudes. After Clarke delivered the memo, the national security advisor's office sent it back, with a note saying, "Wrong answer . . . do it again," Clarke said.[27] In other words, truthful information about Iraq was already being manipulated by the White House within days of the 9/11 attacks.

Six days after 9/11, President Bush gave secret instructions to the Pentagon to start planning options for a military invasion of Iraq, according to Glenn Kessler in the *Washington Post* on January 12, 2003. It was, the newspaper said, "an internal decision-process that has been obscured from public view."[28]

Reports to the president continued to underscore that Iraq and al Qaeda were not connected. The all-important President's Daily Brief (PDB) on September 21, 2001, ten days after 9/11, stated there was no complicity between Saddam and al Qaeda, according to crack investigative reporter Murray Waas in the *National Journal*. "President Bush was told in a highly classified briefing that the U.S. intelligence community had no evidence linking the Iraqi regime of Saddam Hussein to the attacks [of 9/11] and that there was scant credible evidence that Iraq had any significant collaborative ties with al Qaeda," wrote Waas.[29]

Yet, before Thanksgiving, the president personally told the defense secretary that he wanted to see war plans for Iraq, according to writer Bob Woodward on *Frontline*.[30] In December 2001, at a time that intelligence sources still did not believe Iraq was a threat, President Bush began meeting with army general Tommy R. Franks and his war cabinet, said Woodward. The meetings were "to plan the U.S. attack on Iraq even as he and administration spokesmen insisted they were pursuing a diplomatic solution," wrote William Hamilton in the *Washington Post* on April 17, 2004.[31] On March 12, 2002, a year before the Iraq War was initiated, National Security Advisor Condoleezza Rice told British envoy David Manning that the United States was planning a military campaign against Iraq,[32] according to British documents collected and analyzed by the National Security Archive in October 2010.[33]

The evidence continued to show that Iraq was not involved with or connected to 9/11. In June 2002, the CIA reported "no conclusive evidence of cooperation" between al Qaeda and Saddam Hussein, according to the Carnegie Endowment for International Peace. In the summer of 2002— still three-quarters of a year before the Iraq War began—the British head of military intelligence, Richard Dearlove, participated in meetings in Washington, D.C. His description of those meetings, as explained in a briefing to Prime Minister Tony Blair, became known as "The Secret Downing Street Memo" after it was leaked and published in Britain's *Sunday Times* in May 2005. The memo described the White House plans: "Military action was now seen as inevitable [in Iraq]. Bush wanted to remove Saddam, through military action, justified by the conjunction of terrorism and WMD [weapons of mass destruction]. But the intelligence and facts were being fixed around the policy."[34]

Because Iraq had not declared war or used force against the United States, the Bush administration decided to enlist support for the war by claiming that Saddam and Iraq posed a grave and imminent threat to the United States and were responsible in some way for the 9/11 attacks in New York and Washington. Beginning in the summer of 2002, messaging was coordinated by a new White House Iraq Group, or WHIG, to "roll out" the war. "The purpose of these meetings was to garner the intelligence justification for a pre-emptive war to remove Saddam Hussein in order to make a case to the Congress, the American public and the international community," wrote Melvin A. Goodman, a senior Fellow at the Center for International Policy.[35]

Right after Labor Day 2002, the White House began an intensive "marketing" campaign—that is the term used by White House chief of staff Andrew Card Jr.—to pressure the U.S. Congress and the American people to enter into a war in Iraq. "From a marketing point of view, you don't introduce new products in August," Card explained to *New York Times* writer Elisabeth Bumiller on September 7, 2002. The war launch coincided perfectly with the first anniversary of the 9/11 attacks, still a painful memory for many Americans. Bumiller wrote: "A centerpiece of the strategy, White House officials said, is to use Mr. Bush's speech on Sept. 11 to help move Americans toward support of action against Iraq." Karl Rove, the president's political advisor, also commented, saying that September 11 would be a time "to seize the moment to make clear what lies ahead." And, the *Times* noted, "On Capitol Hill, meanwhile, the administration has begun a full-scale lobbying campaign."[36]

Soon, the president, vice president, Secretary of Defense Donald Rumsfeld, National Security Advisor Condoleezza Rice, and others began speaking everywhere—saturating the airwaves with press conferences, interviews, talk-show punditry, and speeches. At this point, the major falsifications of the Bush administration take three-dimensional shape.

Their commentary was spiked by falsified references to weapons of mass destruction, nuclear materials procurement, alliances between the al Qaeda perpetrators of 9/11 and Saddam Hussein, manipulated intelligence, statements from unverified "informers," misrepresentations about the findings of UN weapons inspectors, and more. The Bush team declared that Iraq presented an advancing and immediate threat to the United States on a weekly, and sometimes daily, basis. A vast number of these claims were untrue. The White House "decided to pursue a political propaganda campaign to sell the war to the American people," former Bush press secretary Scott McClellan explained in his 2008 book, *What Happened: Inside the Bush White House and Washington's Culture of Deception.*[37]

A large number of false statements—scores of them—were made personally by President Bush, and evidence has debunked them. In speech after speech, statement after statement, the president spun falsehoods, as a selection of his comments shows. For example, on September 12, 2002, the day after the 9/11 anniversary, the president told the United Nations General Assembly: "Iraq has made several attempts to buy high-strength aluminum tubes used to enrich uranium for a nuclear weapon."[38] This was untrue. In a radio address on September 14, 2002, President Bush said, "By supporting terrorist groups, repressing his own people and pursuing weapons of mass destruction in defiance of a decade of U.N. resolutions, Saddam Hussein's regime has proven itself a grave and gathering danger."[39] This was untrue. In a photo op in Washington, D.C., with Colombian president Álvaro Uribe on September 25, 2002, President Bush said, "You can't distinguish between al Qaeda and Saddam."[40] This was untrue.

In a major address on October 7, 2002, at the Cincinnati Museum Center, the president invoked the 9/11 attacks five times, saying that failure to act against Iraq would "allow terrorists access to new weapons and new resources." At the time, pressure was mounting for Congress to vote immediately on a joint resolution that would give the go-ahead for a war in Iraq. The president told his Cincinnati audience, "Evidence indicates that Iraq is reconstituting its nuclear weapons program." He said, "America must not ignore the threat gathering against us. Facing clear evidence of peril, we cannot wait for the final proof—the smoking gun—that could come in the form of a mushroom cloud."[41] These statements were also untrue.

On February 8, 2003, in a radio address, President Bush said that Iraq has "provided Al Qaeda with chemical and biological weapons training."[42] On March 17, 2003, on the eve of war, President Bush said in a statement addressed to the nation that terrorists could obtain nuclear weapons from Iraq and "kill thousands or hundreds of thousands of innocent people in our country."[43]

President Bush was joined in this frenzy of deceptive commentary by a cohort of other administration officials, speeding from forum to forum. For example, Vice President Cheney said on August 26, 2002, in a speech to the Veterans of Foreign Wars that Iraq was "as grave a threat as can be imagined" and "a mortal threat." The vice president added, "Simply stated, there is no doubt that Saddam Hussein now has weapons of mass destruction. There is no doubt he is amassing them to use against our friends, against our allies, and against us."[44] On *Meet the Press* on September 8, 2002, Vice President Cheney said, "We know with absolute certainty that he [Saddam] is using his procurement system to acquire the equipment he needs to enrich uranium to build a nuclear weapon."[45]

National Security Advisor Condoleezza Rice insisted on *PBS News Hour* on September 25, 2002, that there was a "relationship" between al Qaeda and Iraq,[46] and on September 27, Secretary Rumsfeld told the Atlanta Chamber of Commerce that he had "bulletproof" evidence of Saddam–al Qaeda links.[47] Secretary of State Colin Powell told the UN Security Council on February 5, 2003, that a "sinister nexus" existed between Saddam and "the al Qaeda terrorist network."[48]

All of these statements were untrue.

In fact, the all-important October 2002 National Intelligence Estimate (NIE), an authoritative document consolidating the opinions of all the intelligence agencies, gave the rating of "low confidence" to the possibility that Saddam would share weapons with al Qaeda, according to the authors of "WMD in Iraq," published by the Carnegie Endowment for International Peace.[49]

The International Atomic Energy Agency (IAEA) released a report in January 2003 stating that there was no evidence of a nuclear threat. UN inspectors had entered Iraq on November 27, 2002, conducted more than six hundred inspections in the four months leading up to the war's inception,[50] and found no evidence of weapons of mass destruction of any sort.[51]

On January 29, 2003, just six weeks before the launch of the war, the CIA found an absence of evidence that Iraq had provided training to al Qaeda, according to declassified documents released by Senator Carl Levin on April 15, 2005.[52]

On January 31, 2003, President Bush as much as acknowledged to British prime minister Tony Blair that no weapons of mass destruction were in Iraq, reported a memo later leaked to international lawyer Philippe Sands, author of the book, *Lawless World*. The president suggested other ideas to Blair for inciting war, such as painting planes to look like UN aircraft in hopes that Iraq would shoot them down and create a pretext for war.[53]

On March 7, 2003—less than two weeks before the U.S. military marched into Iraq—Director-General Mohamed ElBaradei of the International Atomic Energy Agency (IAEA) repeated the assessment that there were no weapons of mass destruction in Iraq.[54] Responding, Vice President Cheney belittled the UN inspectors on NBC's *Meet the Press* on March 16, 2003, and said that the IAEA had been wrong before.[55]

These statements by Bush administration officials are a small chunk of a vast edifice of deceptions and misrepresentations. The Center for Public

Integrity, a nonprofit journalism organization, meticulously documented 935 false statements in the two years following 9/11 about the supposed security threat presented by Iraq in "Iraq: The War Card."[56]

On March 18, 2003, President Bush certified in a letter to Congress that a war in Iraq was a "necessary" action against those who "planned, authorized, committed, or aided the terrorist attacks that occurred on September 11, 2001."[57] This document was required by Congress before war could start. The day after he sent the letter, the president sent military planes and tanks roaring into Iraq.

Those who have sifted through the evidence and made findings about what was known during the time period that these statements were being made by the president, vice president, and others have found a multitude of deceptions. "It is now beyond dispute that Iraq did not possess any weapons of mass destruction or have meaningful ties to Al Qaeda," wrote investigative reporters at the Center for Public Integrity. "The Bush administration led the nation to war on the basis of erroneous information that it methodically propagated and that culminated in military action against Iraq," they said.[58]

"In making the case for war, the Administration repeatedly presented intelligence as fact when in reality it was unsubstantiated, contradicted, or even non-existent," said Senator Jay Rockefeller, chair of the Senate Intelligence Committee, on June 5, 2008, after completing a report on prewar intelligence and information. "As a result, the American people were led to believe that the threat from Iraq was much greater than actually existed. . . . Top Administration officials made repeated statements that falsely linked Iraq and al Qaeda as a single threat and insinuated that Iraq played a role in 9/11. Sadly, the Bush Administration led the nation into war under false pretenses."[59]

In retrospect, another thing is clear. A pattern emerges in this intensive campaign to launch the war. The president and his team made the hyped-up statements on television, on radio, in speeches, in public forums—places where criminal claims of deceiving Congress would not apply. If a member of Congress read the newspaper or watched a Sunday-morning talk show, or listened to a speech at the United Nations, so much the better for the Bush team. The communications were meant to deceive but, as public commentary, would not fall within the definition of Section 1001 on false statements to Congress or Section 371 of the federal code on defrauding

Congress. For the majority of these communications, carefully manicured and crafted messaging was used to avoid areas in which the White House could be caught lying to Congress.

But on at least two occasions, the president directly addressed Congress, potentially running smack into the United States Criminal Code.

The president's 2003 State of the Union address and his March 18, 2003, letter of determination to use military force in Iraq were direct communications to Congress made personally by the president. If they were deliberately deceptive, violations of federal law appear to be possible. Despite the deceptions the White House may have blunted prosecution under Section 1001; still, the same deceptions may add up to a case for conspiracy to defraud Congress under Section 371, and there, the White House may have been knocked off course a bit.

FALSE STATEMENTS IN THE 2003
STATE OF THE UNION MESSAGE

President Bush's 2003 State of the Union message, a mere fifty-one days before the attack on Iraq, enters the realm of possible criminal law violation because it contained a series of untrue statements that, available evidence indicates, the president knew to be false or deceptive. President Bush raised the specter that Iraq was arming with nuclear, chemical, and biological weapons and conspiring with Osama bin Laden, as he had in public speeches for the prior four and a half months. While the assertions in this speech were familiar, the venue was not. This was a speech that the president made directly to both houses of Congress, and the law against making false statements to Congress may be relevant.

The president's speech was intended to convey that the United States faced severe threats from Iraq and dire consequences would follow unless the country attacked Iraq first. He called Iraq "evil," just as he had called al Qaeda "evil." The president of the United States said:

> Evidence from intelligence sources, secret communications and statements by people now in custody reveal that Saddam Hussein aids and protects terrorists, including members of Al Qaida. Secretly, and without fingerprints, he could provide one of his hidden weapons to terrorists, or help them develop their own.

Before September the 11th, many in the world believed that Saddam Hussein could be contained. But chemical agents, lethal viruses and shadowy terrorist networks are not easily contained.

Imagine those 19 hijackers with other weapons and other plans, this time armed by Saddam Hussein. It would take one vial, one canister, one crate slipped into this country to bring a day of horror like none we have ever known.

This frightening scenario was based on a catalog of untruths. The president already knew from his briefings that there was no connection between Iraq and al Qaeda, and he knew that there was no evidence that Iraq had any weapons of mass destruction.

The president said:

Our intelligence sources tell us that he [Saddam] has attempted to purchase high-strength aluminum tubes suitable for nuclear weapons production.[60]

But on January 27, 2003, the day before the president's speech, the IAEA reported to the UN Security Council that the aluminum tubes—a necessary component of nuclear weapons technology—were for other, non-nuclear uses.[61] Anticipating the UN report, the *Washington Post*, in an article titled "U.S. Claim on Iraqi Nuclear Program Is Called Into Question," on January 24, 2003, stated: "After weeks of investigation, U.N. weapons inspectors in Iraq are increasingly confident that the aluminum tubes were never meant for enriching uranium." The article noted that the British government had dismissed the claim in a white paper five months earlier, saying that there was "no definitive intelligence" that the tubes were destined for a nuclear program.[62]

Two key U.S. intelligence agencies with expertise on nuclear weapons—the State Department and the Department of Energy (DOE), which houses the government's main experts on the subject—had also informed the president in October 2002 that the aluminum tubes in question were not suited for nuclear weapons, according to partially declassified information released in July 2003. The president gave no sign that his statement was seriously questioned by the "intelligence sources" that knew the most. The Department of Energy specialists are described as saying, "DOE . . . assesses that the tubes probably are not part of the [nuclear weapons] program." The State Department experts concluded: "The tubes are not intended for use in Iraq's nuclear weapons program." While the assessment by the CIA—by no means expert on the complexities of nuclear technology—differed, the nuclear scientists who had actually measured the tubes had concluded that they were not designed for nuclear purposes, but for standard rockets.[63] Tubes intercepted en route to Iraq were too heavy and too thick for nuclear uses, the former top State Department intelligence analyst Greg Thielmann told *60 Minutes* in February 2004. "Key evidence cited by the administration was misrepresented to the public," said Thielmann.[64]

According to investigative reporter Murray Waas, a one-page classified "President's Summary," written expressly for the president in October 2002, three months before his speech, gave direct warning that the accuracy of the tubes claim was in serious doubt. "Bush had been specifically advised that claims he later made in his 2003 State of the Union address—that Iraq was procuring high-strength aluminum tubes to build a nuclear weapon—might not be true," Waas wrote in the *National Journal* on March 20, 2006.[65] The president failed to give Congress a truthful assessment of the aluminum tubes.

The president also told Congress:

The British government has learned that Saddam Hussein recently sought significant quantities of uranium from Africa.

These words—they became the infamous "sixteen words"—were later acknowledged to be incorrect by the president and his advisors, but only after the war in Iraq had been initiated and was well under way. On July 9, 2003, press secretary Ari Fleischer, speaking to a White House press pool in Pretoria, South Africa, said, "This information should not have risen to the level of a presidential speech."[66]

The president undoubtedly knew the words were false at the time that he spoke them to Congress. The CIA, the State Department, and the International Atomic Energy Agency had already found the same claim about Iraq's procuring uranium from Niger to be baseless. The State Department wrote a memo two weeks before the speech, on January 12, 2003, explaining that the uranium claim was bogus—it was based on a badly forged letter with a fake letterhead. The State Department head of intelligence, Carl

Ford Jr., said he was confident that the reservations about the Niger intelligence made their way to President Bush, Vice President Cheney, and Secretary of Defense Donald Rumsfeld, according to an article by Jason Leopold in April 2006.[67] The high-level National Intelligence Council gave a definitive and unequivocal judgment to the White House in January 2003 that the uranium claim was untrue, information that "arrived at the White House as Bush and his highest-ranking advisers made the uranium story a centerpiece of their case for the rapidly approaching war against Iraq," wrote Barton Gellman and Dafna Linzer in the *Washington Post* on April 9, 2006.[68]

The White House conceded that the statement was false only months later when former ambassador Joseph C. Wilson IV revealed that he had gone to Niger in February 2002 at the behest of the CIA to investigate whether nuclear-grade uranium was being purchased by Iraq. He found out that there were no such transactions and reported his findings to the CIA in March 2002, ten months before the president's State of the Union speech and a year before the start of the war. In an op-ed in the *New York Times* on July 6, 2003, three months after the Iraq invasion, he made this information public. Wilson said that the president had "twisted" the facts about the need for war.[69] (These events also led to a campaign of retaliation against Wilson, including leaks traced to the White House that "outed" Wilson's wife, Valerie Plame, as a CIA agent. I. Lewis "Scooter" Libby, a top aide to the president and Vice President Cheney, was tried and convicted of perjury for trying to cover up Cheney's role in this scheme, although his prison sentence was quickly commuted by President Bush.)

Previously, CIA director George Tenet had removed the fake claim about uranium procurement from a Bush speech, according to his 2008 book *At the Center of the Storm*. "The vision of a despot like Saddam getting his hands on nuclear weapons was galvanizing," he said, adding that it "provided an irresistible image for speechwriters, spokesmen, and politicians to seize on."[70] Apparently for the president, as well.

At first, Tenet took the blame for the sixteen false words in the State of the Union speech, as reported on CNN on July 16, 2003.[71] Then the press learned that Tenet had insisted on removing the same language from an earlier Bush speech. So, within days, deputy national security advisor Stephen Hadley stepped forward to say, no, *he* was to blame for the sixteen admittedly false words, said the BBC in "Aide Takes Blame for Uranium Claim" on July 22, 2003.[72] (Hadley was later promoted to national security advisor, and Tenet was awarded the Presidential Medal of Freedom.)

Clearly, the White House was frantic over the disclosure of the sixteen false words. After all, Congress might want to inquire. It was beginning to look as if the president was speaking of himself and not Saddam Hussein when he said in that same State of the Union speech, "[He] has not credibly explained these activities. He clearly has much to hide. . . . he is deceiving."

Looking closely at Section 1001 of the federal code on false statements to Congress, how do the elements of the criminal code match up with President Bush's 2003 State of the Union address?

The president's 2003 State of the Union speech, a major address delivered to the nation's top decision makers, contained many falsehoods that constituted "false and material" statements, including the infamous "sixteen words," and more. These falsehoods were a central part of the speech and its intended message—to convince Congress of the necessity for war, one of the most critical decisions a nation can make. According to the 1988 decision of the U.S. Supreme Court in *Kungys v. United States*, a statement meets the "materiality" test if it has a "natural tendency to influence or be capable of influencing the decision making body to which it is addressed." Clearly, the State of the Union address meets the "false and material" test.[73]

The law also requires that a statement must be made "knowingly and willfully," a condition that is met if an individual "knew that his statement was false when he made it or—which amounts in law to the same thing—consciously disregarded or averted his eyes from the likely falsity," wrote the Congressional Research Service in a report, *Obstruction of Congress*.[74] The president knew that the information in the speech was not correct from presidential briefings, and if he did not, it is because he disregarded the briefings, the intelligence, or both—that is, he "consciously disregarded or averted his eyes." A prosecutor would not have difficulty meeting the "knowingly and willfully" test.

But did the State of the Union address meet the standard of Section 1001, which requires the false statements to be presented in a *form* prohib-

ited by the law? Section 1001 has built-in limits on when criminal prosecution may be deployed. Only certain types of communications to Congress
may be subject to prosecution, even if false. This element of the Section
1001 could present a prosecutor with a serious headache.

In passing the new Section 1001 in 1996, Congress limited the types
of communication that could be prosecuted. It didn't want to create "an
intimidating atmosphere" or to "undermine the free-flow of information"
from constituents, Representative Bill McCollum explained in a speech
before the House on September 25, 1996. Not every letter from an angry
constituent or odd conspiracy theory sent to a member of Congress is subject to prosecution for lying, even if it is untrue. Nor did Congress intend
to permit prosecution for "routine fact gathering" or advocacy, according to debate in the House.[75]

As a result of these concerns, false statements may be prosecuted under
Section 1001 only if contained in "a document required by law," as part
of an authorized "investigation or review," or an "administrative matter."
Does the State of the Union address fall within one of those categories?

On the first point, the State of the Union message is "required by
law"—actually, by the U.S. Constitution, which states in Article II, Section
3 that the president "shall from time to time provide Congress Information
about the State of the Union, and recommend to their Consideration such
Measures as he shall judge necessary and expedient."[76] But even though
President Bush gave an oral and written presentation to Congress, it is not
clear that the Constitution "requires" that the message be in writing, and
a prosecutor will have to work harder to show that the State of the Union
address fits within that definition in the law.

As for whether it is an "investigation or review," the State of the Union
address is not the same as a hearing to gather information for new legislation or fact finding to fulfill oversight responsibilities, which is the sense
of that phrase. And the term "administrative matters"—murky, at best—is
meant to cover things like false payroll requests by members of Congress.

In truth, the State of the Union message is not a document, an investigation, or an administrative filing, but a policy statement filled with goals
and warnings, aspirations and opinions, as well as suggestions for future action by Congress. Although President Bush manipulated this venue to shill
for a war and present a false picture to the Congress, in general, the State of
the Union address represents the kind of communication that the framers

intended for presidents to provide freely and without inhibition. Presidents frequently puff, exaggerate, overpromise, and shade the truth in their State of the Union addresses. The framers undoubtedly knew this would occur, but nonetheless believed that the value of the information outweighed the danger of misstatements—and even untruths.

President Bush and his team, no doubt, knew the wording of the "false statements" law. They may have even chosen this venue and this event as a safe harbor to showcase their truth-straining and deceit-laden case for war, perhaps knowing full well that they probably could not be charged with any violation of Section 1001. In any case, stretching the carefully limited provisions of Section 1001 to encompass the president's State of the Union address is not a good use of the law or, despite the many falsehoods, an appropriate prosecution under Section 1001. If the president's team was keeping score, they won on this one.

While justice may have been cheated in this instance, all may not be lost: the deceits about Iraq contained in the State of the Union address, combined with other statements and acts, may fold into a criminal conspiracy to defraud the government.

FALSE STATEMENTS IN THE LETTER OF DETERMINATION TO GO TO WAR

The president's second communication to Congress that brings Section 1001 of the criminal code into view is the "letter of determination," sent only seven weeks after the 2003 State of the Union. This communication to Congress does not fall prey to the same problems with the false statements law as the State of the Union address—although its application, unfortunately, may encounter other obstacles.

On March 18, 2003, President Bush sent identical, personally signed letters to the president pro tem of the Senate, Senator Ted Stevens, and the Speaker of the House, Representative Dennis Hastert. The letter of determination was submitted under the requirements of a joint resolution passed by Congress in October 2002—the so-called "Authorization for Use of Military Force."

Asserting their role regarding war powers under the Constitution, both houses of Congress had passed the "Congressional Joint Resolution to Authorize Use of Military Force Against Iraq," Public Law 107–243. Known as the AUMF on Iraq, it authorized the use of military force against Iraq—

if certain conditions were met, including a requirement that the president make available to the Senate and the House his determination that

> (a) reliance on diplomatic and peaceful means alone either (1) will not protect the national security of the United States against the continuing threat posed by Iraq or (2) is not likely to lead to enforcement of all relevant UN Security Council resolutions regarding Iraq; and (b) acting pursuant to this resolution is consistent with the United States and other countries continuing to take the necessary actions against international terrorists and terrorist organizations, including those nations, organizations or persons who planned, authorized, committed or aided the terrorists attacks that occurred on September 11, 2001.[77]

The president's letter of March 18, 2003, to the Speaker of the House said:

> Dear Mr. Speaker:
> Consistent with section 3(b) of the Authorization for Use of Military Force Against Iraq Resolution of 2002 (Public Law 107–243), and based on information available to me, including that in the enclosed document, I determine that:
> (1) reliance by the U.S. on further diplomatic or other peaceful means alone will neither (A) adequately protect the national security of the United States against the continuing threat posed by Iraq nor (B) likely lead to enforcement of all relevant United Nations Security Council resolutions regarding Iraq; and
> (2) acting pursuant to the Constitution and Public Law 107–243 is consistent with the United States and other countries continuing to take the necessary actions against international terrorists and terrorist organizations, including those nations, organizations or persons who planned, authorized, committed or aided the terrorist attack that occurred on September 11, 2001.
> Sincerely,
> George W. Bush[78]

The letter of determination spit back the exact language of the Authorization of Military Force (AUMF) on Iraq. But there was a distinct flaw: it wasn't true. The president could not verify the preconditions for entering the war, and he knew this.

Since not all false statements made to Congress can start the jail keys jangling, some questions need to be addressed by a prosecutor. Does the letter meet the standards for making a false statement to Congress (false, material, knowing)? Is this letter, unlike the State of the Union address, a type of communication that is covered under Section 1001?

On the question of "false and material statement," in two short paragraphs, the letter of determination managed to pack in a multitude of falsehoods. It was untrue that Iraq was involved in planning, authorizing, committing or aiding the terrorist attacks of September 11, 2001. Also untrue was the claim that a war against Iraq was a "necessary" action in response to 9/11.

The president was unable to say truthfully that "peaceful means" alone would not protect the United States since weapons inspectors were still working in Iraq and were willing to continue. It was the U.S. invasion itself that forced them to leave. On the eve of the war, the UN ordered fifty-six inspectors and staff to get out of Iraq, the Associated Press reported on March 18, 2003;[79] a total of 119 inspectors had worked in Iraq from November to March, said the Carnegie Endowment for International Peace.[80] The inspectors were answering questions and solving critical concerns, wrote David Corn on *Politics Daily*.[81] And they had found no evidence of the existence or development of weapons of mass destruction.

Nor could the president truthfully say that other peaceful means would result in inadequate protection of the United States. Carne Ross, a British diplomat at the United Nations in 2003, told a British commission investigating the war in Iraq in 2010 that it was a "disgrace" that all peaceful options had not been exhausted, reported the *Guardian* newspaper.[82] The UN Security Council had passed Resolution 1441 on November 8, 2002, calling for Iraq to comply with inspectors or face "serious consequences," but by carefully hammered-out terms of the resolution, a second Security Council resolution was required to authorize a war. President Bush refused to seek the second resolution after it became clear that it would be vetoed, and he declared war without it. International lawyers were near unanimous in their objections, pointing out that there was not an "imminent threat" that would provide an excuse for ignoring the second resolution, wrote Richard Norton-Taylor in the *Guardian* on March 14, 2003.[83] President Bush, however, slammed the door on the diplomatic process and peaceful means, and, on top of that, the clear obligations of the United States under the UN Charter.

There was also no truth to the statement that Iraq posed a "continuing threat" to the United States, since the intelligence agencies had determined that Iraq was not likely to attack or to provide weapons of mass destruction to terrorists and, according to all available research, did not even have weapons of mass destruction to provide. The letter of determination clearly meets the "falsehood" test.

The element of "materiality" requires that the false statement have a "natural tendency to influence or be capable of influencing the decision making body." The false statements by the president in the letter of determination went to the heart of the matter—embroiling the United States in a war and occupation in Iraq. The members of Congress had predetermined the exact conditions that would influence them to agree to a war. The president had to certify that these conditions had been met in order to engage in war. The president's statements that he had met the preconditions set by Congress were not only an influence, but also a determinant of the decision by Congress. The "materiality" test is undoubtedly met.

On the matter of whether Bush made these false statements "knowingly and willfully," it's clear the president knew very well that Iraq was not involved in the 9/11 attacks and, therefore, an attack on Iraq had nothing to do with undertaking "necessary actions" against those responsible for 9/11. He had been told that Iraq was not involved in person by the White House expert on terrorism, in writing, and in intelligence briefings. He knew that Iraq was not a security threat to the United States and was not a continuing threat. He knew that he had not pursued all peaceful means to resolve any questions about Iraq's intentions since he had not waited for weapons inspectors to complete their work, or for the United Nations to vote on a new Security Council resolution. The elements of "knowingly and willfully" are met.

The final element of the law that must be met is whether the letter was "required by law or any investigation or review duly authorized by Congress." The president's letter of determination certainly falls under the definition of "a document required by law." He was required to submit it before invading Iraq. Had President Bush simply ordered troops into Iraq without sending a letter of determination in compliance with the AUMF, Congress might have responded with his impeachment and removal from office. Defying a congressional resolution on military action would have entailed grave constitutional and political risks, including an outcry that democracy was under assault.

On the other hand, President Bush's deceptive letter of determination, filled with false statements, does the equivalent job of destroying our constitutional system. President Bush acted with callous disregard for the criminal law—and his oath of office—by signing a document submitted to Congress filled with falsehoods. This letter certainly takes the form of a statement covered by the "false statements" law.

The false statements in the letter of determination, personally signed by the president, meet all the elements of Section 1001 of the federal law, which makes it a crime to present false statements to Congress. But before a prosecution could proceed, what defense would the president have?

Defense #1 to Prosecution for False Statements in the Letter of Determination: It's Too Late

Despite clear evidence that President Bush violated Section 1001, he and his defenders can now point to the statute of limitations—five years. Since the letter of determination was dated March 18, 2003, the five-year limit for prosecution under the False Statements Accountability Act expired on March 18, 2008—while President Bush was still in office. Although it fails to serve justice, the president has a viable defense.

Because of this aspect of the law, President Bush may have dodged a bullet under the false statements law. Since a president probably cannot be prosecuted while in office (impeachment was possible and would have been a good idea), by getting elected to a second term, the president was able to avoid criminal consequences, letting the statute of limitations expire while he still held office.

President Bush seemed to have this view of his accountability too. After being reelected in fall 2004, the president was asked about accountability for the war, as reported in the *Washington Post* on January 16, 2005. President Bush responded: "We had an accountability moment, and that's called the 2004 election. And the American people listened to different assessments made about what was taking place in Iraq, and they looked at the two candidates, and chose me, for which I'm grateful."[84]

To avoid repetition of this scenario, the law should be reformed to extend the statute of limitations for crimes committed by a president while in office.

But, as with the 2003 State of the Union address, this obstacle to prosecution does not close off the possibility of proceeding on the basis of conspiracy to defraud the United States for falsifications in the letter of determination, and there the statute of limitations is longer.

CONSPIRACY TO DEFRAUD THE UNITED STATES

A coterie of individuals—inside the White House and the Pentagon—participated in the deceptive campaign to launch a war against Iraq. Section 371 of the federal code provides an antidote and permits prosecution for such a conspiracy.[85]

Section 371 has a powerful history. People in the presidential inner circle and cabinet have been charged with conspiracy to defraud the government for their illegal acts in the past.

In the Watergate era, Section 371 was used prominently in an indictment of H. R. Haldeman, President Nixon's top aide. The charges against Haldeman arose from a series of conversations he had with President Nixon in the White House, described in the 1974 report of the House Judiciary Committee on the impeachment of Richard M. Nixon.[86] After the arrest of White House–connected operatives caught breaking into the Democratic headquarters in the Watergate office complex, President Nixon and his aides tried to cover any tracks that led to them. Haldeman and Nixon met in the Oval Office to discuss what to do. One plot was to get the CIA to stop the FBI investigation into the break-in on the grounds of national security, a pretext concocted by Nixon and Haldeman. This conversation was picked up on a taping system that the president had installed in the White House, seemingly for archival purposes. Called the "smoking-gun tape," the discussion proved beyond a doubt that Nixon himself had been involved in the cover-up. Once it became known, Nixon's impeachment and removal from office were guaranteed. To avoid those consequences, President Nixon resigned from office shortly after the tape became public.[87]

Haldeman was convicted of conspiracy to defraud the United States, obstruction of justice, and perjury.[88] Others were also charged—former attorney general John Mitchell, presidential aide John D. Ehrlichman, special counsel Charles Colson, and three other men, as described in the indictment filed in federal district court.

President Nixon was named as an unindicted co-conspirator on the charge of obstruction of justice, as explained in the 1975 report of the

Watergate Special Prosecution Force.[89] If Nixon had not been president at the time, the grand jury would have indicted him, as well, as part of this conspiracy. (The special prosecutor believed that, while in office, the president could not be indicted.) After he left office, Nixon was pardoned by President Ford, preventing criminal charges from being brought against him for the behavior evidenced in the tapes. The need for the pardon highlights that a president can be subjected to criminal prosecution once out of office.

Another case that sheds light on the interpretation of Section 371 comes from the Iran-Contra scandal in 1986, during the presidency of Ronald Reagan. This scandal, as described in depth in the final report of the independent counsel filed with the court, involved two schemes executed by top National Security Council officials in the Reagan administration. The NSC officials first hatched a plan to sell arms to Iran—despite U.S. laws prohibiting the sales—in exchange for freeing several American hostages taken by Hezbollah, a terrorist organization in Lebanon with close ties to Iran. The second plan involved using funds from the arms sales to provide financial and military support for the Contras, who were fighting the elected leftist Sandinista government in Nicaragua. Aid and support for the Contras was barred by law. Regardless, the arms were sold to Iran for an inflated price with the money going into a slush fund that was used to support the Contras. To cover up and avoid detection, the Reagan officials involved—National Security Advisor Robert McFarlane, his successor, Admiral John Poindexter, and their subordinate, Lieutenant Colonel Oliver North—made false statements to Congress in written documents and oral testimony.

An independent special prosecutor, former judge Lawrence Walsh, was appointed to investigate the Iran-Contra scandal and eventually fourteen people were charged with criminal offenses. North, Poindexter, and others were indicted for conspiring to defraud the United States under Section 371, among other charges. North was also charged with obstruction of congressional investigations, making false statements to a congressional committee, and the shredding of official documents.

In the final report of the independent prosecutor, Walsh provided a valuable analysis of the meaning of conspiracy to defraud Congress, and these explanations resonate with the conspiracy inside the Bush White House as well.

Walsh wrote: "The conspiracy . . . involved activities that were shielded by a campaign of lies and deceptions from Government officials who could have disagreed with those activities and might have sought to stop them." The activity in the Reagan era—providing military assistance to the Contras—was carried out, Walsh wrote, "in a way calculated to defeat legal restrictions governing the conduct of military and covert operations and congressional control of appropriations."

Said Walsh: "Because [the conspirators] . . . feared that Congress would stop them if it knew of their activities . . . they deceived Congress . . . By so doing the conspirators obstructed Congress' legitimate functions of regulating governmental expenditures and overseeing foreign covert action."[90]

A similar conspiracy grew inside the Bush White House, one designed to obstruct, deceive, and conceal: to obstruct the legitimate function of Congress with respect to the initiation and funding of a war; to deceive those who might disagree with launching a war in Iraq and might try to stop them; and to conceal their behavior.

Do the actions by President Bush and others inside his administration permit a prosecution under Section 371 of the federal criminal code? A conspiracy under the law involves two or more people acting in concert to try to accomplish an unlawful plan. Members of the Bush administration, including the president, worked together to strategize on a plan—based on a series of deceits—to "sell" the war. While government officials are expected to work together, they are not expected to deceive together. Elizabeth de la Vega, a prosecutor who has carefully studied this topic, wrote in a 2005 article in the *Nation* that, in such situations, "[a] pattern of double-dealing proves a criminal conspiracy."[91]

Among those who "acted in concert" with President Bush and Vice President Cheney, were Defense Secretary Donald Rumsfeld, Deputy Secretary of Defense Paul Wolfowitz, Secretary of State Colin Powell, National Security Advisor Condoleezza Rice, deputy national security advisor Stephen Hadley, co-chair of the White House Iraq Group Karl Rove, special presidential advisor I. Lewis "Scooter" Libby, and a host of other individuals who worked for the White House. A prosecutor will easily be able to meet the element in the law of identifying two or more people who formed the conspiracy.

Section 371 refers to "defrauding," which is defined in the statute as "deceit, craft, trickery or dishonest means." The conspirators in this case used all of those methods—and more—to characterize Iraq as a threat to the United States. As de la Vega noted in her 2005 *Nation* article, "When they chose to overcome anticipated or actual opposition to their plan by concealing information and lying, they began a conspiracy to defraud."

Defrauding can clearly be shown by a prosecutor.

The president and his team, after deceiving the Congress into authorizing a war in Iraq, continued their pattern of concealment and fraud for years. They made a concerted effort to cover up the false statements in the president's State of the Union address, including attacks on former ambassador Joseph Wilson when he challenged the truthfulness of the claims about attempted uranium purchases by Iraq. E-mail records in the critical war period that could have shown the trail of information and authorization—these records are required by law to be archived and retained—were lost or disappeared, according to the Citizens for Responsibility and Ethics in Washington, a nonprofit think tank and advocacy organization that was still fighting for their release in 2011.[92]

The president continued to assert that Iraq had refused to allow in weapons inspectors. On July 14, 2003, months after the war was launched, he said: "We gave [Saddam Hussein] a chance to allow the inspectors in and he wouldn't let them in," reported CNN.[93] In an "exit" interview with ABC's Charlie Gibson on December 1, 2008, the president said, "Saddam Hussein was unwilling to let the inspectors go in to determine whether or not the UN resolutions were being upheld."[94] In his 2010 book *Decision Points*, President Bush claimed that Hussein had not cooperated with weapons inspectors.[95] In response, Walter Pincus of the *Washington Post* wrote on November 15, 2010, "Bush fails to mention two subsequent Blix [director of UN inspections Hans Blix] pre-invasion reports in February and early March, weeks before U.S. bombs struck Baghdad. Those show Iraq cooperating with inspectors and the inspectors finding no significant evidence that Hussein was hiding WMD programs."[96]

Vice President Cheney also continued to conceal the truth and repeat false statements. The *Boston Globe* carried an article on June 16, 2004, quoting a speech by Vice President Cheney at the Madison Institute in Orlando earlier that month. The vice president falsely told his audience that Saddam "had long-established ties with al Qaeda." Asked about it, President

Bush backed him up, according to the *Boston Globe*.[97] In 2009 in a speech to the American Enterprise Institute, Vice President Cheney, referring to the wars in Afghanistan and Iraq, declared that they were conducted "to confront the regimes . . . that had the capacity to build weapons of mass destruction, and might transfer such weapons to terrorists."[98] Since no allegation has ever been made that Afghanistan had WMD, Cheney was simply repeating the same Iraq falsification.

For a prosecution under Section 371 to proceed, the government itself must be the target of the fraud. Of course, Congress is a branch of the U.S. government, and the Bush administration aimed its expansive conspiracy at defrauding Congress into signing off on a war in Iraq. The war "marketing" campaign targeted Congress using "full-scale lobbying." Karl Rove, the president's political advisor, said in a book he released in spring 2010, "Congress was very unlikely to have supported the use-of-force resolution without the W.M.D. threat."[99]

President Bush, Vice President Cheney, and the many officials inside the Bush administration who collaborated with them had good reason to fear that Congress would say no if the truth were known about why they intended make war on Iraq. Instead, the president and his team decided to defraud Congress so that they could do what they wanted to do—enter into a war and the occupation of Iraq.

In lying, they not only committed the crime of conspiring to defraud Congress, they slashed away at our democracy. The framers of the Constitution attempted to protect against unnecessary war making and military adventurism by refusing to give the executive branch the right to start a war on its own (except to repel an imminent attack, not a factor here). Deceiving Congress into issuing an authorization to go to war on false pretexts unravels the Constitution and obstructs, disrupts, and undermines our democracy. A prosecutor will have no difficulty proving that the target of the conspiracy was the Congress.

Nor will a prosecutor have any problem meeting the final element of Section 371—"overt acts." The people inside the Bush administration committed not one, but many overt acts as they engaged in the serial falsification of statements, information, and documents to deceive Congress. The conspirators, all powerful people, used their positions of trust to drive the nation into a war in Iraq come hell or high water, and without regard to the law, the Constitution, or the truth.

Defense #1 to Conspiracy to Defraud:
It Was the Bad Intel, Not Us

President Bush and Vice President Cheney have pointed the finger at bad "intel" from the CIA and other government intelligence agencies for their misrepresentations, claiming, in effect, that they are innocent victims of others. To defend themselves from accountability and prosecution for conspiracy to defraud, they will likely play the same blame game that they have used numerous times to protect themselves by setting up others as the culprits.

In an interview with Charlie Gibson on ABC's *World News* on December 2, 2008, the president said, "The biggest regret of all the presidency has to have been the intelligence failure in Iraq. A lot of people put their reputations on the line and said the weapons of mass destruction is [*sic*] a reason to remove Saddam Hussein."[100]

In his book, President Bush wrote that he was completely surprised that there were no WMD in Iraq. "No one was more shocked or angry than I was when we didn't find weapons of mass destruction. I had a sickening feeling every time I thought about it."[101] But the president recognized six weeks before the invasion of Iraq, in a meeting with British prime minister Tony Blair, that there were no weapons of mass destruction and another pretext for war might be needed.[102]

This is not, however, the same information that the president gave to the nation on March 17, 2003, days before the entering Iraq. Then he declared, "Intelligence gathered by this and other governments leaves no doubt that the Iraq regime continues to possess and conceal some of the most lethal weapons ever devised. . . . The danger is clear."[103]

Other intelligence information was manipulated and falsified, as well. The Senate Intelligence Committee said that the suggestion of an Iraq–al Qaeda connection, repeatedly made by the Bush administration, was "contradicted by available intelligence information."[104]

Human intelligence was seriously misrepresented in at least three cases. A statement from one detainee, Ibn al-Shaykh al-Libi, about a supposed al Qaeda training camp sponsored by Iraq, was delivered after he was subjected to torture, reported *Newsweek* writer Michael Isikoff.[105] The statement was retracted by al-Libi, and it was determined to be untrue by Defense Department analysts as early as February 2002. But that didn't stop the president and others from using it as "evidence" of a connection between al Qaeda and Iraq. On October 7, 2002—eight months after analysts concluded that the al-Libi comment was false—President Bush used him as the sole "source" for a statement in a major speech in Cincinnati. "We've learned that Iraq has trained al Qaeda members in bomb-making and poisons and deadly gases," the president said.[106] *New York Times* reporter Douglas Jehl wrote in December 2005, "The Defense Intelligence Agency had identified Mr. Libi as a probable fabricator months before the Bush administration began to use his statements as the foundation for its claims about ties between Iraq and Al Qaeda."[107]

A second piece of manipulated intelligence came from a man codenamed—incredibly—"Curveball." During a period in which anthrax raised red alerts for Americans, President Bush, Vice President Cheney, and Secretary of State Colin Powell all described, with great fanfare, information about mobile biological weapons labs operating in Iraq. The source was a single Iraqi expatriate interviewed by German agents. Before the start of the war, Tyler Drumheller, the head of the CIA in Europe, repeatedly warned top U.S. officials in Washington that the man was not reliable, but Drumheller's alerts were rebuffed. Later, "Curveball" (real name: Rafid Ahmed Alwan al-Janabi) admitted to the *Guardian* newspaper that he had lied.[108]

Intel was also falsified to assert that Mohamed Atta, one of the 9/11 hijackers, colluded with Iraq. Vice President Cheney made this claim on *Meet the Press* on September 8, 2002, a half year before the Iraq invasion. Cheney said that Atta had met in Czechoslovakia with "a senior Iraqi intelligence official a few months before the attacks on the World Trade Center."[109] But intelligence agencies had completely discredited the Atta meeting six to nine months before the vice president's TV appearance, according to Michael Isikoff in "The Phantom Link to Iraq."[110] The FBI found that Atta was in Florida at the time of the supposed Prague meeting.

The president's team disregarded the intelligence that didn't fit the plan for marketing the war, while at the same time, intelligence failures that did emerge were, in large part, a result of White House pressures on intelligence agencies to support the case for war. In a comprehensive assessment of prewar intelligence on Iraq, the Carnegie Endowment for International Peace determined that the intelligence on Iraq when President Bush first took office was "generally accurate" and that it reported no immediate threats. Beginning in 2002, the assessments changed—but not because the situation on the ground had changed, the Carnegie Endowment said. Instead, some errors seem to have emerged because the intelligence community was politicized by repeated visits to CIA headquarters by Vice President Cheney, the establishment of a separate intelligence operation in the Department of Defense operated by Bush appointees without intelligence experience, and an environment in which agencies likely felt pressure to reach more threatening judgments.

Even then, the Carnegie Endowment found, the available intelligence information was distorted, conflated, and misrepresented by the Bush administration. "Administration officials systematically misrepresented the threat from Iraq's nuclear, chemical and biological weapon programs, beyond the intelligence failures noted," the report said.[111] As Senator Rockefeller said, "There is a fundamental difference between relying on incorrect intelligence and deliberately painting a picture to the American people that you know is not fully accurate."[112]

The president's efforts to blame faulty intel for his repeated deceptions and misrepresentations will not hold up to the light of day, or serve to protect him from prosecution.

Defense #2: Congress Agreed with Us, So What Is the Problem Anyhow?

After deceiving Congress with false information, the president and vice president used the success of their fraudulent scheme as another alibi, claiming that they had the full backing of Congress.

In his speech to the nation on March 17, 2003, two days before the invasion of Iraq, President Bush said, "Recognizing the threat to our country, the United States Congress voted overwhelmingly last year to support the use of force against Iraq."[113] But he failed to mention that the Congress had demanded that certain preconditions be met, and that they had not been met.

On November 11, 2005, in a speech in Pennsylvania, President Bush said, "Democrats and anti-war critics are now claiming we manipulated the intelligence and misled the American people about why we went to war. . . . More than a hundred Democrats in the House and the Senate—who had access to the same intelligence—voted to support removing Saddam Hussein from power."[114] Of course, the Congress did not vote to remove Saddam Hussein from power; Congress voted to permit military intervention against terrorists who had attacked the United States on 9/11 and Saddam Hussein was not on that list. Aside from that, Congress did not have the same access to intelligence information as the president, who refused to declassify some of the most important documents, leaving Congress in the dark.

Senator Rockefeller, in an introduction to the Senate Intelligence Committee Report of June 2008—five years after the war had begun—wrote that "members of Congress did not have the same ready access to intelligence as senior Executive Branch policymakers."[115]

In the Senate Intelligence Committee report, Senator Rockefeller describes how Congress had to demand the National Intelligence Estimate (NIE) on Iraq, and got it in October 2002, only ten days before a vote on the authorization to go to war. "During the course of its investigation, the Committee uncovered that the October 2002 National Intelligence Estimate on Iraq's alleged weapons of mass destruction was based on stale, fragmentary, and speculative intelligence reports and replete with unsupported judgments. Troubling incidents were reported in which internal dissent and warnings about the veracity of intelligence on Iraq were ignored in the rush to war."[116]

The full NIE was classified, so even if members of Congress were shown it, they were not permitted to refer to it or quote from it. The version that was unclassified skipped over important details, in particular, dropping references to analysts who dissented from the summaries given and turning uncertain information into declarative certainties. "The intelligence community was far from unified. The administration concealed that fact by classifying the dissents in the intelligence community until after the war and continuing to make false claims about the immediacy of the danger," wrote the late senator Edward Kennedy in a letter to the *Los Angeles Times* on March 15, 2004.[117]

A *New York Times* editorial on November 15, 2005, summed up the situation. In "Decoding Mr. Bush's Denials," the editors said, "To avoid having to account for his administration's misleading statements before the war with Iraq, President Bush has tried . . . to share the blame, claiming that Congress had the same intelligence he had," wrote the *Times*. "Congress had nothing close to the president's access to intelligence," wrote the paper, and some information, like the National Intelligence Estimate, was "sanitized," it said. "The president . . . did not allow the American people, or even Congress, to have the information necessary to make reasoned judgments of their own. It's obvious the Bush administration misled Americans."[118]

Finally, the question of whether members of Congress had the same information or could have been more aggressive in their search for information is a sideshow: it does nothing to relieve the president and vice president of their own culpability for conspiracy to commit fraud under Section 371.

Defense #3: The Clock Ran Out

This time, the Bush team may have run out of luck. The statute of limitations in a conspiracy runs from the date of the last overt act in furtherance of the conspiracy. In this case, the conspiracy's objective, at a minimum, was to deceive Congress into authorizing and funding a military invasion so that the president and his team could launch an attack on Iraq, occupy the country militarily, remove Saddam Hussein from power, install a new regime, secure "victory," and establish a "stable" Iraq, a claim President Bush made in announcing the commencement of the invasion on March 17, 2003. In his book *Decision Points*, the president acknowledged that the United States would be responsible for replacing Saddam's tyranny and "helping a fractured country rebuild."[119]

After the invasion, President Bush and his team spent the remainder of his presidency continuing the occupation, sending additional troops to counter opposition, and spending hundreds of billions on rebuilding Iraq and maintaining a U.S. presence. As president and commander in chief, Bush continued to preside over the 100,000 U.S. troops stationed in Iraq, as well as military contractors and nonmilitary U.S. personnel, until he left office on January 20, 2009, the earliest point at which the overt acts of the Bush administration can be said to have ended. The time for prosecution under the statute of limitations on the conspiracy to defraud the government would not end before January 20, 2014. Of course, the cover-up—repeated lies—continued even after President Bush left office. And an investigation may disclose other long-term objectives of the conspiracy—such as plans to control Iraqi oil revenues or to establish permanent military bases—that extend the time for prosecution further.

A prosecution against former president George W. Bush and his top aides for conspiring to defraud the United States in violation of U.S. Code Title 18, Section 371 is not only possible, but necessary, to prevent future presidents from similarly trampling our democracy.

———————

In Watergate, former White House counsel John Dean cautioned President Nixon about the spreading criminality inside the White House. "We have a cancer within—close to the presidency, that's growing," Dean said, according to the Nixon tapes transcript.[120] The lies and fraud committed by President Bush and others in his administration in order to start, pursue, and fund a war and occupation in Iraq metastasized into a hundred tumors, a thousand cancers, not merely on the presidency, but on our democracy.

The predetermination of President Bush and Vice President Cheney to embroil the country in war in Iraq and to do so under a cloak of lies and deceit is the original flaw of the Bush administration. It led to a vicious and tangled web of secrecy, suppression of evidence, obstruction of justice, misguided policy, imperial behavior, and the ravaging of people, property, privacy, and our own values.

Once President Bush and Vice President Cheney committed themselves to war by deception, and abandoned law, reason, evidence, analysis, and the Constitution, they embarked upon a course of expanding illegality and immorality to cover their tracks. In that sense, the Bush administration mirrored the ugliest parts of Watergate and those dark times when President Nixon engaged in covert activities.

This toxic approach spread throughout administration activities. Fake intelligence information was leaked to reporters by the White House. Individuals who told the truth were pushed aside or fired. General Eric Shinseki, who—accurately, as it turns out—told Congress that two or three times more troops would be needed than the number projected by the secretary of defense, was sidelined and a successor named, as *Time* magazine recalled in a 2008 profile.[121] And the *Christian Science Monitor* reminded readers in 2007 about Lawrence Lindsey, the president's chief economic advisor, who was shown the door in December 2002 after he riled the White House by estimating the costs of the war at what the president's team said was an excessively high $100 billion to $200 billion—low compared to the still-mounting tally of more than $750 billion, but far beyond the $50 to $60 billion that Secretary of Defense Rumsfeld had proclaimed as the cost.[122]

The ever-expanding tangle of lies about Iraq led to illegal surveillance and also to the illegal use of torture on detainees. Al-Libi, who died in prison under suspicious circumstances, was subjected to torture, not to protect Americans from terrorist attacks, but to eke out a story, any story, that could be used to make the case for war in Iraq. Other detainees experienced brutal questioning by the CIA in an effort to force a statement linking al Qaeda and Iraq, according to an FBI agent who was interviewed by Jane Mayer for her book *The Dark Side.*[123]

The Bush administration unleashed a web of deceit at a time that Americans were vulnerable and worried after the 9/11 attacks. Speaking of the war in Iraq to the McClatchy Newspapers on September 2, 2010, Defense Secretary Robert Gates said, "The problem with this war for, I think, many Americans, is that the premise on which we justified going to war proved not to be valid—that is, Saddam having weapons of mass destruction." He added: "It will always be clouded by how it began."[124]

Although no specific laws make it a crime to drive the nation to war based on fraud, lies, and deceit, the Bush administration brought itself to an indictable place by breaking criminal laws against conspiring to defraud the Congress. These laws must be used to protect the Congress from those who would seek to obstruct its role in the future, and to protect the Constitution from those who seek to ignore or trample on it—essential safeguards for democracy and the American people.

The lives lost and damaged and the billions expended on the war in Iraq can never be recovered, but the United States can say, "Never again." If we do not act now, we risk the danger of another president, at another time, driving the nation into another war, another occupation, based on similar lies and deceptions. Prosecution now is the way to safeguard the nation's future.

TWO

Wiretapping Americans

In a memorable scene in *Little Murders*, a 1960s play and subsequent movie by cartoonist Jules Feiffer, a quirky character played by Elliott Gould believes that the FBI is opening his mail. Letters arrive bent, corners torn, sealing undone, as if, Gould's character says, the FBI doesn't care one iota if he knows. Gould's character devises a scheme to taunt the FBI officer who is assigned to this task, writing letters addressed to himself with messages to the agent: "Yours cannot be a happy task—reading another man's mail. It's dull, unimaginative. A job—and let's not mince words—for a hack. . . . Have you ever wondered why they stuck you with this particular job?" Eventually, the FBI officer is pushed to the edge and begs Gould's character to stop.[1]

Americans have never been comfortable with secret surveillance by the government. The founders put a clause in the Constitution to protect against "unreasonable searches and seizures," and the prohibition on surveillance without a warrant was refined by court decisions over the years. After abuses by President Nixon and others at the highest levels of the government in the name of "national security," a new law—the Foreign Surveillance Intelligence Act, or FISA—was passed in 1978.[2]

President Bush decided to break the FISA law. Under a veil of secrecy, he authorized spying, completely refusing to use the FISA warrant procedures. His actions were exposed by the *New York Times* in a front-page article on December 16, 2005. "President Bush secretly authorized the

National Security Agency to eavesdrop on Americans and others inside the United States to search for evidence of terrorist activity without the court-approved warrants ordinarily required for domestic spying, according to government officials," wrote journalists James Risen and Eric Lichtblau.[3] Within days, President Bush admitted that he had violated the law for nearly three years, and, belligerently, said he planned to continue.[4] Then, before leaving office, the president and vice president went on a fierce campaign to change the law, apparently in hopes of immunizing their illegal acts and protecting themselves from prosecution.

The president had authorized at least two separate surveillance programs; many details about them are still unknown. It is known that the president permitted the government to read private e-mail, sweep through Internet interactions, listen to phone conversations, track phone numbers, and otherwise conduct surveillance on Americans, all unlawfully.[5]

Even in this day of Facebook, Twitter, and Tumblr, voluntary information sharing and social networking, Americans are entitled to be free from unwarranted government surveillance.

Data collected or scooped up by the government may remain in its files forever. The situation can be seen in its gravest light when the people under surveillance are journalists, public leaders, or those who protest official government policies.

If not carefully limited, government surveillance has a corrosive effect on our liberties. Because it is invisible, secret government wiretapping can be especially insidious. The harm is abstract—people don't necessarily know if they have been victims and the issue seems remote.

The framers of our Constitution understood the dangers of unbridled government surveillance. They knew that democracy could flourish only in spaces free from government snooping and interference, and they put restraints on government overreaching in the Fourth Amendment of the Bill of Rights: "The right of the people to be secure in their persons, houses, papers, and effects, against unreasonable searches and seizures, shall not be violated, and no Warrants shall issue, but upon probable cause."[6]

These protections require, at a minimum, a neutral arbiter—a magistrate—standing between the government's endless desire for information and the citizens' desires for privacy. Because there is no adversarial process when surveillance is initiated—the potential targets cannot be informed lest they take measures to foil the surveillance—the neutral arbiter acts as a stand-in for those affected and tries to ensure that the government's request is reasonable and justified.

Without the arbiter, there is no check on the government's appetite, and little, or no, protection for the people who are subjected to surveillance. President Nixon, for example, decided that he didn't need to obey the laws on surveillance. In 1969, he ordered the FBI to wiretap the telephone of William Beecher, a reporter for the *New York Times* who wrote an exposé about the secret bombing of Cambodia by the United States, something President Nixon wanted to hide from the American people. Nixon wanted to uncover the source of the leak, recounted Seymour Hersh in the *Atlantic Monthly* in May 1982.[7] Nixon then ordered the wiretapping of another journalist. He also placed bugs on the phones of his own National Security Council staff, and conveniently kept one going when the NSC staffer left to work for Senator Edward Muskie, a potential rival for the presidency. Without restraint, it was easy for the wiretaps to multiply and to target political opponents.

In 1973, as a newly elected member of Congress, I was assigned to the House Judiciary Committee, which was asked to investigate Watergate and the possible impeachment of President Nixon. Although the name "Watergate" came from the effort by White House operatives to break into and bug the Democratic National Committee headquarters in the Watergate building in 1972, the investigation encompassed years of illegal activity, abuse of power, and dirty tricks by President Nixon. The second article of impeachment passed by the House Judiciary Committee in July 1974 designated illegal wiretapping as one of the reasons to remove President Nixon from office.

After Nixon resigned, Congress went on to address overarching concerns about invasions of the privacy of Americans. The FBI's secret COINTELPRO (an acronym for counterintelligence program) had conducted surveillance on domestic activists from 1956 to the early 1970s. The program's stated mission was "protecting national security, preventing violence, and maintaining the existing social and political order." This involved extensive illegal government surveillance, especially of people in the civil rights and antiwar movements, reported a committee chaired by Senator Frank Church of Idaho that conducted comprehensive hearings and completed a multiyear study in 1976.[8]

Following on the heels of Watergate and the Church Report, Congress passed the Foreign Intelligence Surveillance Act of 1978 (FISA) to strike a balance between the need for foreign intelligence and the right to privacy of Americans.

Foreign intelligence surveillance differs somewhat from standard police surveillance. Foreign intelligence surveillance is aimed at a broad goal: collecting information to protect America against foreign governments, agents, international terrorists, or associated parties. FISA did not affect the collection of foreign intelligence in other countries. When foreign surveillance is conducted in the United States, however, it provided some safeguards to make sure that the rights of Americans were protected from unwarranted wiretapping of their communications. If a U.S. citizen or resident were to be subjected to electronic surveillance in the course of foreign intelligence or counterintelligence work in the United States, the government needed to apply for a FISA warrant.

The FISA law set up a special court to approve wiretapping warrants. To get a warrant, the government needed to provide much less information than in a typical law-and-order case. It needed to show only that the surveillance would serve an intelligence or counterintelligence purpose. If the target was a U.S. citizen or resident, the government had to state a national defense need and probable cause to believe that espionage or criminal activities were involved. "This process can be very speedy," noted Majors Louis A. Chiarella and Michael A. Newton, authors of a "how-to" article in *Army Lawyer* in October 1997.[9]

The special FISA court met in private sessions and their proceedings were confidential to protect sensitive intelligence data; the Chief Justice of the Supreme Court selected its judges from the federal bench. Congress believed that the act of requiring a warrant application and the approval of the court would keep rogue presidential or other executive-branch spying in check. The FISA law ensured that a president could not simply order up wiretapping of Americans under the pretext of foreign surveillance. The FISA law specifically stated that it was to be the "exclusive" means for conducting foreign intelligence surveillance in the United States.

Upon signing it, President Carter said, "It will assure FBI field agents and others involved in intelligence collection that their acts are authorized by statute and, if a U.S. person's communications are concerned, by a court order."[10]

The FISA law permitted retroactive applications in emergency situations—surveillance could begin and the application need not be made for twenty-four hours (adjusted to seventy-two hours in 2002 when the law was amended). The FISA law specifically addressed wartime conditions, permitting the requirement for court approval to be suspended for fifteen days after a declaration of war. But, in adding this wartime exception, the law made it clear that war did not suspend the law in any other way. The legislative history shows that Congress actively rejected the idea that the president held any "inherent authority" to authorize wiretaps in the United States: in times of peace or war, court approval for foreign intelligence surveillance was required.

Violations of the FISA law carry a penalty of up to five years in prison and a fine of $10,000 for each incident. Use of information obtained in violation of the law is a crime, too, if the user has reason to know that the information was obtained by electronic surveillance "not authorized by statute."

In order to address national security needs, all of the records are sealed and the target may never know about the surveillance. A yearly report tells how many warrants were issued. FISA warrant applications were almost never rejected—in the year prior to President Bush's first year in office, FISA records listed 1,005 warrant applications; all were granted. All of the 13,095 surveillance applications in the time period from 1979 (when the court started) until President Bush took office were granted, although apparently in one case, the government was asked to amend its warrant application, and a handful of others were approved with modifications, according to the Federation of American Scientists, which tracks and maintains a list of FISA reports.[11] Some privacy advocates argued that the FISA court was nothing but a rubber stamp for government surveillance and objected to it on civil libertarian grounds.

The original FISA law was updated multiple times. Updates incorporating new technologies, such as trap/pen registers that record telephone numbers like caller ID boxes, or additional categories of searches (such as physical searches of property), occurred in 1994, 1998, 1999, 2000, and thereafter.[12] The original FISA law became the "gold standard of legality" in counterintelligence, wrote the authors of a 1996 book, *Main Justice*.[13]

In any case, FISA worked fairly smoothly for twenty-three years, from 1978, when it was first enacted, through the tenures of Presidents Jimmy Carter, Ronald Reagan, George H. W. Bush, and Bill Clinton, and through a series of international conflicts and wars, including the first Gulf War waged by the first President Bush.

Since President Nixon's time, some hard-liners inside the government had been rankled by limitations on executive power—and that included the FISA law. "Cheney in particular had been chafing at the post-Watergate reforms, and had longed to restore the executive branch powers Nixon had assumed," commented investigative journalist and author Jane Mayer in an interview with Scott Horton in *Harper's Magazine*.[14] After 9/11, President Bush decided to break the FISA law—more than three dozen times.

While breaking the law serially, President Bush and his team lied about these actions. In a speech in Buffalo, New York, on April 20, 2004, two and a half years after the secret warrantless surveillance began, President Bush said: "Anytime you hear the United States government talking about wiretap, it requires—a wiretap requires a court order. Nothing has changed, by the way. When we're talking about chasing down terrorists, we're talking about a court order before we do so."[15] This statement was false: it was not what President Bush was doing.

In January 2005, Alberto Gonzales, the president's White House counsel, was asked in congressional hearings whether the Bush administration would ever consider warrantless wiretapping of U.S. citizens. The situation was "hypothetical," he told Congress, even though it had been going on for real and not hypothetically for four years. As recounted by *Washington Post* writers Dan Eggan and Amy Goldstein, after the questioner, Senator Russ Feingold, persisted, Gonzales added: "It is not the policy or the agenda of this president to authorize actions that would be in contravention of our criminal statutes."[16] Both of his statements were false.

The president ordered the National Security Agency to wiretap solely on his say-so. He did this forty-three times. Each time, he violated the FISA law, since FISA was the exclusive means by which the federal government could engage in foreign intelligence surveillance during times of war or peace—and FISA required a court order.

A review by the inspectors general of the top intelligence agencies, published as the *Unclassified Report on the President's Surveillance Program, 10 July 2009*, gives the most complete picture of the Bush surveillance programs, although many aspects are still hidden. A top-level official inside an agency, an inspector general investigates or audits internal activities and procedures; the five involved in preparing this surveillance report were from the Department of Defense, the Central Intelligence Agency, the National Security Agency, the Office of the Director of National Intelligence, and the Department of Justice, which also included analysis from the FBI. According to their combined report, "the President authorized the NSA [National Security Agency] to undertake a number of new, highly classified intelligence activities. All of these activities were authorized in a single Presidential Authorization that was periodically reauthorized." One program was called the Terrorist Surveillance Program; another, simply dubbed "Other Surveillance Program" in government reports, has been kept completely under wraps. Combined, these programs are called the President's Surveillance Program.[17]

These authorizations began in 2001—Vice President Cheney pinned the date at October 4, 2001, in a letter to Senator Arlen Specter, chair of the Judiciary Committee, on June 8, 2006.[18] President Bush reauthorized the illegal programs roughly every forty-five days. The president personally signed the orders.

Reports indicate that the Bush warrantless surveillance involved wholesale monitoring of communications of Americans going through routers in the United States. Many of the routed calls may not have been international at all. Mark Klein, a retired AT&T technician-turned-whistleblower, reported a wholesale data-mining dragnet of all AT&T customers' calls and e-mails, local and international, according to a 2006 article by Ryan Singel in *Wired* magazine.[19]

The programs may have extended much further, to a "total information awareness" system that collected a variety of data—communications, banking, financial transactions. "The National Security Agency has been secretly collecting the phone call records of tens of millions of Americans," wrote Leslie Cauley in an exposé in *USA Today* in May 2006, in a "program [that] reaches into homes and businesses across the nation by amassing information about the calls of ordinary Americans." Billions of calls were being entered into "the largest database ever assembled in the world."[20]

Each order signed by the president was accompanied by a rote red alert that attempted to justify the need for the illegal surveillance. Added by the White House to CIA assessments, the boilerplate statement said the United States was under threat from global terrorists who "possessed the capability and intention to undertake further terrorist attacks within the United States," according to the 2009 surveillance report by the five inspectors general. The "scary" threat assessments were relied upon as a basis for continuing the program: "if a threat assessment identified a threat against the United States the PSP [President's Surveillance Program] was likely to be renewed," the report said.[21] Later, a memo by Jack Goldsmith in the Office of Legal Counsel revealed that the orders also relied upon confessions wrung from detainees;[22] since many detainees were subjected to torture or cruel treatment, their statements were highly unreliable.

While the president's team said that only the communications of those connected to terrorists were being surveilled, no evidence has been offered to show how the programs were limited. A West Coast foundation and its lawyers learned that they had been the subject of surveillance when the government accidentally sent a classified wiretapping report to one of the lawyers—and then ordered the lawyers to return it and to forget it, that is, to never repeat or refer to its contents, noted Charlie Savage and James Risen in the *New York Times* on March 31, 2010.[23]

After the existence of the President's Surveillance Program became public in December 2005, President Bush went on the radio. He admitted that he had disregarded the law. The president confessed that he had authorized the National Security Agency to intercept the international communications of Americans—and that he did not bother getting legal approval from the FISA court. "I have reauthorized this program more than 30 times since the September the 11th attacks, and I intend to do so for as long as our nation faces a continuing threat from al Qaeda and related groups," he said in the broadcast on December 17, 2005.[24]

His violations continued for another eighteen months. The last authorization of the Terrorist Surveillance Program expired on February 1, 2007, according to the inspectors general who reviewed the program later.

To prevent himself from being held accountable, the president took the unprecedented step of blocking an inquiry into the program by the Office of Professional Responsibility in the Justice Department. The president personally refused to grant requests for security clearances to conduct the investigation. "Since its creation 31 years ago . . . OPR [Office of Professional Responsibility] has never been prevented from initiating or pursuing an investigation," H. Marshall Jarrett, the Office's chief lawyer wrote in a memo quoted in a *Washington Post* article by Dan Eggan on July 19, 2006.[25]

The president's team attempted to set up legal defenses. The president and the vice president claimed that a legal memo written by a lawyer close to the White House—John Yoo—concluded that they were entitled to conduct warrantless wiretapping, although what the actual memo said was kept secret. David Addington, counsel for Vice President Cheney, had to approve every government official who was told about the program, according to an article by Scott Shane—"Cheney Is Linked to Concealment of C.I.A. Project"—in the *New York Times*: "High-level N.S.A. officials who were responsible for ensuring that the surveillance program was legal, including the agency's inspector general and general counsel, were not permitted by Mr. Cheney's office to read the Justice Department opinion that found the eavesdropping legal."[26]

In his June 2006 letter to Senator Arlen Specter, Vice President Cheney responded to the senator's inquiry about the legal basis for the surveillance programs and whether remedial legislation might be appropriate. The vice president said: "While there is no need for any legislation to carry out the Terrorist Surveillance Program, the Administration will listen to the ideas of legislators. . . . The Department of Justice has set forth in detail in writing the constitutional and statutory bases, and related judicial precedents, for warrantless electronic surveillance."[27] A copy of the claimed "constitutional and statutory bases, and related judicial precedents" was not provided.

But to protect themselves against charges of criminality, the president and vice president made a U-turn before they left office and engaged in an aggressive blitz to alter completely and undermine the existing FISA law with new legislation that could roll over it. Temporary legislation called the Protect America Act of 2007,[28] permitting vastly expanded surveillance without the need for court review or approval of a warrant, was pushed through Congress in August 2007 as legislators were hankering to leave for their summer recess.[29]

When the temporary legislation ran out in 2008, the president warned that the country faced "more danger of attack" if Congress failed to act immediately, according to a February 15, 2008 report on CNN, and he pressed for the passage of another new law.[30] An editorial in the *New York Times* urged Congress to stand up to the White House demands: "The real reason this bill exists is because Mr. Bush decided after 9/11 that he was above the law," the editors wrote on July 8, 2008.[31] But Congress did not stand up.

The FISA Amendments Act of 2008 (FAA) passed, and was signed on July 10, 2008.[32] This new law destroyed much of the original architecture of the FISA law. Under the new law, the attorney general authorized foreign intelligence warrants with the stroke of a pen—much like the system in place under President Nixon. The definitions of who could be surveilled under these foreign intelligence surveillance programs expanded enormously, and the role of the FISA court was hollowed out, mostly to reviewing biannually the procedures used by the attorney general, or to approving the increasingly rare cases in which a warrant was needed.

At the time it was being considered, public discussion about the new FISA Amendments Act of 2008 largely focused on telecom companies and a provision giving immunity to corporations that cooperated in wiretapping American customers under the illegal program. Petitions flew across the Internet in opposition. This provision was passed, as well. What was largely overlooked, however, is how the clause would help the president and his team escape liability from prosecution for illegal activities. Shutting down civil litigation against telecoms offered a handy way to hide details of presidential actions that broke the law. If the cases had continued, discovery and evidence collection might have shown the extent of illegality emerging from the White House.

The president had another motive in getting a new law passed. The new FISA Amendments Act of 2008 allowed many of the surveillance practices that Bush had illegally authorized in the past, possibly leading the president to believe that he wouldn't be prosecuted for crimes that had been abolished. At the very least, the "decriminalization" would confuse prosecutors. But it's clear that the law wasn't in effect earlier, and Bush had broken the law that was in effect. In addition, analysis by the Electronic Frontier Foundation in *Beyond FISA* indicates that many of the illegal activities Bush undertook would still not be legal under the new law.[33] Finally, it seems that even the new law was violated by the Bush administration in its remaining months in office. In an article in the *New York Times* on April 15, 2009, by reporters Lichtblau and Risen, a Justice Department spokesperson confirmed that "concerns" had been detected with the National Security Agency's compliance with the 2008 FISA Amendments Act. The *Times* reported: "Several intelligence officials, as well as lawyers briefed about the matter, said the N.S.A. had been engaged in 'overcollection' of domestic communications of Americans" in the months following the enactment of the 2008 FAA, practices that were "significant and systemic."[34]

President Bush's flagrant refusal to follow the surveillance law could have been grounds for impeachment. Although he was not impeached for this activity, he still can be prosecuted for it. The president of the United States is sworn to enforce the law, not violate it. Because his criminal activities in illegal warrantless wiretapping were so damaging to the fabric of the nation, he should be held accountable under the criminal provisions of the FISA law.

Even as he defiantly admitted that he violated the law, President Bush came up with a revolving series of justifications, each weak in itself, and no stronger when strung together. In these defenses, the president and Vice President Cheney variously claimed that it was within the job of the president to conduct warrantless wiretapping, that a lawyer had approved it, and that the surveillance worked to protect the United States from another 9/11-type attack (although there is no evidence that it ever did). Anyhow, their defenders say, the law was changed, making much of what was labeled as illegal fall within the new designation of what is legal . . . so no need to create a fuss about it.

Other defenses and justifications for these blatant repeated violations of the law have been put forward as well. The question is: do any of these possible defenses exonerate the president and others in the administration from accountability under the law? An item-by-item review of the president's central justifications and defenses finds him standing on a wafer-thin plank.

Defense #1 against Prosecution for Violation of the FISA Laws: 9/11 Makes It Okay to Break the Law

The president, defending his violations of the law, said that he needed to act without following the law because of 9/11. As part of this claim, the president insisted that the surveillance actions that he authorized improperly—had they been undertaken before 9/11—could have prevented the attacks.

In a radio address on December 17, 2005, President Bush said: "Two of the terrorist hijackers who flew a jet in [sic] the Pentagon, Nawaf Alhazmi and Khalid al-Midhar, communicated while they were in the United States, to other members of Al Qaeda who were overseas. But we didn't know they were here until it was too late. . . . The [surveillance] activities I have authorized make it more likely that killers like these 9/11 hijackers will be identified and located in time."[35]

But this claim—not a defense to the violation of the law in any case—is simply not supported by the facts. Intelligence operations had successfully gathered significant information about the 9/11 events in advance of the attacks under the framework of the existing FISA law. The president had been warned weeks in advance.

Five weeks before the attack, the president was given a daily security briefing known as a PDB (President's Daily Brief) by intelligence agencies. It was titled: "Bin Laden Determined to Strike in US." The document, delivered to the president and described in person to him while he vacationed in Crawford, Texas, followed a summer of intense activity by al Qaeda to which the CIA was listening with growing alarm, noted David E. Sanger in the *New York Times* on May 16, 2002.[36] The PDB mentioned the hijacking of planes among the al Qaeda plans. According to investigative journalist Ron Suskind, in his book *The One Percent Doctrine*, the president, after listening to the briefing about the al Qaeda threat and being handed the PDB, told the CIA briefers, "You've covered your ass, now," and he then went fishing for the rest of the day. The fact of the August 6, 2001, PDB was not even acknowledged by the White House for nine months.[37]

The 9/11 Commission Report noted that the White House took no further action on the briefing information. The report also states that President Bush actually had forty face-to-face warnings about al Qaeda's striking in the United States prior to 9/11—an average of one every six days, although they were delivered with unprecedented intensity in the summer of 2001.[38] Yet, the president did not mobilize top-level officials or convene the cabinet even once. Neither did his national security advisor, Condoleezza Rice, or others in the White House. So unconcerned were top-level officials about a terrorist attack that Attorney General John Ashcroft tried to slice $500 million out of the counterterrorism budget shortly after taking office in January 2001, according to analysis by the Center for American Progress,[39] and only two days before 9/11, Secretary of Defense Donald Rumsfeld tried to shift hundreds of millions of dollars out of counterterrorism to a pet ballistic missile defense project, wrote *Newsweek* reporter Michael Hirsh on May 27, 2002, in "What Went Wrong."[40] Yet despite a distinct lethargy inside the Bush administration regarding the al Qaeda threat, President Bush tried to blame both his inaction and his later violations of FISA law on some mythical obstacle in surveillance that held him back. There was no such thing.

If the president had in any way deemed that more surveillance information was needed following the August 6, 2001, briefing in which the CIA tried urgently to get his attention, the FISA process was readily available. Had the president determined after 9/11 that more intelligence gathering was needed to prevent further attacks, he could have used the FISA process then, too, and if emergent needs took precedence, could have sought retroactive approval under it. And if the president had found the FISA law insufficient, he could have gone to Congress to ask for changes. Instead, he chose to violate the law. His attempted use of 9/11 to justify his later violations of the law is without foundation, and certainly is no defense against prosecution.

Defense #2: An Authorization to Go to War
Clears the Way to Override Any Law

After the existence of the Terrorist Surveillance Program became known to the American public—four years after the president began the illegal program—President Bush insisted in his radio address on December 17, 2005, that he was permitted to violate the FISA law on surveillance because Congress had authorized him to deploy the armed forces to fight against terrorism. The president said: "I'm using authority vested in me by Congress, including the joint authorization for use of military force, which passed overwhelmingly in the first week after Sept. 11."[41]

This claim, made repeatedly by the Bush administration, is an empty shell. It was specifically mandated that the FISA law applied in peacetime and wartime, and the law provided a sensible exception for a fifteen-day period after Congress declared war. President Bush, however, chose to ignore this provision of the law.

The "Authorization for Use of Military Force" (AUMF), passed right after 9/11 and before the war in Afghanistan, states: "The President is authorized to use all necessary and appropriate force against those nations, organizations, or persons he determines planned, authorized, committed, or aided the terrorist attacks that occurred on September 11, 2001, or harbored such organizations or persons, in order to prevent any future acts of international terrorism against the United States by such nations, organizations or persons."[42]

Nothing in the military authorization mentions overriding the FISA law, and—especially without a specific statement to that effect —a law cannot simply be steamrolled over. Members of Congress did not believe that they were overriding FISA. Even Senator Lindsey Graham, a conservative Republican, said that when he voted for the AUMF, "I never envisioned that I was giving to this president or any other president the ability to go around FISA carte blanche."[43] Senator Tom Daschle, Democratic majority leader, wrote an opinion piece in the *Washington Post* explaining that before passage of the AUMF, the White House had tried to insert additional language that would extend its authority to activities in the United States—possibly including wiretapping. The clause was flatly rejected, Daschle noted.[44] The AUMF did not invite the president to break laws of any sort.

Barton Gellman and Jo Becker, in an article in the *Washington Post* about Vice President Cheney, wrote that the AUMF was drawn up instantly after 9/11 inside the White House with further plans in mind. "In fact, [they] knew very well what would come next: the interception—without a warrant—of communications to and from the United States. Forbidden by federal law since 1978, the surveillance would soon be justified, in secret, as 'incident to' the authority Congress had just granted. . . . It was an extraordinary step, bypassing Congress and the courts, and its authors kept it secret from officials who were likely to object."[45]

Judge Ronald Gilman of the Sixth Circuit U.S. Court of Appeals later addressed the claim that the AUMF overrode the FISA law in the appeal of a civil lawsuit brought by the American Civil Liberties Union that challenged the president's surveillance programs. In a carefully reasoned opinion, Judge Gilman wrote that the Bush argument flies in the face of well-established rules of statutory interpretation. He noted that FISA carries a very specific provision about how the law is to apply in the event of a declaration of war, and that specificity would be given preference over the general one-paragraph language of the military authorization.[46]

The claim that the military authorization permitted the president to violate the FISA law has no validity. It cannot form the basis for a defense of his unlawful actions.

Defense #3: Anyhow, Some Members of Congress
Were Briefed on the Program

President Bush sought to justify his actions by arguing that some members of Congress knew about what he was doing. He claims that the administration told about eight of the 535 senators and representatives. In his December 17, 2005, address, the president put it this way: "Leaders in Congress have been briefed more than a dozen times on this authorization and the activities conducted under it."

What the president did not say is that these leaders were briefed under a raft of restrictions: they could not bring aides, could not take notes, and could not discuss the program even with their own staffs, according to Douglas Jehl of the *New York Times* in a December 21, 2005, article, "Spy Briefings Failed to Meet Legal Test, Lawmakers Say."[47] This made it impossible to address the concerns that arose.

Nor were the leaders told the truth about the program, according to at least two members of the group. House Intelligence Committee ranking member Jane Harman told Fox News Sunday on January 6, 2006, that the White House never disclosed that it was ignoring FISA to conduct wiretapping on Americans without warrants.[48] Senator Bob Graham, Chair of the Senate Intelligence Committee, agreed. He told ABC's *Nightline* that White House briefings had skipped over the fact that it was conducting surveillance without following the court procedures: "The assumption was that if we did that, we would do it pursuant to the law, the law that regulates the surveillance of national security issues," said Graham. "There was no reference made to the fact that we were going to use that as the subterfuge to begin unwarranted, illegal—and I think unconstitutional—eavesdropping on American citizens."[49] Senator Jay D. Rockefeller and House Minority Leader Nancy Pelosi told *Times* reporter Jehl that they had expressed reservations about the Bush program, and Rockefeller produced a copy of a handwritten note he had sent to Vice President Cheney on July 17, 2003, describing his concerns about the wiretapping program after being briefed on it.

Even if they had been fully briefed, eight or ten or fourteen members of Congress cannot ratify the president's illegal acts, and they cannot amend the law. The law stands on its own, impervious to the will of a single individual or a tiny group of elite persons summoned to a meeting by the White House. As then Senator Arlen Specter of Pennsylvania emphasized, "You can't have the administration or a select number of members alter the law."

In addition, the president had a legal obligation under the National Security Act to keep all of the members of the House and Senate Intelligence Committees fully informed of White House intelligence activities—this he did not do. The reporting provision—the reports were to be in writing—was passed "as part of an effort to compel the executive branch to provide more specificity and clarity," wrote the *Times*.[50]

The meetings with congressional leaders—held under rigid controls—were a clear tactic used by the president and vice president to justify their actions and set up a defense against prosecution. Vice President Cheney continued to insist that their illegal actions were legal because some members of Congress had been told about it. Just weeks before he left office on December 21, 2008, Cheney told Fox News, "We briefed them on the program and what we'd achieved and how it worked, and asked them, 'Should we continue the program?' They were unanimous, Republican and Democrat alike. All agreed—absolutely essential to continue the program."[51]

Immediate and direct retorts came from pundits and bloggers. *ThinkProgress* quoted earlier remarks by Senator Rockefeller, who said: "The record needs to be set clear that the Administration never afforded members briefed on the program an opportunity to either approve or disapprove the NSA program."[52]

This flimsy defense, attempting to use a small group of congressional members as a human shield for illegality, also fails to protect the president from liability for his acts in breaking the law. If anything, it shows more convincingly that the president and vice president knowingly intended to violate the law and bamboozle Congress in the process.

Defense #4: A Lawyer Said It's Okay, So It's Okay

If a lawyer tells someone it's okay to commit a crime, may a defendant rely upon that as a defense against prosecution? The answer, it would seem, without hesitation, is no. Yet, "defense of counsel" is a subject that frequently arises with reference to President Bush's actions both on surveillance and torture (I'll say more about that in the next chapter).

But is it valid? Actually, in some cases, it may be. The good-faith reliance upon the independent judgment of a lawyer, known as a "mistake of law," is sometimes recognized as a defense in criminal prosecution—mostly in tax cases. For example, when the crime requires that the defendants know that their actions violate the law, they are permitted to present evidence that they relied, in good faith, on the independent advice of counsel, and the jury can consider that defense. The mere involvement of a lawyer is not enough—the keys are "good faith" and "independent advice" and "reliance." This defense is impermissible, as the federal Court of Appeals for the Ninth Circuit wrote in *U.S. v. Shewfelt*, when defendants retain counsel "to insure the success of their mendacious scheme, not to secure legal advice."[53] If the lawyer is merely hired to "bless" a preexisting scheme, there is no good-faith reliance on counsel's advice.

In the case of the illegal warrantless wiretapping programs, President Bush and his team engineered a wholly cynical scheme to insulate themselves from prosecution. What emerges is a picture of the White House "gaming" the system—rigging the procedures to secure a fake justification for what it wanted to do, and then turning around and waving this justification to deflect criticism. The legal opinion was not sought or given in "good faith" and it was not "independent advice." It was not even given before President Bush started the wiretapping program. According to the surveillance program report by the five inspectors general in 2009, "The first OLC [Office of Legal Counsel] opinion explicitly addressing the legality of the PSP [President's Surveillance Program] was not drafted until after the program had been formally authorized by President Bush in October 2001." By definition, then, the president did not act "in reliance" on the legal opinion, which came after his decision point.[54]

This scheme to manufacture a legal opinion had several steps: (a) the president and vice president sought an opinion not before, but after they initiated the illegal wiretapping programs; (b) they arranged for an opinion from a lawyer who they knew would deliver what they wanted; (c) in order to assure that the lawyer's work would not be subjected to unwelcome questioning or outside scrutiny, they created an unprecedented workflow, blocking out standard levels of comment, review, and revision; (d) upon receipt of an opinion that served their needs—though laden with shockingly erroneous legal and factual assertions—they stamped it secret and refused to allow it to be made public or even shown to others who were supposed to rely on it as a policy guide.

To engineer the legal opinion that the president wanted on wiretapping, the task was assigned to John Yoo, the conservative deputy assistant attorney general in the Office of Legal Counsel who also authored memos sanctioning torture. Yoo "became the White House's guy," said Jay Bybee, who came into the Office of Legal Counsel as Yoo's boss.[55]

The memo on the illegal surveillance program written by Yoo was so poor and so full of factual, legal, historical, and intellectual inaccuracies that it was later withdrawn when he left the office and others in the Justice Department's Office of Legal Counsel finally saw it. There were several improprieties. The process was manipulated from the start. In the Office of Legal Counsel the writing of opinions for the creation of an entirely new government policy—to say nothing of attempting to override important laws already in place—usually involves several lawyers who write, read drafts, and engage in rigorous peer review. In this case, Yoo—a trusty Federalist Society lawyer who had served as a clerk to U.S. Supreme Court Justice Clarence Thomas and apparently became known in legal circles for his advocacy of the radically expansive executive authority desired by the White House—was singled out. In a highly unusual process, he alone was given the assignment and he alone handled it.[56]

The Bush administration controlled this situation by refusing to give other lawyers access to the details of the program. Access was known as being "read in" to the program. The president himself made all of the decisions about who would be "read in" to the program, said Alberto Gonzales, counsel to the president. With "all decisions . . . of who has access to the program, the President of the United States makes the decisions, because this is such an important program," Gonzales told the Senate Judiciary Committee on July 18, 2006, reported Neil Lewis of the *New York Times*.[57] Yoo was the only person in his division to be "read in" to the program. Not even Yoo's boss—Bybee—was "read in." As a result, there was no one— no colleagues, no supervisor, no one with the ability to read, analyze, and comment—to engage in peer review. Attorney General Ashcroft was "read in" to the program on the same day he was asked to sign off on it, and Ashcroft's request to consult on the complex legal and constitutional issues with his deputy attorney general was flatly rejected. (The single other lawyer "read in" to the program was the counsel for intelligence policy, James Baker, presumably because he was responsible for interacting with the FISA court on all other FISA matters.) No interest existed in having thoughtful input. Consequently, the president was able to ensure that no other lawyer could interfere with or contradict Yoo's memo.

Yoo's opinion justifying the surveillance program has never been fully released publicly. Even a redacted version released in March 2011 after a lawsuit by the ACLU blacked out all but a handful of words.[58] But commentary on his memo is included in the 2009 surveillance report of the inspectors general. In brief, the commentators were appalled. They found Yoo misstated the facts about the programs, misstated the language of the FISA law, and overlooked the universally recognized major case precedent on executive power—*Youngstown Sheet & Tube Co. v. Sawyer*, decided by the U.S. Supreme Court in 1952.[59] This type of memo by Yoo—a lawyer who attended Harvard University and Yale Law School, a constitutional law professor, and a supposed expert on executive authority—suggests that he was not giving his best independent legal opinion. The Department of Justice officials who later saw the memo declared that it had "serious factual and legal flaws," and refused to accept it.[60]

Yoo cobbled together a series of fake and falsified positions. For example, Yoo wrote that the FISA law did not make a clear statement "that it sought to restrict presidential authority to conduct warrantless searches in the national security area"—when nothing could be further from the truth. Foreign intelligence, by definition, is a matter of national security, and that's what the FISA law is all about. The law was written explicitly to restrict presidential authority and directly addresses it; the legislative history states that the FISA law is intended to restrict presidential authority "in the national security area." An opinion by Steven Bradbury, who came into the Office of Legal Counsel after Yoo left, noted that Yoo's proposition "is problematic and questionable given FISA's express references to the President's authority," and that it is "not supported by convincing reasoning."[61] I later describe other outlandish and untrue claims by Yoo in the wiretapping memo.

But Yoo discussed the still-secret "Other Surveillance Program" only briefly—the memo focused mostly on the separate Terrorist Surveillance Program, the outlines of which became publicly known with the *New York Times* exposé in December 2005. What Yoo did say about the "Other Surveillance Program" was patently wrong, factually and legally. The 2009 surveillance report said that Yoo "did not accurately describe the scope of these activities" and found his analysis "insufficient." As a consequence, there was a "serious impediment" to certifying the "Other Surveillance Program." In fact, those who finally saw the memo when Yoo departed the

Justice Department in 2003 recognized its extreme inadequacies, resulting in a high-stakes showdown with the White House. Acting attorney general James Comey refused to continue signing off on the president's wiretapping in March 2004, and FBI director Robert Mueller followed suit, threatening to quit if Comey were not heeded. The White House rushed Alberto Gonzales to the hospital bedside of the ailing Attorney General Ashcroft on March 11, 2004, to get his consent. Ashcroft refused to discuss it. Something was seriously amiss.

Clearly, a president who was concerned with doing the right thing and not merely having puppet permission to engage in illegal activities would have asked the best lawyers in the government—a bevy of lawyers—to analyze and review his plans, and to do so before he set them in motion. President Bush did none of this. He started his program and then manufactured a situation so that a single, demonstrably sympathetic lawyer would ratify it outside the normal channels of review. This isn't a good-faith reliance on legal advice, and President Bush is not entitled to rely upon the "defense of counsel" argument to protect him from accountability for his illegal actions.

Defense #5: It Worked, So Why Insist on Legalities?

President Bush and Vice President Cheney have repeatedly justified these rogue surveillance operations by saying that, well, so what, the steps they took worked. The president's illegal authorizations of surveillance produced important information that has prevented attacks, they say. In his December 17, 2005, radio address justifying the illegal orders, the president put it this way: "The activities conducted under this authorization have helped detect and prevent possible terrorist attacks in the United States and abroad."[62]

As he was leaving office, Vice President Cheney continued to make this argument. In an interview with ABC News in December 2008, Cheney said: "On the question of terrorist surveillance . . . It's worked. It's been successful."[63]

But this was at some variance from the conclusions of the inspectors general of the nation's major intelligence agencies, which were decidedly more circumspect and ambivalent about the success of the program. They found that the secrecy of the president's illegal surveillance program inhibited its effectiveness, that the information could have been collected in other ways, and that the intelligence was without context, which limited its usefulness for analysts.

For example, the inspector general for the CIA concluded that it was "difficult to attribute the success of [any] particular counter terrorism case exclusively to the PSP [President's Surveillance Program]." Because much of the information collected under the program was vague—apparently because it was sweeping in vast amounts of intercepted calls, e-mails, and data, or the communications were never translated—CIA personnel relied upon other information. The secrecy of the program hindered its effectiveness—there was little legal guidance, and working on-the-ground personnel were not "read in" to the President's Surveillance Program, preventing effective use. The CIA inspector general was "unable to independently draw any conclusion on the overall effectiveness of the program to the CIA."

The inspector general of the Justice Department "found it difficult to assess or quantify the overall effectiveness of the [program] as it related to the FBI's counterterrorism activities." FBI agents were "frustrated" because the sources of information were not provided and many "PSP leads were determined not to have any connection to terrorism." The inspector general said that the illegal surveillance program was only "one tool of many." The program also created problems for agents because of its "exceptionally compartmented nature." The president's programs "played a limited role in the FBI's overall counterterrorism efforts," the Department of Justice inspector general concluded. Similarly, the director of national intelligence viewed the program as "not of greater value than other sources of information."[64]

The intelligence community professionals interviewed about the President's Surveillance Program "had difficulty citing specific instances where PSP reporting had directly contributed to counterterrorism successes."[65] The president and vice president faked the value of the illegal surveillance, just as they inflated its underpinnings with hyped threat assessments.[66]

Despite the puffery and claims of President Bush, the information collected through illegal surveillance was not "crucial," as the vice president proclaimed. The president's illegal surveillance program appears to have provided little useful assistance to U.S. counterterrorism efforts. "It is now clear that many of [the surveillance programs] could have been conducted just as easily within the law—perhaps more effectively and certainly with far less damage to the justice system," wrote the *New York Times* in an editorial, "Illegal, and Pointless," on July 16, 2009.[67]

The claim that "it worked" would not justify the president's lawlessness, but there is scant evidence that it did work in providing uniquely useful information that prevented attacks on the United States. This attempt to divert attention from the president's illegal activity falls flat.

Defense #6: The President Is the Commander in Chief
So He Can Command Whatever He Wants

Another assertion made by the Bush camp holds that the president, in his role as commander in chief of the military, can take whatever actions he wants in order to support a war effort. To defend his illegal electronic wiretapping to the American public, President Bush said in his December 17, 2005, radio address, "I'm . . . using constitutional authority vested in me as commander in chief."[68] This notion is entirely wrongheaded. A preeminent decision of the U.S. Supreme Court, the *Youngstown Sheet & Tube Co. v. Sawyer*—I referred to it earlier—made this utterly clear and did so forty-nine years before President Bush tried to muster this claim. Commander-in-chief powers do not give the president extrajudicial authority. The U.S. Supreme Court ruled in 1952 in *Youngstown*, often called "the Steel Seizure Case," that President Harry Truman could not issue an order seizing steel mills to prevent a strike, even though the cessation of steel production would interfere with making guns, tanks, planes, and other military products needed for the Korean War effort then under way. The respected justice Robert Jackson wrote that the president is commander in chief of the army and navy, not "Commander in Chief of the country, its industries and its inhabitants." Seizing the mills, even during wartime, was beyond presidential powers. The justice added: "No penance would ever expiate the sin against free government of holding that a President can escape control of executive powers by law through assuming his military role."[69] Yet this is exactly the Houdini-style escape of control—and accountability—that President Bush tried to pull off.

In Yoo's legal opinion on wiretapping, the precedent of the Steel Seizure Case was not addressed at all, as I mentioned earlier. Is it possible that Yoo missed this all-important case? Or did he deliberately leave it out because he was told to do so by the White House? Other lawyers were certainly alarmed when they read Yoo's opinion after he left his position in

2003. As well they should have been: a legal opinion that fails to cite the main case on the subject is not worth the paper it is written on—none of its conclusions can be trusted.

Judges who ruled on the president's wiretapping program in civil court challenges reinforced the centrality of the Steel Seizure Case that Yoo overlooked. In August 2006, Judge Anna Diggs Taylor, a federal district court judge in Detroit, directly applied the Steel Seizure analysis to the warrantless electronic surveillance authorized by President Bush in a case brought by the ACLU.[70] She noted, as Justice Jackson had, that the president is only commander in chief of the military—not of all the people.[71]

The same argument, claiming that Congress cannot restrain the president's commander-in-chief powers, was made with respect to the treatment of detainees. But the Supreme Court rejected this, too. In 2004, in *Hamdan v. Rumsfeld*, the U.S. Supreme Court said a president "may not disregard limitations that Congress has, in proper exercise of its own war powers, placed on his powers."[72] The president cannot claim that he is protected from prosecution for his illegal acts in violating the FISA law because he is the commander in chief of the military. Even to think of permitting that broadened interpretation of his powers as a defense insults and endangers our democracy.

Defense #7: If the President Does It, It's Okay

Call this the Nixon defense. "If the president does it, that means it's not illegal," former president Richard Nixon told interviewer David Frost in 1977.[73] The TV moment was even re-created in an entertaining show on Broadway thirty years later, in part because it is so obviously outrageous.

Similarly, President Bush claimed that he was "the decider." His defenders echo Nixon, saying whatever the president does is legal. They crown him with a kind of "inherent authority" to break the FISA law. Yoo said that a reading of FISA that placed limits on the president's behavior "would be an unconstitutional infringement on the President's Article II authorities," referring to that part of the U.S. Constitution that outlines the powers of the president. Additionally, Yoo wrote in his memo attempting to justify surveillance, "we do not believe that Congress may restrict the president's inherent constitutional powers, which allow him to gather intelligence necessary to defend the nation from direct attack," according to the 2009 surveillance report.[74]

But that is exactly what Congress can do and intended to do. The FISA law was designed to limit how the president and other government officials could gather intelligence, even in time of war. FISA "puts to rest the notion that Congress recognizes an inherent Presidential power to conduct surveillance outside the procedures contained in Chapters 119 and 120 [referring to the FISA law]," according to a 1978 Senate Judiciary Committee report cited by the Congressional Research Service.[75] And to make it abundantly clear, FISA explicitly repealed language in a prior federal statute that recognized the president's right to protect the nation in wartime. The repealed language said: "Nothing in this chapter shall limit the constitutional power of the president to take such measures as he deems necessary to protect the nation against actual or potential attack, or to protect national security against foreign intelligence activities." Repealing that provision was done with a purpose: it "eliminat[ed] any congressional recognition or suggestion of inherent Presidential power with respect to electronic surveillance," said the 1978 Senate Judiciary Committee report.

Vice President Cheney, known for his expansive views of executive authority, forcefully claimed in an exit interview with ABC News on December 18, 2008, that the president's spying program was legal. "It's legal. It was legal from the very beginning. It is constitutional. To claim that it isn't, I think is just wrong," he said.[76] But he gave no legal support for this bald statement.

When the government tried to assert that wiretapping Americans was within the constitutional prerogative of the president in a civil case, it was soundly rejected. Federal judge Taylor in the Eastern District of Michigan said in 2006 that the government could not claim that the president had inherent power "to violate not only the laws of Congress, but the First and Fourth Amendments of the Constitution itself."[77]

Unlike a monarch, the president has no inherent authority to make up the law or violate the law or ignore the law. If the president believes the law is wrong, he can go to Congress and seek an adjustment, something President Bush was very good at doing. By his oath of office, the president is sworn to "uphold the law." The president cannot claim that he is outside the law, above the law, or gets his law from some other authority. The defense that the president can violate the law because he is, after all, the president, is utterly invalid and undermines the very Constitution upon which the nation is founded.

Defense #8: The Program Was Changed Later, So Congress Ratified the President's Actions Retrospectively

After the disclosures of the Bush warrantless wiretapping program in 2005, President Bush at first admitted in a grandiose speech that he had ignored the law, and then insisted that it was his right to do so. But before he left office, the president was singing a different tune, and he pressured Congress to change the law.

As described earlier, the FISA Amendments Act of 2008 (FAA), pushed through Congress by the Bush administration, changed the original FISA law radically, eliminating most of the strong protections of FISA and permitting wiretapping without a court order. Under the new law, wiretapping is approved internally in the Justice Department, which then sends a report twice a year to the FISA court. The FISA court can still review requests for warrants, but the situations in which the government must apply for a warrant are pretty meager. Some of what President Bush authorized from 2001 to 2007 in forty-three executive orders that violated the original FISA law might be legal under these new provisions. (Other Bush actions may not be legal even under the new amendments, but because information about the surveillance programs has been held in secret, a full reckoning has been impossible.)

To defend themselves from prosecution for their FISA criminal violations, President Bush, Vice President Cheney, and others are likely to claim that the law has changed, so they shouldn't be accused of violating an old law. Why should they be prosecuted when, in large part, the crimes they committed from 2001 to 2007 were decriminalized later? On a December 16, 2008, interview with ABC News, Vice President Cheney defended the surveillance program, saying, "It's now embodied in the FISA statute that we passed last year. . . . It is legal."[78]

While the new FISA Amendments Act went so far as to provide immunity from civil suits to telecoms that collaborate in wiretapping, it did not provide criminal immunity to President Bush, administration officials, or even telecoms. And to underscore this point, Congress did not change the criminal penalties for violation of FISA. The 2008 change in the law—six years after President Bush began to violate the law—does not erase the fact that President Bush broke the law that existed.

But maybe the Bush team forgot about the savings clause. When a law is changed after the violations have occurred, a provision swings into effect under the United States Code known as the "savings clause" or the "repeal of statutes as affecting existing liabilities" (1 USC § 109). Under it, the prior law is "saved" for the purposes of prosecuting wrongdoers unless the new law explicitly repeals the old law. The new FISA Amendments Act did not repeal the old FISA law. There are technical exceptions to the savings clause, but they do not save the president from prosecution.[79]

An important ruling that shines light on the president's accountability under the original FISA law was issued on March 31, 2010, in a lawsuit brought by the Al-Haramain Foundation and its lawyers,[80] who asserted that they were subjected to illegal surveillance.[81] In 2010, Judge Vaughn Walker, chief judge of the federal district court in San Francisco, noted the "purported January 2007 termination" of the president's surveillance programs, but said that, even if the program had ended, the government could be sued for damages during its period of operation.[82] The court ordered the government to pay damages for its violations of the laws on surveillance. Although this was a civil lawsuit for damages, importantly, some of the same analysis—that the actions were illegal when undertaken—applies to accountability under the criminal law.

In addition, some reports indicate that the Bush administration violated even the new FISA Amendments Act. The Electronic Frontier Foundation, a watchdog and litigation organization in California, believes that the National Security Agency continued a dragnet of domestic communications without following the simple procedures of the FISA Amendments Act.[83] An article in the *New York Times*, "Officials Say U.S. Wiretaps Exceeded Law," reported that "the N.S.A. was improperly capturing information involving significant amounts of American traffic" for many months after the FAA was passed in the summer of 2008.[84]

Because the president and vice president had repeatedly violated FISA, they were understandably concerned about protecting themselves from prosecution. President Bush and Vice President Cheney tried hard to create a legal environment in which they could not be prosecuted. They tried to cause confusion for a prosecutor and attempted to spin verbally a change in the law as amnesty for themselves. But they did not fully succeed. President Bush broke the law, hid his actions, and tried to cover up—for four years before it was publicly disclosed, and for another two years after that. Our country cannot survive as the democracy our founders envisioned if our highest elected executives can simply ignore the law or attempt to change the law to whitewash their own actions. They cannot escape prosecution for their illegal actions by claiming that the law was later changed.

Defense #9: Sorry, Even If the Law Was Broken (Forty-Three Times), It's Too Late Now

The president, vice president, the head of the NSA, their aides, and others who joined in a conspiracy to violate the FISA law may try to claim that the statute of limitations has run out, so even if they broke the law, it's too late to prosecute them.

The statute of limitations for criminal violations of FISA is five years,[85] and the statute of limitations on a conspiracy runs from the date of the last overt act in furtherance of the conspiracy.

In the conspiracy to conduct illegal wiretapping, the statute of limitations may well run until January 20, 2014, or five years after President Bush left office. That's because illegal wiretapping launched by the Bush warrantless surveillance program continued until the president left office, according to a *New York Times* article by James Risen and Eric Lichtblau on June 16, 2009.[86] Intercepts of phone calls and e-mails in late 2008 and early 2009—while President Bush was still in office—were not legal under the FISA Amendments Act of 2008, the *Times* reported. Representative Rush Holt, chair of the House Select Intelligence Oversight Panel, said that the violations were "flagrant" and couldn't be dismissed as accidental, according to Risen and Lichtblau. Two other intelligence officials confirmed the existence of a National Security Agency program that "routinely examined large volumes of Americans' email messages without court warrants" and that these programs still operated as of early 2009.[87]

The January 20, 2014, date for the expiration of the statute of limitations may apply to the president and his team for other reasons as well. The report by the inspectors general on the president's warrantless surveillance program describes, in brief, a two-year period for the "transition of authority" from unilateral presidential wiretapping authorizations to the use of the FISA court. The inspectors general were critical that the "transitioning" had not begun sooner.[88] Since the last presidential authorization for warrantless surveillance expired on February 1, 2007, portions of the illegal program may have lasted for another two years until the transition was over on February 1, 2009. Again, the five-year statute of limitations would run from the end of President Bush's term on January 20, 2009, to 2014.

There is another reason to believe that the statute of limitations did not begin to run until President Bush's term ended, or nearly so. The data-mining program, still shrouded in layers of secrecy, may have illegally continued to collect vast pools of communications records from Americans during the final two years of President Bush's term. This program may have lasted until at least September 17, 2008, according to documents filed in federal court in the Northern District of California by the Electronic Frontier Foundation as part of a civil lawsuit against President Bush and AT&T.[89] If September 17, 2008, were the very last day of the data mining violations, the statute of limitations would run until September 17, 2013.

If those dates, for some reason, do not resolve the statute of limitations question, there are other events that might mark the last overt act in the conspiracy to violate FISA. As noted, the presidential authorization of illegal surveillance is said to have expired on February 1, 2007. But, even so, some of the wiretaps permitted under that order may have kept going for a year after they were issued, which would move the statute of limitations to five years from February 1, 2008.

If all illegal operations were stopped on February 1, 2007, and there were no ongoing authorizations, no surveillance operating on previously approved authorizations, no continuation of the secret data-mining program, no further use or retention of information collected illegally under the warrantless operations, and no additional presidentially authorized warrantless surveillance, then the statute of limitations could expire, at the earliest, on February 1, 2012. Given the many reports of information collection that started under of President Bush's warrantless wiretapping activities and then carried on after the authorizations stopped, this date seems highly unlikely to hold much water.

The clock is running on this important prosecution, but the statute of limitations is not a bar to seeking criminal accountability for the president's multiple violations of the FISA law.

A special prosecutor should be named immediately to investigate the details of these activities and other crimes related to illicit surveillance. President Bush, Vice President Cheney, and others involved in the illegal surveillance of Americans should be prosecuted for their admitted violations of the law if the evidence warrants it. In addition, as I describe in chapter 4, new oversight of and protections from government surveillance should be passed by Congress to protect the privacy of Americans.

A criminal justice system that operates without accountability by the powerful is destructive of our liberties and of democracy itself. Unless strong steps are taken in response to blatant violations of law, there will be no guard against future presidents who also want to intrude unilaterally upon the lives and communications of Americans.

In the end, Americans must decide whether this is a country with a dual system of justice: one for the powerful and the other for those without power. Holding the Bush administration accountable for its FISA illegalities makes a firm statement that when the president and his team break the law, the president and his team will pay the price.

THREE

Crimes of Torture

At the Guantánamo Bay prison compound operated by the United States, Mohammed al Qahtani, a Saudi, was detained in 2002 in extreme isolation under blinding continuous light for months, while being interrogated twenty hours a day for forty-eight of fifty-four consecutive days. He was led around on all fours with a leash, threatened by an aggressive dog, exposed to life-threatening cold temperatures, and subjected to beatings, prolonged loud music, forced nudity, forced enemas, forced injections, and more, as shown in U.S. government logs published by *Time* magazine on June 12, 2005.[1]

In Syria, Maher Arar of Canada was held for a year in an underground windowless cell akin to a grave and repeatedly beaten with thick electrical cords—this after being detained on a stopover by U.S. officers at JFK Airport in New York in the fall of 2002 and then delivered to Syria for interrogation. He was released as an innocent man, mistakenly identified as a terrorist, wrote Jane Mayer in the *New Yorker* on February 14, 2005.[2]

At Bagram Air Base in Afghanistan in the second half of 2002 and early 2003, Bashir Ahmad, a Pakistani man detained by U.S. forces who admitted to fighting for the Taliban, was left tied to a chain hanging from the ceiling, sometimes by his hands, and sometimes by his feet, after which American soldiers beat him with a wooden rod, according to an investigative series appearing in McClatchy newspapers in June 16, 2008.[3]

In Poland in 2002, Abd al-Rahim al-Nashiri of Saudi Arabia was kept

naked, shackled, and hooded in a secret prison operated by the CIA. A bit-
less power drill was revved near his head, a gun cocked by his ears, his skin
scoured with a stiff brush, and his family threatened with harm, although it
was in another facility in Thailand that he was subjected to near drowning
by waterboarding. His case was described in a report by the CIA inspector
general and in subsequent news reports, including on the CBS News site
on September 21, 2010.[4]

And then there was Abu Ghraib.

Across the globe, the Bush administration operated an international
network of torture sites, a far-flung archipelago of cells and compounds
hidden from the view of the American people. In them, the administration
adopted the desperate methods of despots—the use of torture, the infliction of cruel, inhuman, and degrading treatment, in flagrant abuse of long-
held human rights principles.

Committing or authorizing torture is a crime. It is against the law in
the United States. It is against the international treaties adopted and ratified by the United States. Torture is prohibited up and down the chain
of command—it cannot be authorized, condoned, or implemented; when
reported, it must be investigated and prosecuted. Cruel, inhuman, and
degrading treatment—reprehensible actions that are not as severe as
torture—is also prohibited by international law.

In his book released in November 2010, President Bush recounted that,
when asked by the CIA about using a form of torture—waterboarding—on
one particular detainee, he replied, "Damn right."[5] Key presidential advisor Karl Rove told the BBC on March 12, 2010, that he was "proud" of the
use of waterboarding.[6] And on February 14, 2010, former vice president
Cheney told ABC's *This Week*, "I was a big supporter of waterboarding.
I was a big supporter of the enhanced interrogation techniques."[7]

The use of torture was not the action of just a few freewheeling soldiers
or CIA agents. It was a policy adopted and approved by the Bush administration at the highest levels.

Not all the details of the torture or all of the stories are known, but
what is now known is that President Bush signed a memo that wiped
away the restrictions against torture and cruel treatment of detainees. We
know that the Bush administration drafted and approved harsh interrogation techniques based on those used against American prisoners of war in
the most brutal detention situations. We know, without a doubt, that the

techniques approved by President Bush were considered torture by governments worldwide, human rights organizations, UN monitoring organizations, and even the United States, which had in years prior prosecuted others for torture based on the same acts; at a minimum, the techniques were cruel, inhuman, or degrading.

But what is less known is how the members of Bush administration attempted to immunize themselves from prosecution. In an unprecedented fashion, the president, vice president, and others in the administration used their powers to protect those who violated the law—that is, themselves.

Powerful laws against the use of torture and cruel treatment were in place when President Bush took office; by the time he was flown away from the capital at the end of his second term, the laws were hobbled and, in some cases, rendered completely useless.

I was not prepared for the pictures and stories from the Abu Ghraib prison in Afghanistan. I don't think many Americans were. Torture and cruel treatment of prisoners are associated with the Soviets, the Chinese Communists, the North Koreans, the North Vietnamese, the Nazis. A tool of the most repressive regimes, torture has been condemned throughout history.

One of my earliest memories is hearing my mother talk about Josef Mengele, the notorious Nazi doctor at Auschwitz who performed torture experiments on twins. I was a twin, and my mother, who was born near the city of Kiev in what is now Ukraine, and came to America as a teenager, must have had nightmares about what would have happened had she stayed in Europe. When she mentioned Mengele, she told my twin brother and me how lucky we were, as Jews, to have been born in America.[8]

The Mengele stories were a far-off specter—rather like a scary book that you put down, thinking it would never appear again in your life. But my awareness of torture, sadly, didn't end there. As a member of Congress, I learned about Nazi war criminals in America. One case involved Klaus Barbie, the "Butcher of Lyon," a Gestapo officer infamous for torturing French resistance fighters and sending Jewish children to Auschwitz. I worked to create a Nazi-hunting unit in the U.S. Justice Department, and in 1983 it released the details of how the United States had secretly employed Barbie after the war and then helped him resettle safely in

Argentina. This link between the United States and a torturer was ugly, to say the least.[9]

Like most Americans—and people worldwide—I recoiled at those photographs that emerged from Abu Ghraib prison in Iraq in 2004: naked men forced to assume sexual positions; dogs snarling in the faces of frightened, chained detainees; a person, hooded, forced to stand in a humiliating way, on a small box with wires attached to his body.[10] Information continued to unfurl about the memos and authorizations of torture from the highest offices in our land. I was not prepared for the lying, the scope of abuses, the lack of accountability.

Despite U.S. laws and international treaties that prohibit torture and that stand firmly against cruel, inhuman, and degrading treatment, the United States became involved in perpetuating and inflicting both. It didn't start with a handful of soldiers at the prison—a few "bad apples," as a White House spokesperson said in a containment strategy. The direction, instead, came from the White House, the Pentagon, the National Security Council, the Justice Department. Top people inside our government—a small group—unilaterally took it upon themselves to take our nation down a path of torture.

Facts continued to accrue. Highly respected journalists wrote articles and then books, reports were issued, documentation made its way to the public from some of the most credible sources in the world, such as the International Committee of the Red Cross (ICRC), which monitors the Geneva Conventions. We now know that hundreds of people held in U.S. custody during the time of the George W. Bush administration were exposed to sleep deprivation, painful stress positions, loud noise, extremes of temperature, food deprivation. A list of "approved techniques" read like a memo by Kafka. Reports indicate that prisoners were hung from the ceiling by their arms, slapped, left naked or in diapers only, shackled on concrete floors, bashed into walls. One approved "enhanced interrogation technique" forced a man to crouch in a locked box while a "nonlethal" insect was dropped in. These techniques were often used in combination, and again and again. At least three men in U.S. detention were waterboarded—one 83 times in a month, another 183 times. "Waterboarding" is a form of torture that can be traced back to the Spanish Inquisition.

More than one hundred detainees died in U.S. custody before 2005, at least one-third of them in circumstances suggesting homicide, according to autopsy reports analyzed by the ACLU.[11] Men were "rendered"—lingo for turned over for questioning—by the U.S. to other countries, where it was virtually certain that they would be tortured. In other cases, the CIA flew detainees around the world to hidden prisons that it ran in Poland, Lithuania, Romania, and Thailand (the entire list of places is still concealed), where they could be treated brutally in secret. For the first time in our country's history, a U.S. president embraced cruel, inhuman, and torturous policies of interrogation and detention.

The history of the United States shows how strongly and deeply the framers of our Constitution resisted the notion of torture. Their opposition surfaces not once, but twice in the Bill of Rights. The Fifth Amendment makes it clear that no person "shall be compelled in any criminal case to be a witness against himself." Since the main objective of torture was to obtain confession of a crime, the Fifth Amendment was designed to put a stop to that. The Eighth Amendment prohibits the infliction of "cruel and unusual punishments," which, by definition, includes torture.

There are no exceptions to these prohibitions. There is no loophole for serial murderers, awful crimes, or even war. There is no exception for the need to solve crimes, even when it might save lives. For the framers of the Constitution, there was no compromising this bedrock value. Knowing that torture annihilates human dignity, they did not abide by any ends-justifies-the-means view: torture was simply banned.

The framers understood the problems with torture. Moral revulsion aside, they knew that torture didn't ensure a truthful answer. Torture may produce information, some of which may be true, but there is no way to separate what is true from what the prisoner has made up in order to stop the torture. Because torture doesn't produce reliable information, a statement wrung out by torture can't be used as a basis for prosecution. Think about it. If torture were permitted, it would be the default approach in all cases.

Anti-torture principles are intertwined with U.S. history. In his instructions to the troops in April 1863, President Abraham Lincoln wrote: "Military necessity does not admit of cruelty—that is, the infliction of suffering for the sake of suffering or for revenge, nor of maiming or wounding except in fight, nor of torture to extort confessions."[12]

After World War II, new humanitarian measures around the world and in the United States bolstered the prohibition against torture. In 1948, the

Universal Declaration of Human Rights was adopted by the new United Nations. The United States voted in favor. Article 5 states: "No one shall be subjected to torture or to cruel, inhuman or degrading treatment or punishment."[13]

Two international treaties ratified by the United States prohibited the mistreatment and torture of U.S. detainees: One was the Geneva Conventions;[14] the other was the Convention Against Torture.[15] Two federal laws correspond with these international treaties and make torture or the mistreatment of detainees a crime: the War Crimes Act of 1996[16] and the "anti-torture law" (18 USC §§ 2340–2340A) passed in 1994.[17] There are also prohibitions against conspiracies to commit any of these crimes.

In case any doubt existed about the U.S. perspective on torture, the *Army Field Manual for Intelligence Interrogations* made it clear to interrogators that they were prohibited from "the use of force, mental torture, threats, insults, or exposure to unpleasant and inhumane treatment of any kind"; also rejected were "brainwashing, physical or mental torture, or any other form of mental coercion." The *Field Manual* explicitly republished the Geneva Conventions, described as "definite limits on measures which can be taken."[18]

President Bush repeatedly said, "We do not torture," while the truth is that we did. "We" also engaged in cruel and inhuman treatment—again at the president's initiative and with his approval. Once exposed, the president and vice president lobbied for changes in the law to shield themselves from prosecution. They turned American values on their head.

———————

Shortly after September 11, President Bush issued an executive order permitting the CIA to capture and detain prisoners. Both the Department of Defense and the CIA were involved in interrogating detainees after September 11; sometimes their interrogations overlapped, and sometimes private contractors or the FBI entered the mix.

Most of the imprisonment and interrogation activities fell to the military and the Department of Defense, headed by Secretary of Defense Donald Rumsfeld. The CIA, under the direction of George Tenet, also conducted interrogations on military grounds, at CIA facilities in Iraq and Afghanistan, at "black" sites in countries across the globe, and through proxy jailers in foreign countries.

The first torture subjects are unknown, but "American Taliban" soldier John Lindh, when captured in the fall of 2001, was kept in solitary confinement, naked, cold, and deprived of sleep, according to *The Dark Side* by Jane Mayer.[19]

Other prisoners were captured that fall as well. Ibn al-Shaykh al-Libi was an early target of torture. Captured in November 2001, al-Libi was an al Qaeda trainer in Afghanistan. FBI agents used standard noncoercive interviewing techniques on him, and with some success. To their disgust, FBI agents were shoved aside when CIA interrogators arrived and forcibly removed al-Libi to Egypt, where he was tortured.

Aside from the aggressive treatment, there was another fishy thing going on, as described in the *New Yorker* by Jane Mayer in February 2005. Bush administration officials demanded information from al-Libi—not about September 11 or a possible follow-up attack, but about making a link between Iraq and al Qaeda. "Administration officials were always pushing us to come up with links, but there weren't any," the FBI officer said.[20] An implausible and untrue "confession" given under torture by al-Libi was snatched up by Vice President Cheney and President Bush to claim—falsely—that Iraq was involved in the 9/11 attacks.

Sometime in December 2001, not long after al-Libi was picked up, William J. Haynes II, general counsel of the Department of Defense, began investigating techniques that were used in countries known to torture and were part of the resistance training in the SERE (Survival, Evasion, Resistance, Escape) program of the Department of Defense, according to a 2008 report by the Senate Armed Services Committee.[21]

SERE studied torture by debriefing U.S. POWs in the Korean War who had been subjected to the extremely brutal techniques employed by North Korea; the methods were drawn from those in Communist China. The SERE program then prepared U.S. military trainees—all participants volunteered—so that they would be able to resist similar types of harsh questioning and mistreatment if they were captured by an unsavory enemy.[22] To do this, SERE instructors reenacted the cruel techniques used against Americans and that the United States plainly considered illegal. After the Korean War, the United States had even filed a complaint with the UN alleging that Korea had not complied with the Geneva Conventions, wrote Northwestern University law professor Joseph Margulies in the *Washington Post*.[23]

On January 11, 2002, as the first of 750 prisoners were transferred to Guantánamo Bay, White House officials and the CIA met to discuss interrogation methods. David Addington, counsel to Vice President Cheney, participated; so did John Yoo, deputy assistant attorney general in the Justice Department's Office of Legal Counsel, and Alberto Gonzales, counsel to the president. Then and there, according to a 2007 investigative story by Barton Gellman and Jo Becker in the *Washington Post*, the idea was hatched to break the back of the Geneva Conventions. "The vice president's office played a central role in shattering limits on coercion of prisoners in U.S. custody, commissioning and defending legal opinions that the Bush administration has since portrayed as the initiatives, months later, of lower-ranking officials," wrote Gellman and Becker.[24]

When Secretary of State Colin Powell got wind of what was under way—that the all-important Geneva Conventions for the humane treatment of detainees were being unceremoniously dumped—his office and its top lawyer immediately registered a pointed objection to the White House.[25]

The first official word came on February 7, 2002. On that day, President Bush publicly announced that, in fact, the Geneva Conventions would not apply to Taliban and al Qaeda prisoners. A two-page memorandum shredded decades of careful thinking, U.S. law, military practice, and an international treaty.[26]

The memo said that prisoners should be treated "humanely," which sounds good, but it had a caveat—except for "military necessity." This caveat was huge: a vague and undefined phrase that blasted open the portals to hellish circles and ended well-established limits on the infliction of cruelty and degradation. President Lincoln had used the same phrase, but to march in exactly the opposite direction—"military necessity doesn't admit cruelty," he had said.

President Bush's memo embellishing on his "decision point" soon became institutionalized in the form of "enhanced interrogation techniques" that could be used on detainees in Afghanistan and Guantánamo. The torture and cruel treatment of detainees that drew public attention much later was the direct and foreseeable result of this February 2002 memorandum by President Bush: here was the first and most significant of three critical actions that unleashed, for the first time in U.S. history, the systemic, presidentially authorized use of torture and abuse in detention and interrogation.

The Senate Armed Services Committee in 2008 weighed the full impact of the president's decision to push aside and replace well-established military doctrine. "Following the President's determination, techniques such as waterboarding, nudity, and stress positions, used in SERE training to simulate tactics used by enemies that refuse to follow the Geneva Conventions, were authorized for use in interrogations of detainees in U.S. custody," the committee report said.[27]

As noted, the SERE program gathered its torture techniques from those used against U.S. prisoners of war in the 1950s. More than three dozen U.S. Air Force personnel were subjected to these techniques by the North Koreans, after which each airman made a startling—and completely false—"confession" that the United States was engaged in germ warfare, statements paraded in public as propaganda.

After the war, air force sociologist Albert D. Biderman wrote an article describing the methods, "Communist Attempts to Elicit False Confessions from Air Force Prisoners of War."[28] The methods explained by Biderman became the basis of the SERE program, which operated under highly controlled limitations. Although the SERE program didn't conduct real interrogations with actual suspects—that was the responsibility of a different department of the military—its techniques were "reverse engineered" for use against prisoners held by the United States. "In what critics describe as a remarkable case of historical amnesia, officials who drew on the SERE program appear to have been unaware that it had been created as a result of concern about false confessions by American prisoners," wrote reporter Scott Shane in the *New York Times*.[29]

And so a sick irony emerges from the White House development of torture. In the hands of the Bush administration, the SERE methods were turned into tools of terror to be used by the United States against persons who were captured. "The use of techniques in interrogations derived from SERE resistance training created a serious risk of physical and psychological harm to detainees," the Senate Armed Services Committee said.[30] Exactly why the CIA wanted to use the SERE methods in the first place is a mystery. The CIA was charged with securing the country from attacks; agents needed to get at the truth about al Qaeda—"actionable intelligence"—in order to upend plots and track down real-life terrorists. False confessions were the last thing that the CIA needed. "People say we need intelligence, and we do," said Senator Carl Levin, chair of the Armed

Services Committee. "But we don't need false intelligence," he told Scott Shane of the *Times*.

And, yet, at the request of higher-ups in the Bush administration, SERE trainers put together a menu of proposed enhanced interrogation techniques, described at one point in a convenient guide by the CIA:

> During the walling technique, the detainee is pulled forward and then quickly and firmly pushed into a flexible false wall so that his shoulder blades hit the wall. His head and neck are supported with a rolled towel to prevent whiplash.
>
> In cramped confinement, the detainee is placed in a confined space, typically a small or large box, which is usually dark. Confinement in the smaller space lasts no more than two hours and in the larger space it can last up to 18 hours.
>
> Insects placed in a confinement box involve placing a harmless insect in the box with the detainee.[31]

President Bush said in his memoir that he personally selected the techniques to be used.[32]

———————

In March 2002 a man named Abu Zubaydah was apprehended in Pakistan. The CIA believed he was a real catch and had pegged him as a top al Qaeda figure—in reality, he was a kind of travel agent for jihadists, or more likely, for their wives and children. And, it turns out, he was also mentally unstable, and rather severely injured in the course of being captured. At first, the FBI interrogated him using standard procedures, and with a good deal of success. He identified "the brain" seen in various coded messages and intelligence reports as Khalid Sheik Mohammed, believed to be one of the planners of the 9/11 attacks. But then the CIA arrived with SERE specialists. The CIA aggressiveness so disturbed the FBI agents that they protested to FBI headquarters about the "borderline torture." The agents received instructions to leave, which they did. Abu Zubaydah soon became one of the first targets of a new protocol of torture and cruel treatment.[33]

Around that time, U.S. government leaders began to meet to discuss what would be done to whom. "Members of the President's Cabinet and other senior officials participated in meetings inside the White House in

2002 and 2003 where specific interrogation techniques were discussed. Members of the National Security Council Principals Committee reviewed the CIA's interrogation program during that period," noted the Senate Armed Services Committee.

At 1600 Pennsylvania Avenue, Vice President Cheney, National Security Advisor Condoleezza Rice, Defense Secretary Donald Rumsfeld, Secretary of State Colin Powell, CIA director George Tenet, and Attorney General John Ashcroft would go over the best aggressive interrogation techniques for specific prisoners. Ashcroft, no bleeding-heart liberal, is said to have objected—not because he disagreed with the torture, but because he didn't think they needed to be involved in the nitty-gritty. "Why are we talking about this in the White House? History will not judge this kindly," he said to his colleagues, according to high-level sources who later spoke to ABC News.[34]

On August 1, 2002, torture had lawyers working for it. Two memos—they came to be known as the "torture memos"—were issued carrying the signature of Jay Bybee, assistant attorney general in the Justice Department's Office of Legal Counsel; they were written by a deputy: John Yoo, the same lawyer who justified illegal wiretapping. These documents became the second critical action of the top-down authorization, approval, and institutionalization of torture and cruel treatment. They were aptly described in a subheading of the 2008 report of the Senate Armed Services Committee: "Department of Justice Redefines Torture."

By way of background, the Office of Legal Counsel (OLC) has a unique role in the Justice Department—it is to give independent legal advice to the president and executive branch. "Principles to Guide the Office of Legal Counsel," prepared in 2004 by nineteen former OLC attorneys, explained that OLC lawyers "should provide an accurate and honest appraisal of applicable law, even if that advice will constrain the administration's pursuit of desired policies. The advocacy model of lawyer, in which lawyers craft merely plausible legal arguments to support their client's desired actions, inadequately promotes the President's constitutional obligation to ensure the legality of executive action."[35] In the words of Jack Goldsmith, OLC head in 2003 and 2004, the office has "the most momentous and dangerous powers in the government: the power to dispense get-out-of-jail free cards."[36]

The first of the two torture memos, fifty pages in length and directed to Alberto Gonzales, counsel to the president, was headed: "Re: Standards of Conduct for Interrogation under 18 USC §§ 2340–2340A."[37] Kept secret until June 2004 when it was leaked to the press, it expanded presidential authority, sought to override the anti-torture law in the United States, and attempted to change the long-established meaning of torture. It was accompanied by a six-page letter from Yoo, reminding Gonzales that the president had previously eliminated Geneva Convention protections for al Qaeda and the Taliban.[38]

The second torture memo, eighteen pages in length, was addressed to the acting general counsel of the CIA, John Rizzo. It finally saw the light of day in a redacted form when it was released to the public on April 16, 2009. This memo laid out exceptionally detailed descriptions of ten specific enhanced interrogation techniques that were approved for CIA use on Abu Zubaydah, a prescription that became the pattern for other torture sessions. It put the first torture memo into practical application.[39]

Yoo churned out the memos after meeting with Gonzales and Addington, counsel to the vice president. When Yoo's colleague Patrick Philbin, deputy assistant attorney general, raised a question about one section of the memo, Yoo simply responded that "they" wanted it—"they" implying White House insiders.[40] When the Office of Professional Responsibility tried to review the decision-making process as part of an investigation into the conduct of Yoo and Bybee, many of Yoo's e-mails from that time period were simply missing. For the most part, the torture memos skirted the normal processes of review and skipped the State Department altogether.[41]

As it happens, the memos were filled with legal fantasia. The torture memos aimed to redefine torture under the anti-torture law, a major legal obstacle to the use of enhanced interrogation techniques. The goals were clear: to prevent any prosecutions along the chain of command under the anti-torture law and to permit the CIA to employ the interrogation techniques adapted for the SERE program from the North Korean regime.

Daniel Levin, a later head of the Office of Legal Counsel, was succinct in his evaluation: "[T]his is insane, who wrote this?" he said, according to the report of the Office of Professional Responsibility.[42] Or, as politely stated in 2004 by the inspector general of the CIA, the approach in the memos "diverges sharply from previous Agency policy and rules that govern interrogations by U.S. military and law enforcement officers."[43]

The anti-torture law makes it a crime for anyone acting in a government capacity to commit torture or to conspire to commit torture outside the United States. The torture memos actually came about because CIA officers wanted legal assurances that they wouldn't be prosecuted for the use of the SERE techniques. Abu Zubaydah was already being subjected to several SERE-type techniques when the memos were issued, according to the inspector general of the CIA.

Michael Chertoff, then head of the criminal division of the Justice Department, refused to give any form of advance "declination" to prosecute, the Office of Professional Responsibility investigators found. That's not all. The OPR investigators learned that the FBI said that it would not conduct or participate in any interrogations employing the aggressive techniques, no matter what the Office of Legal Counsel said, and it refused to participate in further discussions.[44]

Yoo was "under pretty significant pressure to come up with an answer that would justify [the program]," John B. Bellinger III, legal advisor to the National Security Council, told investigators from the Office of Professional Responsibility.

The torture memos used three tactics to blunt the anti-torture law: (1) they narrowed the definition of torture so almost nothing qualified as torture; (2) they asserted that anyone creating pain for the purpose of seeking information did not have the specific intent to commit an act of torture (since the objective was getting the information, not inflicting pain); and (3) they created a series of defenses for the president and others if allegations of torture were to arise.

The first memo, dated August 1, 2002, chopped apart the anti-torture law and attempted to assign new, unheard-of (if inventive) meanings to its provisions. Yoo took a scalpel to the definition of torture, narrowing it so greatly that most acts fell *outside* the definition of torture. Only a thin slice of activity was left that could be considered "torture." He did this by taking the definition of torture that existed in the law—"specifically intended to inflict severe physical or mental pain or suffering"—and linguistically savaging every phrase and word.

Particular energy was expended on whipping up an unusual definition of "severe pain"—the basis of torture. Severe pain, Yoo wrote, must be "the equivalent in intensity to the pain accompanying serious physical injury, such as organ failure, impairment of bodily function, or even death."

At first glance, the definition seems to suggest a very high degree of pain; on inspection, it's meaningless, especially as a tool of proof. For example, no one knows what pain accompanies death—it is, after all, the land "from whose bourne no traveler returns," as Shakespeare once said. And so, what could possibly be its equivalent? Even Yoo, when asked by the Office of Professional Responsibility several years later about the pain that death entails, said: "Well I think, I assume that's very painful, but I don't know." Yoo's comment is evidence that his definition was not meant to be intellectually serious but was merely concocted to prevent effective application of the law.

The terms "organ failure" and "impairment of bodily function" do not have standard pain indexes, either—these are vague and unmeasurable descriptions. How can a person possibly prove that being shackled to the ceiling, naked, in an icy environment and deprived of sleep for days on end produces the same pain as the failure of an organ? Yoo pretended to give the words "organ failure, impairment of a bodily function, or even death" some additional legal heft by claiming that he was drawing on a federal statute that provides emergency health benefits. But the emergency health benefits statute that he uses doesn't define severe pain, nor does it even use the words "organ failure, impairment of bodily function, or death." The citation of the health benefits law was another ruse, designed to suggest that there was a precedent or analogy in federal law, when there was none.

This tactic is the template by which Yoo attempted to manipulate the rest of the anti-torture law. Some examples:

- On the subject of severe physical "pain or suffering," Yoo tampered with the definition by deleting the word *suffering*. He claimed that pain and suffering are the same thing, which is a bit like saying that death and destruction are the same because they are combined conversationally into a single phrase. Yoo's elimination of *suffering* as having an independent meaning was a way to immunize waterboarding from prosecution. The reality is that CIA interrogators, referenced in the memo by Yoo, asserted that waterboarding did not cause pain and they did not want to worry about a potential prosecution if it caused suffering, which was a very likely result.

- In an attempt to provide torture with a legal justification, Yoo stated that the anti-torture law is unconstitutional because Congress cannot restrict the president's commander-in-chief powers during wartime. There is no legal basis for this extreme conclusion. Yoo even failed to mention Supreme Court precedent to the contrary or the many powers given by the U.S. Constitution to Congress in the conduct of wars.

Navy General Counsel Alberto J. Mora later met with John Yoo about a follow-up torture memo that Yoo was drafting. Mora recalled the conversation in the 2009 documentary film, *Torturing Democracy:* "As he was talking, I was becoming more concerned and more alarmed, and ultimately I asked him the question, 'Well, John, does this mean the President has the authority to order torture?' And he said, 'Yes.'" Mora was stunned.[45]

The second Yoo/Bybee memo, dated August 1, 2002 (which is frequently called the "Classified Bybee Memo"), laid out the SERE-type techniques of interrogation proposed for use on Abu Zubaydah. Not surprisingly, Yoo found that not one of them constituted torture. This document was also filled with other disconcerting entries. For example, it justified waterboarding but took no account of its history and the fact that the United States had treated it as torture in the past. No mention or acknowledgment was made of the federal prosecution of Texas sheriff James Parker in 1983 and his deputies for using "water torture" against prisoners, or of the prosecution of a Japanese officer, Yukio Asano, in 1947 for waterboarding a U.S. citizen, or the court martial of a U.S. soldier in Vietnam for the waterboarding of a captive in 1968.[46]

The memo, addressed to the CIA, approved a series of brutal techniques. The language in the memo read like this: "In this phase, you would like to employ ten techniques that you believe will dislocate his expectations regarding the treatment he believes he will receive." The techniques were then listed: attention grasp, walling, facial hold, facial slap (insult slap), cramped confinement, wall standing (in which the detainee's fingertips would have to support his full body weight as he leaned into a wall), stress positions, sleep deprivation, "insects placed in a confinement box," and "the waterboard."

Yoo fails to probe any of these techniques in a meaningful way. On the subject of sleep deprivation, approved as an enhanced interrogation technique, Yoo did not consider the methods by which detainees would be kept awake. One CIA/SERE idea of keeping detainees awake involved shackling the individual in a standing position with his arms over his head and naked, except for a diaper. Nor did Yoo discuss the extent to which any of these techniques, when used in combination with one another, could cause severe physical pain. Considered singly, each is found to pass the muster of John Yoo and Jay Bybee. But what happens when they are used together—sleep deprivation, a crouching box, and walling? Alone, the techniques are appalling; combined, the brew is devastating.

Years later, in April 2005, the failure to consider the effects of *combining* these techniques created new agitation inside the Justice Department when James Comey, deputy attorney general, objected vociferously to signing off on "combined techniques," according to a 2009 story on *Truthout*, which also reprinted Comey's e-mails (later archived by the *New York Times*). Referring to the authorization of "combined techniques," Comey wrote, "I could not agree to this because it was wrong."[47]

The thrust of the two Bybee/Yoo torture memos comes to this: over a thirty-day period, a chilled nude man in diapers who is not permitted to use the toilet, who is being fed on semi-starvation rations, who is being kept awake for eleven days at a time by being shackled into a standing position, is taken out of the shackles for incessant interrogation sessions where he is repeatedly smashed into a wall, hosed with frigid water, slapped, and put into other shackled standing, sitting, crouching or confined "stress" positions. And then he is waterboarded. This, according to those who approved it, does not cause severe physical pain or suffering, or mental pain or suffering.

The conclusion flies in the face of human experience, a problem compounded by the failure to consider the substantial medical literature on the impact of these various torture techniques. The memos were not an intellectually honest effort.

The torture memos formed the core justification for other actions and decisions that sanctioned, authorized, and institutionalized torture and cruel treatment. The memos, Jack Goldsmith wrote in his book *The Terror Presidency*, "could be interpreted as if they were designed to confer immunity for bad acts."

Despite being riddled with problems, the memos were important to President Bush and his team. Based on the distorted interpretation of the law in these secret documents, the president, vice president, and their team began to claim that their behavior in authorizing "enhanced" interrogation was "legal."

Almost as soon as the memos were sent off, waterboarding began on Abu Zubaydah. He was subjected to this form of suffocation by water eighty-three times. But that was only a part of his treatment. Singly and in combination, he was forced into standing stress positions for prolonged periods; beatings by use of a collar around his neck from which he was swung around the room and into walls; confinement in boxes, one of which required crouching and broke open stitches from surgery; slapping; nudity; sleep deprivation; elimination of solid food; exposure to cold temperatures; and more. In short, Zubaydah was subjected to all of the techniques "approved" in the torture memos, by the National Security Council Principals Committee, and by President Bush himself.

MILITARY OBJECTIONS OVERRULED

On December 2, 2002, Donald Rumsfeld signed a memo that approved fifteen aggressive techniques pulled from the SERE program for use in the military. These were: yelling; deception; stress positions, such as forced standing; use of fake letters from family or other falsified documents; isolation for up to thirty days; interrogation outside the standard interrogation booth; deprivation of light and auditory stimuli; hooding; twenty-hour interrogations; removal of religious and comfort items; switching from regular rations to ready-to-eat meals; removal of clothing; forced grooming, such as shaving of facial hair; use of individual phobias like fear of dogs to induce stress; mild, noninjurious physical contact, like grabbing, poking, pushing; scenarios to convince the detainee that death or painful consequences were imminent for him or his family; exposure to cold weather or water; use of a wet towel and dripping water to induce the sensation of suffocation.[48]

Waterboarding, of course, became the most controversial torture technique when its approved use became publicly known. Waterboarding is a process of suffocation in which the victim is brought to the very edge of dying and then is revived. The victim experiences drowning. The SERE description said: "The application of the waterboard technique involves binding the detainee to a bench with his feet elevated above his head. The detainee's head is immobilized and an interrogator places a cloth over the detainee's mouth and nose while pouring water onto the cloth in a controlled manner. Airflow is restricted for twenty to forty seconds and the technique produces the sensation of drowning and suffocation." To prove that it was no big deal, Chicago's syndicated shock jock Erich "Mancow" Muller offered himself up for a controlled waterboarding experiment in May 2009. ("They cut off our heads, we put water on their face," he'd joked.) When the water was poured, he threw his emergency signal almost instantly. The experimenters stopped and sat him up. "Absolutely torture," Mancow declared.[49]

On a different radio show in October 2006, Vice President Cheney concurred with a listener who asked what was wrong with "a dunk in the water." Cheney responded, "Well, it's a no-brainer for me." He backtracked later in the week and said that his comments were not about waterboarding, according to the *Washington Post* on October 26, 2006.[50]

Khalid Sheik Mohammed became the most waterboarded detainee. The torture was used on him 183 times, along with other enhanced interrogation techniques. President Bush told a crowd in Michigan on June 2, 2010, he ordered the waterboarding of Mohammed. "I would do it again," the president said.[51]

Lawyers throughout the military warned Rumsfeld against the use of the enhanced interrogation techniques: "crosses the line of 'humane' treatment," wrote one; would "expose our service members to possible prosecution," wrote another.[52] Rumsfeld ignored them. In signing the December 2, 2002, order, Rumsfeld added only one comment: "I stand for 8–10 hours a day. Why is standing limited to 4 hours?"

Rumsfeld's authorization became the third core action that led to the systemic use of torture. The techniques that he authorized violated U.S. law as well as the Geneva Conventions. "Secretary of Defense Donald Rumsfeld's authorization of aggressive interrogation techniques for use at Guantánamo Bay was a direct cause of detainee abuse there," according to the Senate Armed Services Committee. "What followed was an erosion in standards dictating that detainees be treated humanely," the Senate committee wrote.

Immediately after Rumsfeld signed the December 2 order, U.S. personnel at Guantánamo began six weeks of brutal interrogation of Mohammed al Qahtani. "The torture debate centers on the permissibility of things such as waterboarding, yet it never even broaches the topics of solitary confinement, short-shackling, and sleep deprivation," wrote Justine Sharrock, author of *Tortured*, a book about soldiers who were required to participate in brutal interrogations or detention. "But when used in combination, as is often done . . . sometimes daily over the course of years—these techniques are torture," wrote Sharrock.[53] Susan J. Crawford, appointed as the convening authority for Guantánamo military commissions in 2007, put it this way: "We tortured Qahtani," she told Bob Woodward of the *Washington Post*. Crawford, a former judge who was assigned to review and evaluate cases, determined that al Qahtani could not be tried because of the torture. "This was not any one particular act; this was just a combination of things that had a medical impact on him," she said.[54]

After Rumsfeld issued the December 2 list, Navy General Counsel Alberto Mora, who had previously objected to the proposed interrogation techniques, continued to express concerns. He said that the interrogation techniques authorized by Rumsfeld could "rise to the level of torture." He put his objections in a draft legal memo delivered on January 15, 2003, to William Haynes, the Department of Defense general counsel, and warned that he would sign it later that day unless the techniques were withdrawn. Before that could happen, Rumsfeld rescinded the December 2 memo, according to the report of the Senate Armed Services Committee.[55]

Unfortunately, the rescission was not well known at Guantánamo or in Afghanistan, although the original December 2 memo seemed to be everywhere. As a result, little changed. And rather than adjust his intentions, Rumsfeld engineered a way to get around the objections of Mora and his military colleagues. Behind their backs, he got Yoo to write a new torture memo that applied to the military, despite their objections, and replicated the language of the torture memos of August 1, 2002. A new list of enhanced interrogation techniques generated by Rumsfeld in April 2003 included extremes of temperature and light, dietary manipulation, sleep deprivation, removal of clothing, prolonged standing, hooding, slaps, exploitation of aversions. Rumsfeld also suggested that he would consider requests for other methods from interrogators in the field.

When U.S. tanks thundered into Iraq on March 19, 2003, President Bush said that the Geneva Conventions would apply to the Iraq conflict. But, in reality, President Bush's memorandum of February 7, 2002, eclipsed this statement; the poison was not poured back into the bottle. The mistreatment grew.

Prisoner abuse spread readily when interrogation officers from both Afghanistan and Guantánamo who were familiar with the enhanced interrogation techniques or Rumsfeld's December 2 memo were sent to Iraq to oversee operations or to train interrogators. They brought with them the torture techniques they had been authorized to use by Secretary Rumsfeld and their observation of aggressive CIA interrogations.

Deplorable conditions for people detained in the war in Iraq first came to the attention of the International Committee of the Red Cross in its role as monitor of the Geneva Conventions during visits in late 2003. In February 2004, the ICRC reported "systemic" mistreatment of prisoners in U.S. custody in Iraq, including "holding people naked in a completely dark and empty cell," "beatings with hard objects," "slapping, punching, kicking with knees or feet," "pressing the face into the ground with boots." ICRC reports are delivered to the authorities holding the prisoners.

That same month, U.S. Major General Antonio Taguba completed an investigation for his superiors in the military on Abu Ghraib, where the United States crowded seven thousand prisoners into Saddam Hussein's old chamber of horrors. Like the ICRC, Taguba found "systemic and illegal abuse of detainees" by U.S. military personnel including slapping, punching, kicking, rape, use of military dogs, and "sadistic, blatant, and wanton criminal abuses." Taguba delivered this report to his commanders.[56]

On April 28, 2004, when the Abu Ghraib photographs showed up on television, the world got a look at what the International Committee of the Red Cross and Major General Taguba had seen. The images became indelible.[57]

President Bush responded by appointing Secretary Rumsfeld, himself a malefactor, to look into what happened. Not surprisingly, investigations avoided scrutinizing accountability at the top.[58] Nor were examinations conducted of CIA activities. Still, once reports were made, they showed serious and systemic wrongdoing. For example, the Schlesinger Report, released in August 2004, described "widespread" and "serious" abuse of prisoners. It found "fundamental failures throughout all levels of the command," and "institutional and personal responsibility at high levels."[59] Several low-level military personnel were prosecuted, convicted, and sent to jail. No high-level personnel were prosecuted or penalized.

It took another two years, until September 6, 2006, before President Bush publicly acknowledged in an address to Americans that an "alternative" system of interrogation had been used against fourteen "high value" detainees.[60] These prisoners were transferred from undisclosed "black sites" and foreign prisons to Guantánamo Bay.

Without flinching, the president insisted that the interrogation techniques used on the "high value" detainees "were tough, and they were safe, and lawful, and necessary."[61] Videotapes that could support his view, however, were destroyed by the CIA,[62] and the White House refused to release photographs from interrogation and detention centers.

When asked if President Bush knew the details of the interrogation system, former vice president Cheney told *Face the Nation* on May 10, 2009: "I certainly, yes, have every reason to believe he knew—he knew a great deal about the program. He basically authorized it. I mean, this was a presidential-level decision. And the decision went to the president. He signed off on it."[63]

Despite the secrecy that had attempted to hide the torture protocols, a large and growing body of information began to surface into public view. The scope of the abuse has been described—in excruciating detail—by Congressional committees, CIA documents, Justice Department legal opinions, the International Committee of the Red Cross, lawsuits in Italy, Spain, Germany, and England, interviews of released detainees and U.S. employee witnesses, legal filings in the United States, and accounts by journalists or experts, including Jane Mayer, Karen Greenberg, Seymour Hersh, Philippe Sands, Andy Worthington, Mark Danner, and others. Several of those subjected to the torture and cruel treatment—Maher Arar and Khaled El-Masri are two—were completely innocent of any connection to terrorism or wrongdoing. A not insubstantial number of other detainees were bystanders who were turned in for cash bounties that the United States had offered.

In February 2007, the International Committee of the Red Cross completed its investigation of the treatment of the fourteen "high value" detainees. The ICRC concluded that they had been subjected to "an arbitrary deprivation of liberty and enforced disappearance, in contravention of international law. Moreover, and in addition to the continuous solitary confinement and incommunicado detention which itself was a form of ill-treatment, twelve of the fourteen alleged that they were subjected to systemic physical and/or psychological ill-treatment." This treatment, the ICRC said, "either singly or in combination, constituted torture." It expressed concern about possibly ongoing secret prison detention.[64]

The inspector general of the CIA perhaps best described what the mounting piles of information were showing in his report in 2004.

"The EITs [enhanced interrogation techniques] used by the Agency . . . are inconsistent with the public policy positions that the United States has taken regarding human rights," he wrote.[65] But President Bush continued to authorize torture. In July 2007, he signed an executive order permitting the CIA to avoid laws, new and old, that would restrain its handling of detainees or prohibit the use of torture techniques.[66]

In June 2008, Major General Taguba, who investigated detainee treatment at Abu Ghraib, wrote the preface to a report released by Physicians for Human Rights, *Broken Laws, Broken Lives*. Retired by then, General Taguba didn't hold back on his opinion: "There is no longer any doubt as to whether the current [Bush] administration has committed war crimes. The only question that remains to be answered is whether those who ordered the use of torture will be held to account."[67]

PRESIDENT BUSH AND HIS TEAM ACT TO PROTECT THEMSELVES FROM PROSECUTION

As noted above, the two laws that most directly apply to torture and mistreatment of detainees are the War Crimes Act of 1996 and the "anti-torture law."

Confronted with these laws and worried about prosecution, Bush administration officials plotted a course of legalistic maneuvers intended to protect themselves. Rather than enforce the law, as required by the president's oath of office, Bush officials warped the law to conform to their deviant behavior. They succeeded in many ways. Yet, because the president and his team overstepped the bounds of the law so profusely, they may still be caught in their own web.

The federal War Crimes Act of 1996 was a healthy, admirable, and muscular law when President Bush took office in January 2001. It prohibited not only torture, but also degrading treatment of detainees, cruelty, acts of humiliation, and outrages against personal dignity. But by the time that President Bush left office, and at his behest, the War Crimes Act of 1996 had been stripped of meaning and rendered worthless. Revisions that the Bush administration rushed through Congress in 2006 altered the War Crimes Act—retroactively. It was a barely noticed—and widely successful—enterprise designed to protect President Bush and his top officials from the application of the law and the consequences of their acts in sanctioning and unleashing torture and cruel treatment.

The War Crimes Act came about in order to carry out a central obligation of the United States under the Geneva Conventions. The Geneva Conventions, which were adopted by the United Nations in 1949, were a direct response to the horrific experiences of prisoners of war and civilians during World War II. Nations across the globe, including the United States, were determined to prevent a repetition by creating international law to ensure the decent treatment of detainees in conflict situations.[68]

The United States ratified the Geneva Conventions in 1955 during the presidency of Dwight D. Eisenhower. As the commander of U.S. and Allied troops during World War II, President Eisenhower fully understood their military and moral significance and he eagerly embraced them. "The Geneva Conventions are fashioned primarily to meet universal humanitarian aspirations and needs," he wrote. They are intended "for the relief of physical suffering and moral degradation so often in the past experienced by victims of war, both military and civilian."[69] Eisenhower knew that the Geneva Conventions would play a vital role in protecting U.S. troops if they were captured. The Geneva Conventions set standards for treatment of both prisoners of war and persons not taking part in hostilities.

The United States had a powerful tradition of following the Geneva Conventions. As I noted earlier, the Conventions were specifically incorporated into the U.S. Army *Field Manual*.[70] Since they were adopted, the Geneva Conventions have been followed in every armed conflict, including the Vietnam War and the first Gulf War—every war, that is, up to the time of President George W. Bush.

The Geneva Conventions also require each nation that ratifies to take steps to punish those who commit "grave breaches." It was for this reason that Representative Walter B. Jones Jr., a Republican from North Carolina, introduced the War Crimes Act in 1996, which made violations of the Geneva Conventions a part of federal criminal law. Jones represented a large military base, Camp Lejeune, and had been persuaded of the need for the law by a former Vietnam War pilot who had been captured and tortured. Liberal and conservative, Democratic and Republican members of the Congress joined together to support the legislation.

The War Crimes Act stated that war criminals could be prosecuted directly in the United States. It held: "Whoever, whether inside or outside the United States, commits a war crime . . . shall be fined under this title or imprisoned for life or any term of years, or both, and if death results to the victim, shall also be subject to the penalty of death." There is no statute of limitations in death cases.[71]

As passed in 1996, the act defined a "war crime" as any conduct that is a "grave breach" of the Geneva Conventions, which automatically included willful killing; torture or inhuman treatment; and willfully causing great suffering or serious injury to the body or health of a civilian or prisoner of war in the circumstances of an international armed conflict. In 1997, the War Crimes Act was further bolstered at the suggestion of the Defense and State Departments to cover prosecutions for violations of "Common Article 3" of the Geneva Conventions. So, in addition, it criminalizes; "violence to life and person, in particular murder of all kinds, mutilation, cruel treatment and torture . . . outrages upon personal dignity, in particular humiliating and degrading treatment."

Bush administration officials, including the president, undoubtedly violated both the War Crimes Act of 1996 and the Geneva Conventions. As a result, the president sought to immunize himself and his inner circle from the consequences under the law—by changing the law.

As early as January 2002, just months after the invasion of Afghanistan, extreme concern arose in the White House about criminal liability under the War Crimes Act. A January 25 memo from then White House counsel Alberto Gonzales, leaked two years later to *Newsweek*, described this concern in the most urgent terms to President Bush. Gonzales had a solution. He called for the United States to reject the applicability of the Geneva Conventions to the Taliban and al Qaeda. He made several claims, among them that the Geneva Conventions were "obsolete" and "quaint." The much less noticed reason that Gonzales wanted to reject the Geneva Conventions did not make the headlines. Doing away with Geneva, he wrote, "substantially reduces the threat of domestic criminal prosecution" under the War Crimes Act of 1996.[72]

In other words, Gonzales argued for rejecting the Geneva Conventions because the War Crimes Act of 1996, which carried out the conventions in the United States, called for significant criminal penalties for violations that might not feel so quaint if applied to the residents of the White House. Gonzales reasoned that if the Geneva Conventions did not apply, then the War Crimes Act would not apply either. And that would mean no prosecutions under it.

Gonzales noted in particular the possibility that "prosecutors and independent counsels" "may in the future" bring "unwarranted charges" under the War Crimes Act of 1996. The term "independent counsels" had a very particular meaning. "Independent counsels" were special prosecutors appointed by courts to investigate and prosecute presidents and cabinet members and to ensure that elite officials are held accountable for crimes they commit.

The memo to the president makes it clear that President Bush had been briefed previously—and personally—on this subject. Gonzales makes direct note of this. "As I discussed with you," he writes in his memo to the president.[73]

Left unsaid in the Gonzales memo, but surely understood, was that the War Crimes Act also called for the death penalty in cases where death resulted from violations of the act—which, in turn, meant that the statute of limitations did not apply. The War Crimes Act of 1996 could expose President Bush and his top officials to criminal liability for the rest of their lives.

The State Department opposed Gonzales's position. After reading a Gonzales draft, Secretary of State Colin L. Powell sent a crisp objection to the White House on January 26, 2002. In bullet points, he listed pros and cons for doing away with the Geneva Conventions. He found ten "cons" to eliminating Geneva Conventions protection ("will reverse over a century of U.S. policy"; "may provoke some individual foreign prosecutors"). On the other side, he found a single muted "pro" for eliminating Geneva Conventions protection ("an across-the-board approach"). Powell made factual corrections, too: Geneva Conventions protection "was intended to cover all types of armed conflict and did not by its terms limit its application," he wrote.[74]

The legal advisor to the secretary of state, William H. Taft IV, followed up on February 2, 2002, with a memo to the White House with the strong recommendation that the Geneva Conventions apply and emphasizing that other State Department lawyers concurred. On the tender point of criminal liability, he wrote, "The risk of prosecution under [the War Crimes Act] is negligible. Any small benefit from reducing it further will be purchased at the expense of the men and women in our armed forces."[75]

No matter: President Bush knew that the risk was not negligible; he, unlike Taft, knew exactly what the interrogations involved and he was not going to risk the chance of being prosecuted. He accepted Gonzales's recommendation and declared that al Qaeda members would not be covered by the Geneva Conventions, and the Taliban would not be treated as prisoners of war. It was at this point that President Bush, on February 7, 2002, for the first time since U.S. ratification of the Geneva Conventions in 1955, declared them inapplicable.[76]

The torture memos issued by the Office of Legal Counsel on August 1, 2002, were more specifically directed to the anti-torture law than the War Crimes Act, which the White House believed had already been wiped away by the president's memorandum of February 7, 2002.

Despite these core actions by the White House to authorize cruel treatment and torture, concern about the aggressive interrogations continued to emerge from unusual sources, creating stumbling blocks for the Bush administration. In May 2004, the inspector general of the CIA, John L. Helgerson, wrote an extensive top-secret report that was highly critical of the interrogation techniques being used by the agency on detainees between September 2001 and October 2003.[77] A team of twelve people had conducted the inspector general's investigation with site visits, reviews of interrogation videotapes (later destroyed), and interviews of more than one hundred individuals, including the CIA director, general counsel, and senior agency personnel. "In thousands of pages, [the report] challenged the legality of some interrogation methods," Mark Mazzetti and Scott Shane later wrote in the *New York Times*.[78]

This internal assessment showed that the inspector general was distressed about the U.S. failure to follow human rights principles and was troubled by the use of the enhanced interrogation techniques—certainly the repeated waterboarding, but also choking, mock executions, threats to family members, cuts and abrasions caused by stepping on shackles, kicking, knocking down, possible dragging, and deaths at "rendition" facilities. The report concludes that "the Agency faces potentially serious long-term political and legal challenges as a result of the CTC [Counter-Terrorism Center] Detention and Interrogation Program, particularly in the use of EITs [enhanced interrogation techniques]."

This troubling—and important—report was directed to those at the highest levels. The report, said Mazzetti and Shane in the *New York Times*, was "a body blow to the CIA program." It put CIA director George Tenet on high alert and "landed on the desks" of White House officials, said the *Times* reporters. In addition to challenging the legality of the interrogations, the report questioned the effectiveness of the entire program as a tool for information gathering.

Another obstacle—and perhaps more serious because it was in the public eye—arose in 2005. Republican senator John McCain, who, as most people knew, had been a victim of torture as a POW during the Vietnam War, attached language to two major defense bills to ban the cruel, inhuman, and degrading treatment of any detainee. The provisions established the *Army Field Manual* as the standard for interrogation. "Our image in the world is suffering very badly, and one of the reasons for it is the perception that we abuse people we capture," McCain told the Associated Press.[79]

The Bush administration strongly opposed the language and threatened a veto. Vice President Cheney personally lobbied Senator McCain and other key senators against the legislation—"Cheney pulled [senators] into a room off the Senate floor and sternly argued that the provision would usurp the president's authority," according to the *Washington Post*.[80] Cheney's efforts failed, and only a handful of senators opposed McCain's measure. Then the House registered its strong support for McCain as well—in fact, his legislative proposal looked veto proof. Given the frosty congressional landscape, President Bush seemed to back down in mid-December and made a ballyhooed joint appearance with McCain in the White House to declare a reversal of his position and new support for the legislation. He "praised McCain's effort," said the *Washington Post* on December 16.[81]

But, behind the scenes, the Bush administration continued to lobby for changes that it wanted. As a result, the final measure, which was passed as the "Detainee Treatment Act of 2005," contained a loophole that had not appeared in McCain's original proposal. "The administration did gain a provision acknowledging that the advice of counsel defense was available to interrogators," noted the investigative team of the Justice Department's Office of Professional Responsibility in its 2009 report.[82]

This clause offered new defenses to protect those who engaged in torture, the president included. Government employees who committed torture were given a handy way to get off the hook should a courageous prosecutor appear and charge them with criminal activities. Persons charged with violations of the War Crimes Act now would be permitted to claim that they believed their actions were acceptable—for example, if they relied on the advice of a lawyer. The new provision states: "It shall be a defense that such [government officer] did not know that the practices were unlawful and a person of ordinary sense and understanding would not know the practices were unlawful. Good faith reliance on advice of counsel should be an important factor, among others, to consider in assessing whether a person of ordinary sense and understanding would have known the practices to be unlawful."

In other words, the Detainee Treatment Act incorporates the "mistake of law" defense (which I described earlier regarding illegal surveillance) into the law. Putting this directly into the law gives "mistake of law" extra muscle as a protection for anyone accused of violating the War Crimes Act. And to further sweeten the pot, the Detainee Treatment Act promised that the government would provide free legal help to government employees charged with a violation of the law.[83]

The president signed the Detainee Treatment Act on December 30, 2005. But that was not the end. The White House had another trick up its sleeve. The president added a "signing statement" to the law. Previous presidents had used signing statements—infrequently—but when they were used, they were a rather innocuous way of explaining the purpose of the law. In this case, President Bush used the signing statement to try to nullify the very law he was signing and to create more defenses for himself. In odd and authoritarian language (that talks about the "unitary executive branch," a complete fiction), the signing statement asserts that the president has the power to override the law. It says, in part: "The executive branch shall construe [the law] in a manner consistent with the constitutional authority of the President . . . as Commander in Chief."[84]

The intention, an unnamed senior Bush official told reporter Charlie Savage on January 4, 2006, was to reserve the right to waive the law, if need be. New York University law professor David Golove gave this interpretation to Savage: "The signing statement is saying 'I will only comply with this law when I want to, and if something arises in the war on terrorism where I think it's important to torture or engage in cruel, inhuman, and degrading conduct, I have the authority to do so and nothing in this law is going to stop me.'"[85] For President Bush, the Detainee Treatment Act of 2005 became a way to secure a new defense in the event of prosecution, while keeping on with the same practices.

Six months after passage of the Detainee Treatment Act, the Bush administration confronted the most serious blow to its plans to shield its own culpability. On June 29, 2006, the U.S. Supreme Court issued a ruling in *Hamdan v. Rumsfeld*, a case on military trials for detainees. The court not only tossed out the poorly designed plan for trying detainees that the Bush administration had created, but—even more significantly—ruled that Common Article 3 of the Geneva Conventions applied to detainees in the so-called "war on terror."[86] In other words, the Geneva Conventions could not be discarded on the president's say-so, as President Bush had attempted to do with his February 7, 2002 memorandum.

A panic button must have sounded inside the White House. If the Geneva Conventions did apply to the detainees, then the War Crimes Act also applied under the Bush team's own reasoning. The scheme to avoid War Crimes Act liability had come crashing down. The new defenses in the Detainee Treatment Act ("we believed it wasn't a crime") might not be broad enough to protect people in the White House from liability for cruel and inhuman treatment of detainees. President Bush and his team once again faced the possibility of prosecution under the War Crimes Act of 1996; their first line of defense to provide immunity for themselves had just vanished.

Their efforts to craft a new plan aimed at protecting themselves suddenly moved into high gear. The president himself met with a variety of officials to explore options, reflecting his personal awareness of the danger of criminal liability that he now faced and the need to secure protection. After the *Hamdan* decision came down, "officials from the Departments of State, Defense, and Justice met with the President and officials from the CIA and NSC to consider the impact of the Court's decision. It was clear from the outset that legislation would have to be enacted to address the application of Common Article 3 and the War Crimes Act to the CIA interrogation program," according to investigators in the Justice Department's Office of Professional Responsibility.[87] No time was wasted. A team quickly assembled over the summer to come up with ideas for new legislation. In September the Bush administration put forward the Military Commissions Act of 2006, designed to create a new framework for trying Guantánamo detainees.[88] While much of the public was distracted by astounding provisions that would eliminate the right to habeas corpus, steel arrows tucked inside the legislation were aimed at the heart of the War Crimes Act of 1996. They narrowed the War Crimes Act dramatically, in fact, making it virtually unenforceable. The International Committee of the Red Cross, getting wind of the proposed changes, raised objections, according to a story in the *Washington Post*, one of the only articles to mention the topic at all.[89] But since the bill was introduced just before the 2006 midterm elections, few members of Congress would dare to vote against it for fear of being vilified as soft on terror.

Congress passed the law in a record three weeks and President Bush signed it on October 17, 2006. If people merely read the table of contents of the new law, they wouldn't even see the changes to the War Crimes Act listed specifically; they were merely designated as "implementation of treaty obligations." But critical alterations were hiding . . . in full view. In this action—almost astonishing to review—the Bush administration used three unprecedented legal tactics to shred the War Crimes Act and protect itself from criminal liability. This time President Bush and Vice President Cheney wouldn't take any chances.

The Military Commissions Act of 2006[90] essentially gutted the War Crimes Act, making it virtually useless to a prosecutor:

1. It amended the War Crimes Act to narrow the definition of cruel and inhuman treatment, thereby making legal acts that were previously illegal.

2. It made these weaker provisions retroactive throughout the entire time period of the Bush presidency.

3. As extra insurance, it expanded previously enacted defenses in the Detainee Treatment Act of 2005, such as the defense of reliance on a lawyer, to make them retroactive as well.

On the first point, the Military Commissions Act eliminated several provisions of Common Article 3 as crimes under U.S. law. Specifically eliminated were acts that constituted "violence to life and person" and "outrages upon personal dignity, in particular humiliating and degrading treatment." Other acts were redefined, too, removing them from the reach of the law. In particular, prosecution for "cruel and inhuman treatment" was wiped away.

The trick to doing this involved changing the definition of "cruel and inhuman treatment" to make it the equivalent to "torture." The Geneva Conventions list "torture" and "cruel and inhuman treatment" as distinct and separate, making it clear that they are two different forms of behavior and are not equivalent. That's what the original War Crimes Act of 1996 did, too. No longer.

The ramifications of this change of definition might seem minimal on the surface. They aren't. Without a doubt, the enhanced interrogation techniques constituted cruel treatment. No one could seriously dispute this. The stories and pictures from Abu Ghraib—vicious dogs snarling at a naked and shackled prisoner; chaining someone to a cell floor for hours at a time—are cruel and inhuman. But if certain actions can be defined as "merely" cruel treatment, the new War Crimes Act says that they are no longer prosecutable since "cruel and inhuman treatment" was replaced with "torture." This meant that if mistreatment did not rise to the level of torture, it could not be prosecuted under the new War Crimes Act.

Former navy general counsel Alberto J. Mora described the critical legal distinction to the Senate Committee on Armed Services in June 2008. "Many of the 'counter-resistance techniques' authorized for use at Guantánamo in December 2002 constitute 'cruel, inhuman, or degrading' treatment that could, depending on their application, easily cross the threshold of torture," said Mora. "Many Americans are unaware that there is a legal distinction between cruelty and torture, cruelty being the less severe level of abuse. . . . The government could evasively if truthfully claim (and did claim) that it was not 'torturing' even as it was simultaneously interrogating detainees cruelly. Yet there is little or no moral distinction between cruelty and torture, for cruelty can be as effective as torture in savaging human flesh and spirit and in violating human dignity."[91]

Other definitions in the War Crimes Act were "adjusted" by the Military Commissions Act as well, following along in the capricious path of the Bybee/Yoo torture memos of August 1, 2002. Rather than the broad umbrella approach of the Geneva Conventions, the law was narrowed to nine specific behaviors that constitute violation of the law. In a particularly perverse twist, the definition of "mental pain and suffering" is "prolonged mental pain and suffering" for acts occurring before 2006, and "transitory mental pain and suffering" for acts occurring after 2006. The reason for this shift was to create another buffer against prosecution for waterboarding. By 2006, the use of waterboarding seemingly had been stopped; some claim that the mental "pain and suffering" of waterboarding is "transitory" and, under this new writing of the War Crimes Act, is not a prosecutable crime *before* 2006, when the waterboarding occurred.

What does all this mean for a prosecutor? In short, it means that the new law is a mess. The law was chopped and churned, and the U.S. Congress was sadly compliant and complicit.

But there was more. The most extraordinary aspect of the Military Commissions Act of 2006 is a retroactivity provision to the War Crimes Act. (Although one may exist, I cannot think of a single precedent for this.) After the War Crimes Act was changed in ways that make it difficult to interpret and apply, the changes were made retroactive to November 26, 1997, the date of a major amendment that strengthened the War Crimes Act and which is also undone by the new law. In other words, the new War Crimes Act—weakened and hobbled in 2006—was backdated. The old law is simply replaced with the new one for the nine previous years. The effect of this black magic was to give the entire Bush administration a "free pass."

And the Military Commissions Act added yet another retroactivity clause, this one extending the defenses slipped into the Detainee Treatment Act of 2005. These defenses—that individuals in the chain of torture could claim that they did not know the act was wrong or that they relied on the advice of a lawyer—were made retroactive as well, here to September 11, 2001.

In this maze of legal hocus-pocus, the Military Commissions Act of 2006 applied to a provision in the Detainee Treatment Act of 2005, which in itself applied to a potential prosecution under the War Crimes Act of 1996. Defenses that were not in the War Crimes Act when President Bush and his team entered the Oval Office and that were not in place when they committed crimes authorizing cruel and inhuman treatment as well as torture, were now ready and available.

As a consequence, the War Crimes Act, which should have served as a sentry of strength against the lawless Bush administration, was warped and disassembled. Instead of a law expressing the need for humane treatment of detainees, as originally designed, the Bush administration left behind a mangled and shrunken version, essentially issuing pardons to themselves. Rather than accountability, they opted—literally—to fix the books.

CAN PRESIDENT BUSH, VICE PRESIDENT CHENEY, AND THE BUSH OFFICIALS BE CHARGED FOR ACTS OF TORTURE UNDER THE WAR CRIMES ACT?

Top Bush officials, including the president, vice president, secretary of defense, and others, undoubtedly violated the War Crimes Act of 1996 in its original form, that is, as it was written in the legal code when they entered office. Under that War Crimes Act, authorization of torture or cruel, inhuman, or degrading treatment of detainees is a criminal act. The president and vice president were personally involved in these actions.

They went to extraordinary lengths to decimate the law and construct layers of protection against prosecution. It's no wonder that President Bush and Vice President Cheney felt free to talk openly—even brag—about their authorization of torture and cruel treatment. They believed that they placed themselves beyond the reach of the law. As it relates to the War Crimes Act, they are likely right.

Defense #1 against Prosecution under the War Crimes Act (and the Only One Needed): We Fixed the Law and It No Longer Applies

It's true. The primary defense of Bush officials charged with crimes of cruel, inhuman, or degrading treatment under the War Crimes Act would be that the law does not apply to their actions. Since the key definitions under the law were changed and made retroactive, a prosecutor will have to ask: "which definition of torture, or of cruel treatment, applies?"

If a person were charged under the *old* definition in the law, a defendant would argue that the old law had been changed by the new law so that the old definition—legally speaking—did not exist. Charging a person under the *new* watered-down law would be extremely difficult because so many actions are exempted. In short, the law has been made incomprehensible.

Congress should have stopped the tampering with the War Crimes Act. That didn't happen. President Bush succeeded in an insider assault on the War Crimes Act, making it legally nonsensical and virtually useless as a tool for prosecution of cruel or inhuman treatment.

The current tattered state of the War Crimes Act puts the United States out of compliance with the Geneva Conventions, a treaty ratified by the United States. Congress should begin at once to remove the retroactivity clauses, revert the language, remove the prerogative to claim reliance on a lawyer's advice as a defense, and reinstate the law to reflect its original purpose and provisions.

CAN PRESIDENT BUSH, VICE PRESIDENT CHENEY, AND THE BUSH OFFICIALS BE CHARGED UNDER THE ANTI-TORTURE LAW?

The anti-torture law in the United States is the second important law that should cause worry for Bush officials. Under U.S. Code Title 18, Sections

2340–2340A, it is a federal crime for anyone acting in a U.S. government capacity to commit torture or to conspire to do so.[92] The law applies to torture committed outside the United States. Those convicted under the law can be sentenced to prison for up to twenty years, and the death penalty may be imposed if death results from the torture. The law applies to all U.S. nationals, which, in this case, includes the president of the United States and his entire team.

The initial passage of the anti-torture law in 1994 accompanied the U.S. ratification of the International Convention Against Torture and Other Cruel, Inhuman or Degrading Treatment or Punishment (CAT). First adopted by the UN General Assembly in 1984, this important treaty bars torture and specifies that public officials must not only refrain from using torture, but are obliged to prevent it and to intervene actively if they become aware of it.

The Convention Against Torture, as ratified by the U.S. Congress in 1994, is clear: there are no exceptions to the ban against torture. In other words, it carries something akin to strict liability for torture—officials engage in it at their peril. President Ronald Reagan hailed adoption of the Convention Against Torture by the UN in 1984. He urged U.S. ratification, sending a message to the Senate in 1988 that it "will clearly express United States opposition to torture, an abhorrent practice unfortunately still prevalent in the world today." He said the ratification "will demonstrate unequivocally" the nation's desire to end torture.[93]

After the United States ratified the Convention Against Torture in 1994, the anti-torture law also entered the books. It defines torture as an act "specifically intended to inflict severe physical or mental pain or suffering" on a person who is in custody. The anti-torture law also has a special section on "conspiracy"—Section 2340A(c). It says: "A person who conspires to commit an offense under this section shall be subject to the same penalties (other than the penalty of death) as the penalties prescribed for the offense, the commission of which was the object of the conspiracy."

In a bit of irony, the USA Patriot Act extended the statute of limitations in the anti-torture law by adding it to a list of laws for which there is *no* statute of limitations in certain circumstances (the intention was to heighten the punishment for terrorists, but, of course, it applies to all violators.) The absence of a statute of limitations means that there is no time limit on prosecution—as long as the people who committed the torture are alive, they are liable to prosecution.

There is no doubt that the anti-torture law covered acts of brutality carried out by the Bush administration against detainees. Torture occurred at the explicit behest of President Bush and as a result of his loosening the reins on mistreatment of detainees, acts that are covered under this law.

In an attempt to shield themselves from accountability under the criminal law, President Bush's team secured a reinterpretation of the anti-torture law from a Federalist Society lawyer in tune with its sensibilities—John Yoo. The Bush insiders wanted a verbal silo of language to shield their illegal behavior; Yoo delivered. The question, then, is whether that interpretation does, in fact, protect the president and others from prosecution for the torture protocols they adopted. On close examination, the walls of protection they tried to construct come tumbling down.

President Bush explained his administration's use of waterboarding of suspects in custody in an interview with Martha Raddatz of ABC News in April 2008. "We had legal opinions that enabled us to do it," the president said.[94] By this statement, the president, perhaps unintentionally, acknowledged a key element pointing to his culpability for torture: he and his executive staff had not sought out the best legal advice about interrogation, which, if given, might potentially have put the brakes on the harsh interrogation methods they wanted to use, but instead looked for and secured legal "enablers."

I described earlier the multiple problems with the content of the "legal opinions." There is another issue as well—the timing. The president has indicated that he relied on the legal opinions in the memos in authorizing waterboarding and other enhanced interrogation techniques. But the memos were written *after* torture and cruel treatment were already under way. As a result, the president and his team could not have "relied" upon them in deciding to authorize torture. The inspector general of the FBI indicated in a report on detainee interrogations in 2008 that SERE-style interrogations began on Abu Zubaydah between April and June 2002;[95] the torture memos were released on August 1, 2002—two to four months after that.

Other interrogations were already in process, too. Colonel Lawrence B. Wilkerson, the former chief of staff for Secretary of State Colin Powell, wrote in *The Washington Note* blog in 2009 that, in his research, the "administration authorized harsh interrogation in April and May of 2002—well before the Justice Department had rendered any legal opinion." Wilkerson was referring specifically to the case of Ibn al-Shaykh al-Libi,[96] who was delivered by the United States to Egypt for questioning and tortured there. Aggressive interrogations were also occurring at Guantánamo before the August 1, 2002, legal "justifications," according to a report written by the inspector general of the FBI in 2008.[97]

Rather than offering guidance on the best course of action to take to abide by the anti-torture law and fulfill the Constitution, the Yoo/Bybee torture memos were meant to exonerate and offer cover for torture activities that had already occurred, and to greenlight just about anything coming down the pike.

The treatment and interrogation of many detainees violated the law, according to documents and reports that have been uncovered. Government documents released to the American Civil Liberties Union in 2005 showed that twenty-one individuals died of homicide in custody and eight deaths appear to have resulted from abuse, such as "blunt force injuries," "asphyxiation" and "strangulation."[98] In 2008, Human Rights First identified sixty-eight detainees at Guantánamo Bay who may have been abused in its report *Tortured Justice*.[99] A full investigation and release of all documents related to interrogations would permit a complete review of the cases of alleged mistreatment and torture.

But a prosecution need not rest on showing how widespread the torture was or how many individuals were affected. The case of Abu Zubaydah, who was subjected to a wide range of torture and cruel treatment, already illustrates how the actions of the Bush administration undoubtedly broke the law. The CIA destroyed videotapes of his interrogations in 2005. As a result of his treatment and prior injuries, Zubaydah now suffers blinding headaches and permanent brain damage, and experienced two hundred seizures in two years. "Abu Zubaydah's mental grasp is slipping away," his lawyer, Joseph Margulies, wrote in the *Los Angeles Times* in 2009.[100]

There are other cases as well. A military reviewer found that al Qahtani was a victim of torture. In the case of detainee Mahamadou Walid Slahi, the lawyer assigned to serve as prosecutor in 2003, Lieutenant Colonel Stuart Couch, concluded that Slahi had been tortured and refused to handle the case, according to a report of the Senate Armed Services Committee in 2008. His treatment was portrayed as similar to al Qahtani's. Slahi was chained, placed in temperature extremes and a space without light; a masked interrogator told of seeing a grave with him in it and showed him a fictitious letter stating that his mother was being detained. The interrogations continued even after a psychologist reported that Slahi was hearing voices. It "seems a bit creepy," the psychologist said in an e-mail to a supervisor, according to the Senate Armed Services Committee report.[101]

The Bush administration admits that it engaged in waterboarding. U.S. courts have "made it clear" that waterboarding "is indeed torture," wrote law professor Evan Wallach, a former member of the U.S. Army's Judge Advocate General's Corps, in a law review article.[102]

Waterboarding by the CIA ended by 2004, according to an analysis by Mark Mazzetti and Scott Shane in the *New York Times*, as CIA officials became "acutely aware that the agency would be blamed if the policies lost political support."[103] The highly critical report by the CIA inspector general, released in May 2004, and the Detainee Treatment Act passed by Congress the next year, reinforced its demise.

President Bush has insinuated that waterboarding was inconsequential because it involved only three detainees (but 268 waterboarding incidents). He wrote in his memoir, "Of the thousands of terrorists we captured in the years after 9/11, about a hundred were placed into the CIA program. About a third of those were questioned using enhanced techniques. Three were waterboarded."[104] (At least one other detainee was waterboarded in "rendition.") But one is enough to violate the law. It does no good for a criminal to say, "Look at all of the people I didn't beat up"—criminal prosecutions are predicated on individual violations of the law, not percentages.

The use of waterboarding and other abusive interrogation methods authorized by President Bush inflicted severe physical pain, as well as severe suffering, on many detainees, and violated the anti-torture law. Violating the law is a federal crime, and conspiring to violate the law is a federal crime as well. President Bush, Vice President Cheney, Secretary of Defense Rumsfeld, and those who aided and abetted them should be criminally investigated for their deliberate and willing violations of the law.

The remaining question is whether the president and his team have a defense for their violations of the anti-torture law. The answer, in short, is no. One by one, the defenses fall away.

Defense #1 against Prosecution under the "Anti-Torture" Law:
The President and His Team Made Only Policy Decisions;
They Didn't Personally Hurt Anyone Physically or Mentally

The president's office blamed a "few bad apples" in low-level positions for the abuse at the Abu Ghraib prison. In fact, the orchard, the barrel, and the shipping container were all rotten, and it was the president and his team who were the overseers and the planners. Those who set the torture policy are culpable for the actions that followed.

Historically, where torture has been used, the top leaders, whether civilian or military, bear responsibility. The United States executed Japanese general Tomoyuki Yamashita, head of the Japanese armies in the Philippines during World War II, for the brutal treatment of prisoners of war and civilians caused by his troops. Slobodan Milosevic, the former president of Serbia, was charged internationally with permitting atrocities (he died in prison before the completion of the proceedings). Far from being exempted from the laws as the commander in chief (as the Yoo/Bybee torture memos absurdly tried to assert), the president as well as others at the top of the chain of command are responsible for ensuring that the laws against torture are scrupulously followed.

In this case, President Bush, Vice President Cheney, Defense Secretary Donald Rumsfeld, and their lawyers and advisors were deeply involved in planning and implementing the torture protocols and the use of cruel, inhuman, and degrading treatment. They engaged in a conspiracy that spread across departments and agencies of the government, that went from the top down, and they cannot defend themselves by asserting that they did not personally engage in "walling" individuals or shackling them in painful positions.

The president, vice president, and cabinet members are responsible for their own personal participation in authorizing torture and for their conspiracy to commit torture; this defense will not succeed.

Defense #2: A Lawyer Said We Could Do It

A favorite smokescreen of President Bush is that a lawyer told him that the enhanced interrogation techniques were okay. When examined in light of the anti-torture law, this claim simply doesn't hold up. It is, without a doubt, a sham by which the Bush officials tried to shift the blame, absolve themselves, and buffer their actions, but it won't protect the president, vice president, and others from accountability under the anti-torture law.

President Bush explained this line of thinking in an interview with Matt Lauer on November 8, 2010, on NBC. "Why is waterboarding legal, in your opinion?" asked Lauer. President Bush replied: "Because the lawyer said it was legal. He said it did not fall within the Anti-Torture Act. I'm not a lawyer, but you gotta trust the judgment of people around you and I do," the president said. Lauer says, "You say it's legal. 'And the lawyers told me.'" And, as transcribed by NBC, Bush replies: "Yeah."[105]

But the president, as he liked to say, was "the decider," and his book is called *Decision Points*, not *My Lawyer's Decision Points*. As the president, the buck stopped at his desk, not at the desk of a lawyer across the way. The president and his team made active choices. At each step along the road to torture there were dissenting voices, and the president chose to ignore them. Secretary of State Colin Powell, as well as the lawyer for the State Department, objected vociferously to the February 7, 2002, memo that withdrew Geneva Conventions protections. Powell was the former chair of the Joint Chiefs of Staff and had more military experience than any other person in the cabinet.

In December 2002, as Secretary Rumsfeld prepared to sanction enhanced interrogation techniques, military lawyers across the spectrum raised concerns. Navy General Counsel Alberto Mora repeatedly objected.

Referring to the Yoo/Bybee torture memos, Jack Goldsmith, special counsel in the Department of Defense and later head of the Office of Legal Counsel, said that "never in the history of the United States had lawyers had such extraordinary influence over war policies as they did after 9/11. The lawyers weren't necessarily expert on al Qaeda, or Islamic fundamentalism, or intelligence, or international diplomacy, or even the requirements of national security."[106]

In a prosecution (as I described earlier in chapter 2), in order to raise a defense of "reliance on counsel" when charged with criminal law violations, as here, a defendant must rely in good faith on the independent advice of counsel. None of these elements are present here. The Yoo/Bybee torture memos were not sought in good faith, but were sought to provide cover for the president. They did not constitute the independent advice of counsel but were written to justify a policy. The opinions came nine months after the first U.S. detentions, and two to four months after SERE-type inter-rogations began on Abu Zubaydah.

And as for reliance, as I noted earlier, the president did not, in fact, rely on memos, having authorized brutal interrogations prior to their writing. But the president was not entitled to rely upon the torture memos, which were patently poor legal work—called "insane" when reviewed by a succes-sor to Yoo at the Justice Department. Since, as the president notes, he is not a lawyer, he had a higher obligation—and that was to secure an honest opinion about the law. What the president sought instead was a legal opin-ion that would provide a shield—a golden shield to protect himself from the application of the criminal law.

It should be noted that John Yoo was later investigated by the Justice Department's Office of Professional Responsibility to determine whether he had engaged in professional misconduct in writing the torture memos. Despite the lack of cooperation of most high-level staff, including former attorney general John Ashcroft and Cheney's lawyer and advisor, David Addington, the professional responsibility officers determined that the memos showed blatantly bad lawyering by Yoo, poor logic, the failure to refer to important cases, and intentionally false statements.[107] The decision to cite him for professional misconduct was overruled by a Justice Depart-ment bureaucrat,[108] who said that it was a "close question" whether Yoo's memos were intentionally misleading but decided that they merely showed poor judgment. More central here, this determination does not relieve Yoo or Bush or Cheney or others along the chain of decision making from legal liability under the anti-torture law.

(Lawyers themselves are not immune from prosecution for torture or war crimes, either. One of the Nuremberg trials—the "Justice Trial"—charged sixteen judges and prosecutors with war crimes for their part in enforcing Nazi edicts.[109] As I discuss in chapter 5 on international law, sev-eral human rights groups have sought to bring charges in Spain against six Bush administration lawyers for their role in authorizing torture.)

As was established with Nixon and Watergate, the president is sworn by his oath of office to "take care that the laws are faithfully executed," not to manipulate the system to secure an inauthentic justification and then go ahead and break the law.

The issue of good-faith reliance upon a lawyer's advice is a very limited one, and for good reason. It's most often used in tax cases. In torture cases, in which the physical and mental health of other people is at risk, as well as the nation's moral stance on human rights and its reputation in the world, it is utterly inappropriate and insufficient as a defense for the president of the United States.

Defense #3: It Wasn't Torture

President Bush and Vice President Cheney have repeatedly defended their activities by saying that they did not commit torture. "The United States does not torture. It's against our laws, and it's against our values," Bush stated in 2006 when fourteen "high value" detainees were transferred to Guantánamo from secret CIA prisons (black sites) around the world.[110] In a speech before the American Enterprise Institute in 2009 Vice President Cheney said, "Torture was never permitted."[111]

Waterboarding is clearly considered torture. "There is no question in my mind—there's no question in any reasonable human being, there shouldn't be, that this is torture. I'm ashamed that we're even having this discussion," said Richard Armitage, deputy secretary of state in the Bush administration, about waterboarding in the film *Torturing Democracy*.[112] The U.S. government itself has prosecuted cases of waterboarding as torture, even against a sheriff in Texas and a U.S. soldier in Vietnam. Even President Bush refused to answer whether he would consider waterboarding torture if it were used against U.S. personnel when asked by interviewer Matt Lauer in 2010.[113]

And it's not just waterboarding. The enhanced interrogation techniques, used in combination and repeatedly, also constituted torture in the eyes of human rights observers.

The techniques by themselves had brutal origins. As the report by the Senate Armed Services Committee said, "It is particularly troubling that senior officials approved the use of interrogation techniques that were originally designed to simulate abusive tactics used by our enemies against our own soldiers."[114]

Using these techniques, American interrogators inflicted severe pain and suffering and prolonged mental harm. Prisoners experienced harm— Abu Zubaydah, al-Qahtani, and Slahi are but three. The International Committee of the Red Cross, a monitoring body, found torture, and the U.S. government itself, in the Taguba report, found "systemic and illegal abuse" of detainees. Some of it was apparently so bad that the United States refused to release photos depicting the treatment of detainees, which, in the words of Vice President Cheney, would be "incendiary."[115]

Individuals observing the treatment of detainees understood the treatment to be torture as well. Joseph Darby blew the whistle on the degrading treatment of detainees at Abu Ghraib in Afghanistan. FBI officers "separated themselves" from aggressive interrogations, according to a 370-page report by FBI inspector general Glenn Fine.[116]

Although the president and his team secretly attempted to redefine torture in a way that would exclude their behavior, they cannot wash away their legal violations with linguistics. Unlike the War Crimes Act, the anti-torture law was in full force and effect, and was not modified by Congress.

The president and vice president would have us believe that actions recognized as torture by observers of all sorts—cabinet officials, FBI agents, enlistees, human rights observers, international monitors—are not, in fact, torture. But this is not a sustainable argument. As Justice Felix Frankfurter wrote in a 1949 case on abusive interrogation, *Watts v. Indiana*, such a conclusion would require us "to shut our minds to the plain significance of what here transpired."[117] The evidence of torture is potent, even overwhelming. The president, vice president, and their team can repeat "it's not torture" as often as they like, but they can't shut off the minds of ordinary people to the plain significance of what happened to detainees in U.S. custody. A defense that no torture occurred will certainly fail.

Defense #4: So What? It Worked

While President Bush has denied that his administration engaged in torture, he and Vice President Cheney—perhaps feeling safe from prosecution—also have taken the opposite tack and claimed in subtle and more direct ways, with a wink and a nod, that the torture "worked."

In his 2009 speech to the American Enterprise Institute, Vice President Cheney said, "Intelligence officers of the United States were not trying to rough up some terrorists simply to avenge the dead of 9/11. . . . They were trying to prevent future killings. From the beginning of the program, there was only one focused and all-important purpose. We sought, and we in fact obtained, specific information on terrorist plans."[118]

When announcing the transfer of "high value" detainees to Guantánamo from hidden black sites on September 6, 2006, the president said the prisoners in this special program had "given us information that has saved innocent lives by helping us stop new attacks—here in the United States and across the world."[119] He went on the describe examples of how lives were saved. He talked about Abu Zubaydah at length, claiming that a plethora of leads had come from an "alternate set of procedures"—something disputed by agents who were present. The president described Khalid Sheikh Mohammed and other "high value" detainees, too, and said that attacks "to kill innocent Americans" and others had been prevented—by anthrax, a car bomb in Karachi, attacks on a Marine base in Djibouti, on Heathrow or Canary Wharf in London. These same descriptions wound their way into his 2010 memoir, where he said that the detainees who were waterboarded revealed "more than half of what the CIA knew about al-Qaeda," and that it "helped break up plots" to attack "multiple targets."

But intelligence officers have come away with a different view. While it was true that the detainees often talked—if nothing else, to stop the mistreatment—they did not necessarily provide useful information, and, in some cases, sent armies of investigators racing to far-flung places to check out false leads.

FBI supervisory special agent Ali Soufan and his team secured actionable intelligence from Abu Zubaydah through noncoercive questioning before the CIA entered the picture with its SERE techniques, Soufan said in an op-ed in the *New York Times* in 2009.[120] But there it ended. The CIA's enhanced interrogation techniques were useless in extracting actionable intelligence.

A former U.S. intelligence officer said in an investigative article by Tim Lassetter of McClatchy Newspapers in 2008, "As far as intelligence value from those in Gitmo [Guantánamo], I got tired of telling the people writing reports based on their interrogations that their material was essentially worthless."[121] *Vanity Fair* writer David Rose quoted a longtime FBI counterintelligence officer in an extensive investigative report in December 2008. "Torture has made it harder," the agent said. He estimated that 30 to 50 percent of the leads from enhanced interrogation techniques were completely worthless.[122] "You get burned out, you get jaded. And you think, 'Why am I chasing all this stuff that isn't true?'"

The CIA inspector general was also dubious about the success of the enhanced interrogation program using the SERE techniques. He said that, while detention of the suspects removed them from possibly destructive activities, "[m]easuring the success of the EITs [enhanced interrogation techniques], however, is a more subjective process and not without some concern." The inspector general said the "the overall effectiveness of the EITs is challenging."

Similarly, there is not "the tiniest shred of evidence" to support the assertion that the torture of Khalid Sheikh Mohammed saved lives, said Dan Froomkin, Washington correspondent for the *Huffington Post* in a detailed story on November 22, 2010.[123] Reviewing all the claims of actionable intelligence collected through enhanced interrogation techniques, he found that every one had been "thoroughly debunked."

When asked about the value of intelligence secured from the enhanced interrogation techniques, FBI director Robert Mueller was loath to answer, wrote David Rose in *Vanity Fair*. "I ask Mueller: So far as he is aware, have any attacks on America been disrupted thanks to intelligence obtained through what the administration still calls 'enhanced techniques'? 'I'm really reluctant to answer that,' Mueller says. He pauses, looks at an aide, and then says quietly, declining to elaborate: 'I don't believe that has been the case.'"

Jay Rockefeller, Chair of the Senate Intelligence Committee, concurred. "I have heard nothing to suggest that information obtained from enhanced interrogation techniques has prevented an imminent terrorist attack. And I have heard nothing that makes me think the information obtained from these techniques could not have been obtained through traditional interrogation methods used by military and law enforcement interrogators. On the other hand, I do know that coercive interrogations can lead detainees to provide false information in order to make the interrogation stop," he said.

Torture apologists came out of the woodwork after Osama bin Laden was killed in a raid by U.S. special forces on May 2, 2011.[124] They claimed that torture led to identification of his whereabouts, something that has been completely refuted by those in the know. The basis for this spurious claim is that tortured detainees mentioned the name of a bin Laden courier. But none of the "high value" detainees subjected to enhanced interrogation techniques revealed important information about the courier. Khalid Sheikh Mohammed mentioned the courier's nickname only in response to "standard interrogation" techniques and "many months" after being waterboarded, according to an article by the Associated Press.[125] In any case, the CIA actually had that same information—the courier's nickname—long before Mohammed was captured in March 2003.

CIA director Leon Panetta said that the first mention of the bin Laden courier was made in 2002 by a detainee who was in another country and not in CIA custody.[126] Senator John McCain said, "Not only did the use of enhanced interrogation techniques on Khalid Sheik Mohammed not provide us with key leads on bin Laden's courier, Abu Ahmed, it actually produced false and misleading information." In reality, it took the CIA nine years to find bin Laden, and eight years from the time that Mohammed was interrogated. As Senator McCain noted, "In short, it was not torture or cruel, inhuman and degrading treatment of detainees that got us the major leads that ultimately enabled our intelligence community to find Osama bin Laden."[127]

In many instances, the intelligence agencies were frustrated with the false leads. The "leads" were sometimes used as evidence for war propaganda. Interrogators say that they were pressured to get information linking al Qaeda to Iraq, a particular interest of the Bush-Cheney team in making a case for war in Iraq. "The Bush administration based a crucial prewar assertion about ties between Iraq and Al Qaeda on detailed statements made by a prisoner while in Egyptian custody who later said he had fabricated them to escape harsh treatment," wrote Douglas Jehl in the *Washington Post* in December 2005.[128]

In fact, the torture techniques may have "worked" against the United States. The torture of detainees has made it impossible to bring cases against many of them. The images of Guantánamo and Abu Ghraib became recruiting tools for terrorists. Former navy general counsel Alberto Mora reported in a statement to the Senate Armed Services Committee on June 17, 2008, that officers serving the United States maintained that the first and second identifiable causes of U.S. combat deaths in Iraq were the symbols that emerged from the harsh treatment at Abu Ghraib and Guantánamo. McCain described the images of torture as the best aid for al Qaeda: "It serves as a great propaganda tool for those who recruit people to fight against us," he said.[129]

Officials in the State Department found that the use of enhanced interrogation techniques strained relations with allies as well. "If you just look at how we are perceived in the world and the kind of criticism we have taken over Guantánamo, Abu Ghraib and renditions . . . whether we believe it or not, people are starting to question whether we're following our own high standards," former secretary of state Colin Powell said in the *Washington Post* in 2006.[130]

Even CIA agents worried. The CIA inspector general wrote in a report on interrogations in 2004: "The EITS [enhanced interrogation techniques] used by the Agency . . . are inconsistent with the public policy positions that the United States has taken regarding human rights. This divergence has been a cause of concern to some Agency personnel involved with the program."[131]

When President Bush claimed in his 2010 memoir that lives in England had been saved because waterboarding uncovered terrorist plots, his statements were quickly contradicted by British authorities. "There were real plots . . . but where I doubt what President Bush has said is that this, what we regard as torture, waterboarding, actually produced information which was instrumental in preventing those plots in coming to fruition," said Dr. Kim Howells, the former chair of the Intelligence and Security Committee, which oversees the work of the intelligence community, on BBC Radio.[132] "He needs to justify what he did to the world; we think waterboarding is torture," said Howells.[133]

British prime minister David Cameron, interviewed two days later on his travels to Seoul by Andrew Porter of the *Telegraph*, added his own opinion: "Look, I think torture is wrong and I think we ought to be very clear about that," the prime minister said. "And I think we should also be clear that if actually you're getting information from torture, it's very likely to be unreliable information." He continued, "I think there is both a moral reason for being opposed to torture—and Britain doesn't sanction torture—but secondly I think there's also an effectiveness thing . . . if you look at the effect of Guantánamo Bay and other things like that, long-term that has actually helped to radicalise people and make our country and our world less safe."[134]

In the end, the defense that "it worked" is both untrue and irrelevant to saving the Bush team from prosecution. The Convention Against Torture is absolutely plain: torture is unacceptable for any reason—whether it "works," or not. Declaring that the techniques worked does not absolve President Bush and his team from prosecution; indeed, it is merely an admission that its use was intentional. These attempted justifications and defenses do not protect the president and his team from accountability under the law. What is even more chilling is that, rather than delivering security and protection, the torture has caused long-lasting harm to the moral authority of the United States around the world.

Defense #5: It's Too Late

The statute of limitations for torture under the anti-torture law is eight years after the date the offense was committed (18 USC § 3286). But there is no statute of limitations on prosecution if the torture resulted in death or serious bodily injury to another person, or if it "created a forseeable [*sic*] risk" of death or serious bodily injury.

Serious bodily injury and death were both foreseeable risks of the torture, and were the actual results as well. Abu Zubaydah, who was waterboarded and subjected to multiple other SERE-type techniques, has suffered two hundred seizures. At his Combatant Status Review Tribunal hearing in March 2007, another detainee, al-Nashiri, said: "Before I was arrested I used to be able to run about ten kilometers. Now I cannot walk for more than ten minutes. My nerves are swollen in my body."[135] According to the Physicians for Human Rights in its 2008 report, *Broken Laws, Broken Lives*, several aspects of the enhanced interrogation techniques, including stress positions and sleep deprivation, create the foreseeable risk of serious bodily injury.[136] Detainees suffered "severe and long-lasting physical and/or mental harm," the group said. Allen Keller, director of the Bellevue/NYU Program for Survivors of Torture, described the Guantánamo and Iraq victims he has observed as "some of the most damaged individuals I have ever examined."[137]

Waterboarding, personally approved by the president and vice president, carries a well-known and *foreseeable risk* of death, which would remove any time bar to their prosecution. The risk was described by the CIA's Office of Medical Services in its 2004 "Guidelines on Medical and Psychological Support to Detainee Rendition, Interrogation and Detention." It said one of the risks of waterboarding is "drowning"; hypothermia and aspiration pneumonia are also described as known risks of death from waterboarding.[138] The risk of death was well understood: a medical doctor was required to be present at all waterboarding sessions by the CIA, unlike sessions where other interrogation techniques were used, and procedures were changed to reduce some of the risks of death, for example, putting the detainee on a liquid diet beforehand so that he would not aspirate his vomit and die. Equipment needed to perform an emergency tracheotomy and allow breathing to resume was kept at hand, as described by Steven Bradbury, principal assistant attorney general in the Office of Legal Counsel, in a May 2005 memo to the CIA.[139]

Human Rights First also identified dozens of cases of deaths in custody that appear to be homicides. Iraqi Abed Hamed Mowhoush died in U.S. custody at the Al-Qaim facility in Iraq after abusive interrogation.[140] Gul Rahman died at the "Salt Pit," a secret CIA black site in Afghanistan, allegedly of hypothermia after being kept partially, or perhaps completely, naked in a cell overnight. The United States has refused to turn over an autopsy report or his remains to his family.[141]

Because of the foreseeable risk of deaths and actual deaths of detainees in U.S. custody, the statute of limitations for torture will not expire until one of two things happen—either those who are responsible for the torture are prosecuted, or they die.

———————

Swaddled with the legalisms, cloaked in secrecy, stocked with deceits, Bush administration officials perverted the law in brand-new ways. They seemed to feel confident that they had put into place the legal protections that would make it impossible for a prosecutor to pursue them. In the end, these barriers cannot and will not hold.

Torture stands in opposition to a guiding principle of democracy, that is, to enshrine the humanity of each person. Accountability for torture is needed to wash the terrible stain away, to establish the rule of law, to educate Americans about the innate dignity of all people, to restore our moral authority worldwide, and to prevent any repetition in the future.

President Bush and Vice President Cheney have admitted that they authorized and implemented actions that constitute torture, and they were aided and abetted by key appointees and staff in their administration. All of their claimed defenses are paltry, and certainly none is strong enough to protect them from prosecution under the anti-torture law for their roles, individually and in conspiracy, in the torture campaign. An independent prosecutor should be appointed at once to open an investigation into the violations of the anti-torture law by President Bush, Vice President Cheney, and those who aided and abetted them.

FOUR

Accountability at Home

Redressing Bush
Administration Misdeeds

Accountability is defined by Webster as "the quality or state of being accountable; especially: an obligation or willingness to accept responsibility or to account for one's actions." The dictionary dates the word to 1794—a mere two years after the inauguration of George Washington as the first American president.

Accountability was the hallmark of President Bush's education agenda, a subject that brought him to Sarasota, Florida, on September 11, 2001. Who can forget the image of his appearance at an elementary school on that day, sitting while the children read *The Pet Goat*? Several months later, on January 8, 2002, only weeks before signing an order suspending the Geneva Conventions and paving the way for detainee torture, the president signed the No Child Left Behind legislation. "Accountability is an exercise in hope," he said, in comments posted on the Department of Education website. "When accountability for our schools is real, the results for our children are real."[1]

This is not exactly the same standard that President Bush has applied to himself. In a rare prime-time press conference on April 14, 2004, more than one year after the United States attacked Iraq without finding any WMD and within weeks of the appearance of shocking photos of cruel and inhuman treatment of detainees at the Abu Ghraib prison, President Bush was asked what mistakes he had made. His response was reported by Reuters: "American President George Bush grimaced, sighed, rambled and chuckled under his breath . . . before saying he could not think of a single mistake he had made since the September 11 attacks. 'I'm sure something will pop into my head here in the midst of this press conference, with all the pressure of trying to come up with [an] answer, but it hadn't [*sic*] yet.'" Nothing ever did come.[2]

Nothing ever came of the supposed WMD, either. After President Bush left office, NBC's Matt Lauer asked him about the nonexistent WMD. "Was there ever any consideration of apologizing to the American people?" Bush gasped quietly and shook his head. "I mean, apologizing would basically say the decision was a wrong decision, and I don't believe it was the wrong decision," the president said.[3]

Clearly, President Bush is not as big on accountability for himself as for schoolteachers. While in office, he worked hard to create legal mazes and dead ends to accountability for his own acts. Despite the tremendous losses in lives, injuries, and costs, he found it more convenient to blame lawyers, intelligence officers, and speechwriters when his horrific blunders and illegal actions were uncovered.

The American people can demand accountability for his misdeeds. While prosecution is preferable where crimes have been committed, additional tools are also available for reckoning with the misdeeds of President Bush and his team, and recovering from the damage inflicted. The illegal acts of the president and vice president must be exposed and publicly repudiated to reestablish our values and to warn off those who would follow in their footsteps.

Here are some ways.

EMPOWERING A SPECIAL PROSECUTOR

A special prosecutor—also called an independent counsel—has the power to investigate wrongdoing by top government officials. In 1978, after the Watergate debacle, Congress adopted legislation to ensure that a special prosecutor would be named if high officials were suspected of crimes. President Nixon and his co-conspirators engaged in a catalog of criminality, but initially the Justice Department rolled over and looked in the other direction.

In retrospect, it should have been no surprise that the Justice Department did not fully investigate. People, including presidents, are rarely eager to probe into and prosecute themselves; instead, individuals can be counted on to protect themselves at all costs. Despite the apparent involvement of the White House in the break-in, only the attorney general—who was chosen by Nixon—could appoint a special prosecutor to investigate Nixon, and that wasn't going to happen. When a new attorney general, Elliot Richardson, was named in 1973, the Senate secured a commitment before confirming him that he would name a special prosecutor. The work of the special prosecutor—first, Archibald Cox, and then Leon Jaworski—resulted in the prosecution and conviction of numerous top Nixon administration officials, and the naming of the president as an unindicted co-conspirator in a criminal case involving the Watergate cover-up. When the special prosecutor obtained court approval to get the tape recordings of conversations in the Oval Office from a system installed by the president, the whole house of cards began to fall. The tapes captured the president discussing the cover-up of illegal acts. Impeachment looked imminent, and President Nixon resigned.[4]

Congress learned a lesson, too—that presidential accountability should not be left to chance or to the Justice Department, where appointees would be under the thumb of the president. As a member of the Judiciary Committee in Congress at the time, I coauthored with chair Peter Rodino, a special prosecutor law, and Congress enacted it. Under the law, serious suspicions of criminal activity by the president or other high-level officials required the naming of a special prosecutor (later called an independent counsel). To avoid having the president or his attorney general pick a biased prosecutor, the law empowered a specially convened three-judge court to make the selection.[5]

The law functioned well until the matter of Whitewater, a real estate deal gone bad, arose during the Clinton presidency. A three-judge court picked an independent counsel, Kenneth Starr, a partisan who expanded his probing from the real estate deal into a sexual relationship with an intern. After endless investigations, the independent counsel released a lurid report and made a recommendation for impeachment—although this was not at all the job of an independent counsel. Many Americans were disturbed by this spectacle.[6] When the independent counsel statute expired in 1999, Congress let it lapse. This, however, left a giant escape hatch for members of the Bush administration, and they not only used it but blasted a doublewide corridor through it.

Nothing is now in place to require the appointment of an independent prosecutor in the event of presidential or cabinet member criminality, and nothing was in place during the entirety of the Bush presidency. As in Nixon's era, the attorney general could use discretionary power to name a special prosecutor, but it took substantial pressure to make that happen. In the summer of 2003, the CIA was furious when one of its covert agents, Valerie Plame, was "outed" and demanded that the Justice Department appoint a special prosecutor to investigate and take action. Attorney General John Ashcroft, facing a possible conflict of interest, turned the job over to his deputy, James Comey, who named Chicago prosecutor Patrick Fitzgerald. In a serious and professional investigation, Fitzgerald found that Plame had been targeted by enraged White House insiders who considered her fair game after her husband, Joe Wilson, exposed the president's falsehoods about Iraq's WMD program. Fitzgerald prosecuted and convicted top White House aide I. Lewis "Scooter" Libby (his prison sentence was later commuted by the president).[7]

The appointment of Fitzgerald as a special prosecutor turned out to be a fluke. The last attorney general appointed by President Bush, Michael Mukasey, simply refused to investigate incidents that might incriminate the president or vice president. He even refused to enforce congressional subpoenas for White House staff, reported CNN.com in 2008, undermining the ability of Congress to investigate and correct illegalities.[8]

Under pressure from the CIA inspector general, Mukasey did name one special prosecutor, John Durham, on January 2, 2008, to investigate missing CIA videos of detainee interrogations. But Durham's assignment was carefully limited; he was not granted the same independent powers as Patrick Fitzgerald. Fitzgerald was designated "special counsel independent of the supervision or control of any officer of the Department," and was accorded "all the authority of the attorney general." Durham, by contrast, was to report to the deputy attorney general, as do all United States attorneys. In other words, he was asked to do a special assignment for his boss—he was not given the independence to go where the investigation might take him.[9]

In fact, for more than two and a half years, Durham seemed to let the investigation languish. Finally in November 2010, just as the statute of limitations appeared to be expiring, Durham issued a press release saying that he did not have the evidence to prosecute. He issued no report, no document, no guide to what he had investigated or how he had come to this conclusion, noted the *New York Times* in an editorial on January 25, 2011.[10]

By way of contrast, the special prosecutor law that existed until 1999—U.S. Code Title 28, Section 595(a)(1)—required that a report of findings be made to Congress.[11]

In any event, Durham picked up another assignment from the Obama administration. In August 2009, President Obama's attorney general, Eric Holder, asked Durham to look into specific cases of torture, as reported in the *Washington Post*.[12] From the start, Holder narrowed the investigation, calling it a "preliminary review," and gave Durham only the authority to report to higher-ups in the Justice Department. The inquiry was to investigate select situations overseas in which interrogators may have gone beyond what was permitted under the enhanced interrogation techniques approved by President Bush.[13] The investigation was not authorized to look into the actions of policy makers, decision makers, the authorizers, facilitators, and people at the top of the heap who approved torture techniques—that is, the president, the vice president, the secretary of defense, the lawyers, or the group of National Security Council Principals who met to discuss how torture should be applied to detainees in black sites around the world.

On June 30, 2011, Attorney General Holder announced that 99 of the 101 cases reviewed by Durham were being dropped, and two involving death in custody would be subject to "full criminal investigations" of the CIA interrogators who allegedly went beyond the enhanced interrogation techniques approved by President Bush.[14] By refusing to consider cases involving harm from the EITS, the Justice Department essentially condoned those who adopted the torture rules and left unquestioned those who authorized them.

This review does not prevent a further inquiry. An independent and detailed investigation of the possible crimes of President Bush and Vice President Cheney is needed. The attorney general should designate a special prosecutor—one with the same independent powers that Patrick Fitzgerald had—to investigate the criminal behavior of higher-ups in authorizing torture.

To protect the country against future transgressors, Congress should dust off the special prosecutor law and reenact it. A revived law will vindicate the public's right to accountability—it might even be used to bring about justice and accountability for the Bush administration.

A new special prosecutor law should follow the model of the three-judge panel with some modifications. This time around, the panel should be prohibited from picking anyone with an appearance of a conflict, and the law should include safeguards against the appointment of a biased or over-zealous prosecutor. A revived law also should prohibit the special prosecutor from straying into unrelated allegations or questions of impeachment.

The seeming criminality and gaming of the system of the type that the Bush administration employed would be less likely to happen if our highest officials knew that a special prosecutor were available to take action when needed.

RESTORING THE WAR CRIMES ACT

To protect themselves from prosecution, the Bush officials deliberately hobbled the War Crimes Act of 2006, as I described in chapter 3. Prior to their manipulation, the War Crimes Act provided a clear path of accountability for those who mistreated detainees or permitted their mistreatment in violation of the Geneva Conventions.

The War Crimes Act in its present form is decimated and drained of meaning. The law as it stands does not meet the U.S. obligations under the Geneva Conventions, putting the United States starkly out of compliance. For example, the Geneva Conventions require countries to make it a crime to violate "grave breaches" of their provisions, and now the United States has something that doesn't do the job.[15] This is no minor matter: the Geneva Conventions, as an international treaty, are the "supreme law of the land" under the U.S. Constitution. Failure to have a law properly enforcing the Geneva Conventions shows continuing contempt for the Conventions by the United States—and that is a stain that should be erased.

The important provisions of the law need to be reinstated so that, in the future, it can be used as intended and required—a tool for prosecuting war criminals.

RECLAIMING PROTECTIONS AGAINST UNCHECKED SURVEILLANCE

After the president had broken the law dozens of times with warrantless wiretapping, the Bush administration pushed through Congress a revision of the Foreign Intelligence Surveillance Act of 1978. The FISA Amendments Act of 2008 (or FAA) turned upside down the previous law's careful plan for electronic surveillance. While the original FISA created a court to act as a neutral arbiter to review government requests for surveillance of U.S. citizens and residents, the FISA Amendments Act of 2008 substantially eliminated the neutral arbiter role.[16]

Under the old law, the government had to apply to the FISA court for a warrant to wiretap Americans for foreign intelligence or counter-intelligence purposes. For certain kinds of mass surveillance, the new law limits the role of the FISA court to approving the procedures being used for surveillance instead of reviewing the details of the proposed surveillance itself. This allows for the wholesale acquisition of communications with almost no FISA court scrutiny. Exactly whose communications are being "acquired" by the government in these processes isn't divulged to the FISA court, even when it involves diverting a vast amount of private communications to government computers—possibly all e-mail traveling in or through the United States or sent to and from other countries.

As a glancing accommodation to people concerned about the abuses of surveillance, intelligence agencies were required to report on how Americans' privacy is being maintained under the law. But the information has been delivered at less than lightning speed, and what's been reported is downright discouraging.

Semiannual reports by the National Security Agency and other government intelligence bodies "assessing compliance with the targeting and minimization procedures" seemed to vanish into thin air. The American Civil Liberties Union sued for copies under the Freedom of Information Act, and finally, on November 29, 2010, secured nine hundred heavily redacted pages. Between the blacked-out lines and words, the documents gave glimpses into the program's operations, and nothing about them was very comforting. The conclusion from the redacted semiannual reports showed that "[t]he federal government has repeatedly violated legal limits governing the surveillance of U.S. citizens," wrote the *Washington Post*'s Spencer H. Hsu.[17] The reports showed that a large number of surveillances did not comply with the law, and minimization requirements were not followed ("minimization" is a procedure that is supposed to make sure information that is not pertinent to the investigation isn't misused).

"It is clear," the ACLU wrote in releasing the documents, "that violations continued to occur on a regular basis." It noted: "Every internal semiannual assessment . . . conducted from the enactment of the FAA through March 2010 [the date of the last report released] finds violations of the FAA's targeting and minimization procedures. This likely means that citizens' and residents' communications were either being improperly collected or 'targeted' or improperly retained and disseminated."[18] But exactly what the agencies did and how were all big unknowns. Nor was it known what would happen to the information that was improperly collected. Is it retained in some giant computer file? Has it been destroyed?

Eighteen months before the document release to the ACLU, the *New York Times* had also reported on similar problems with surveillance and the failure to comply with the law. "The National Security Agency intercepted private e-mail messages and phone calls of Americans in recent months on a scale that went beyond the broad legal limits established by Congress last year," wrote Eric Lichtblau and James Risen in April 2009. The Justice Department acknowledged problems with what was termed "overcollection" of Americans' communications. In addition, the *Times* reported on a whistleblower's accusations of "significant misconduct" in FBI surveillance, apparently targeting Americans for warrantless surveillance under the guise of "foreign intelligence" when there was no rationale connecting the Americans to terrorism, and then seemingly retaining or disseminating information improperly.[19]

In other words, reports from inside the government were showing one thing: surveillance operating under minimal oversight posed serious problems that endangered the privacy and liberty rights of Americans.

The FISA Amendments Act of 2008 expires in 2012. This is an excellent opportunity for the nation to review the law objectively and to see if it is balancing the privacy needs of Americans and the government's need for foreign intelligence. This will be the time when it can—and should—be revised.

All government agencies will not scrupulously follow the law—as noted, several have already admitted that they do not. Stronger protections are needed. Despite the efforts of Congress to build detailed reporting requirements into the 2008 law, it is nearly impossible to assess whether surveillance has better protected the country against terrorist attacks or has simply resulted in wholesale violation of Americans' privacy with nothing much to show for the effort. Unredacted versions of the agency reviews need to be made available to public experts so that there can be a complete understanding of how the law is working to help or to harm. And instead of requiring citizens to rely on lawsuits under the Freedom of Information Act to find out what the government is doing, the next version of the law should make the reports automatically available (in a redacted form, at least) to the public.

Concerns raised in 2008 by then senator Russ Feingold, something of an expert on this subject because of his membership on both the Senate Judiciary and Intelligence Committees, provide good guidance on what provisions should be analyzed closely and—if the law isn't working—fixed.[20] He identifies possible problem areas, including the broad scope of collection of all communications between the United States and the rest of the world, the potential for "reverse targeting" that uses a foreign target as a pretext to wiretap a U.S. citizen or resident, and insufficient procedures for minimization of surveillance of U.S. persons so that communications acquired illegally are not retained or used improperly for other purposes.

Americans whose information is part of the material that is "overcollected" under the law should have an opportunity to know about it and clear it out of government files. The next version of the FISA Amendments Act should include a "freedom of information" clause that allows Americans to find out whether their information was unlawfully overheard or collected under FISA, and to remove or otherwise "minimize" the record. This adjustment, while not fully reining in executive branch excesses, will provide some measure of relief to Americans whose constitutional rights are improperly infringed.

Most claims of wrongful collection of information have been foreclosed in court because the individuals suing cannot show that they have been secretly surveilled under the law, and they can't show it because all of the activities under the law are secret. A federal appeals court ruling on March 21, 2011, in the case *Amnesty v. McConnell* finally allowed a consortium of news organizations, attorneys, and human rights advocates who worried that their international communications might be wrongly intercepted to proceed with a legal action to challenge the FISA Amendments Act of 2008.[21] In revision, however, the law itself should include a provision that allows people to seek relief from the government if they have a reasonable suspicion that their privacy has been invaded.

The next version of the foreign intelligence surveillance law should keep all the needs of America in mind—those of intelligence agencies to gather the information to protect national security, as well as those of citizens to enjoy the fruits of liberty from living in a democratic society.

RECOVERING MISSING RECORDS

Records are evidence. Any fan of television crime programs knows that letters, mail, and video- and audiotapes can be central to determining criminal liability and fixing accountability. But pivotal records of the Bush administration have gone AWOL, including records that might illuminate actions relevant to torture and war deceptions.

These are not trivial matters. The Watergate investigations of President Nixon were rocked by two key instances of evidence destruction. One was the "18½-minute gap"—a portion of a taped conversation between President Nixon and his aide H. R. Haldeman that was erased. The second involved a White House safe that was emptied and the contents burned. Both were part of the overall Watergate cover-up and stand as enduring symbols of criminality by a president and co-conspirators.

Hiding or mutilating federal records may be considered a crime under federal law in some cases. For example, under U.S. Code Title 18, Section 2071, it is a federal crime if anyone "willfully and unlawfully . . . mutilates, obliterates, or destroys any record . . . paper, document or other thing . . . filed or deposited in any public office, or with . . . any public officer."[22] Violation of the law carries a prison term of up to three years and a fine. Other laws, such as obstruction of justice, might come into play as well.

Among the missing records are videotapes of interrogations of detainees that were destroyed by the CIA. Some of the tapes were of interrogations of Abu Zubaydah, who was subjected to waterboarding and other cruel and inhuman interrogation techniques, as noted by the *New York Times*. The tapes could have shown criminal liability. The CIA destroyed ninety-two tapes in 2005, even though a federal court, ruling in a Freedom of Information case brought by the ACLU, had ordered the agency to retain all the tapes. "The tapes were destroyed in part because officers were concerned that video showing harsh interrogation methods could expose agency officials to legal risks," according to the *Times*. In 2008, Assistant U.S. Attorney John H. Durham was assigned to investigate the tape destruction, but did not file any charges.[23] The Justice Department should require Durham to report findings from his investigation.

In addition, it's imperative that courts apply sanctions when evidence is demolished. "The C.I.A.'s decision to destroy the tapes—rather than submit them to the judge for a decision on whether to order their public release—was a serious affront to the court and the rule of law," wrote the *New York Times* editors on January 25, 2011.[24]

Right after the Durham decision, the National Archives renewed a

2007 request to the CIA seeking an explanation about why the tapes were destroyed, reported Michael Isikoff for NBC News.[25] Under the Federal Records Act, "no federal records may be destroyed" without prior approval of the National Archives and Records Administration—and the archives obviously had not approved the destruction of the tapes.[26] While the power of the National Archives to enforce the law is limited, it could call for the CIA inspector general to do a complete investigation, or it could hold public hearings on the videotape destruction and create a public record of their contents by verbal testimony. In the future, tougher remedies, including personal fines, should be enacted to help people think more seriously about the possible consequences before destroying similar federal records.

E-mails from the Bush administration during critical time periods are also missing. One batch includes millions of White House e-mails that Special Prosecutor Patrick Fitzgerald discovered were missing in his investigation of the "outing" of CIA agent Valerie Plame. In connection with his 2006 prosecution of White House aide I. Lewis Libby, Fitzgerald revealed to the court that there might be e-mails missing from both the vice president's office and the executive office, as described in a 2010 report by Citizens for Responsibility and Ethics in Washington (CREW), "The Untold Story of the Bush White House Emails."

"The Bush White House had little or no interest in preserving emails that likely would cast a less than favorable light on its actions," wrote CREW. Along with the National Security Archives, CREW sued the Bush White House to recover the missing e-mails. The Obama White House eventually agreed to restore ninety-four days of Bush e-mails and to turn them over to the National Archives so it could determine public accessibility under existing laws.

Overall, the Bush White House had a very poor system for backing up and retrieving data. Even though the National Archives, which was responsible for the preservation of presidential papers, pointed out problems, nothing was done to correct them, CREW said.[27] Because of this, Congress should pass legislation to permit the National Archives to install and implement a proper electronic data retrieval system for the White House. In that way, future presidents will not be able to thwart accountability by hiding or destroying the public record.

The third area of missing records concerns John Yoo's e-mails during the key period in which he wrote the torture memos. The e-mails were reported "deleted" and supposedly "non-recoverable," according to the Office of Professional Responsibility in an investigative report written on July 29, 2009.[28] In February 2010, the National Archives asked the Justice Department to explain the deletions of Yoo's e-mails, and some, but not all, were subsequently recovered, according to CREW.[29]

To resolve the matter, the inspector general for the Justice Department should also begin a full investigation to determine what happened to the e-mails and if any misconduct was involved. Recovering all of Yoo's e-mails might show whether the White House participated directly in writing the memos on enhanced interrogation techniques.

The government should take whatever steps are possible to find and release missing documents and e-mails. Missing Bush records, or some of them, might be retained in computer files, archives, electronic backup systems, or backrooms. Thorough and sophisticated searches for them might yield results. Only with records accountability can the public begin to understand firsthand the truth about the "decision points" that led to war, torture, cover-ups, perjury, and other misconduct by President Bush and his team.

CHANGING THE STATUTES OF LIMITATIONS
FOR GRAVE ABUSES OF POWER

A president probably cannot be prosecuted while in office—impeachment is the only remedy during that time period. What has not been tested is when the statute of limitations would begin to count down for presidents— from the time of the commission of the crime, or the last act in a conspiracy? Or does it only begin on the date that the president leaves office?

For the gravest crimes, a ticking clock should not govern whether or not accountability is applied. A change in the federal statute of limitations laws could adjust this. Congress should pass a law holding the statutes of limitations in abeyance while the president is in office, and extending it for another five to eight years after tenure in office has ended. The statutes of limitations should be abolished for certain crimes, such as illegal surveillance, torture, war crimes, and lying to embroil the country in war, when committed by presidents, vice presidents, and other top officials of the government. These officials should not feel that they can be free of the law simply because they successfully block prosecutions while they are in office, and then claim that the time has expired when they are out.

Quite simply, waiting out the statutory time period and writing a memoir to confess—or celebrate—law breaking is unacceptable; top officials
must be held accountable for grave crimes whenever they are discovered.

PURSUING THE CIVIL LITIGATION PROCESS

Civil lawsuits offer a routine but powerful means of accountability. When
people whose constitutional rights have been violated by the government
sue those responsible, the lawsuits serve important functions. They may
secure financial and other redress for the victim. They also reveal governmental misconduct, and public attention may force reform. And they
educate the public about government misbehavior, in this way playing a
vital role in democracy.

A number of civil lawsuits filed in American courts have attempted to
seek accountability from the Bush administration, particularly on allegations of torture and illegal surveillance. Other civil litigation matters have
addressed telecom collusion on wiretapping, freedom of information, conditions of detention, retaliation against whistleblowers, and the constitutionality of new laws or executive orders by the White House. But with
some rare exceptions, cases that would shed light on accountability for
the stark breach of the law by the president, vice president, and others—
particularly on war crimes, torture, and illegal surveillance—haven't gotten
very far in the United States. In fact, legal actions by torture victims have
gotten nowhere. Most have been stopped dead in their tracks at the earliest stages of the proceedings, especially because of the Bush administration's constant invocation of the "state secrets" privilege, which I describe
in the next section. Courts have retreated behind the skirts of "national
security"—even though the claim of national security may be bogus. During Watergate, President Nixon repeatedly raised fake claims of national
security to cover up criminal misconduct.

But the court deference to national security claims in recent years has
been exceptionally high, even in situations where the claim seems invalid
because the "secret" has become public. For example, a claim that the CIA's
program to turn people over to other countries for torture is a state secret
is peculiar, at best; it is especially odd when the program has been documented in books, films, television programs, and government reports that
have become public, and even in lawsuits filed in other nations. As a result
of the extremely expansive use of the state secrets doctrine, President Bush,

Vice President Cheney, and others have managed to escape facing the accountability that comes from depositions, document discovery, testimony, and trials, and civil litigation, for the most part, has been shut down.

And yet, lawsuits seeking information about missing e-mail and unreleased documents, sometimes incident to another case, have succeeded in bringing forward information that can help the public piece together some of the criminal actions of the Bush administration. Other lawsuits have provided insight into government practices, such as extraordinary rendition to black-site prisons in other countries. *Arar v. Ashcroft* was filed by the Center for Constitutional Rights on behalf of Maher Arar, a Syrian-born engineer and Canadian citizen who was traveling back to Canada from a trip to Tunisia in September 2002 when he landed at JFK Airport to change planes.[30] Based on a faulty tip from the Canadian police, U.S. officials detained him. After being questioned about ties to al Qaeda, he was forcibly transported to Syria.

Arar's treatment was described later in an appellate court opinion: "During his first twelve days in Syrian detention, Arar was interrogated for 18 hours per day and was physically and psychologically tortured. He was beaten on his palms, hips and lower back with a 2-inch-thick electric cable. His captors also used their fists to beat him on his stomach, his face and the back of his neck. He was subjected to excruciating pain. . . . He was placed in a room where he could hear the screams of other detainees being tortured and was told that he, too, would be placed in a 'spine breaking chair, hung upside down in a tire for beatings and subjected to electric shocks.' "[31] He was finally released with no charges.

Arar's lawsuit, brought against Attorney General John Ashcroft and other Bush administration officials in the federal court for the eastern district of New York in 2004, was dismissed and the Second Circuit Court of Appeals upheld the dismissal in 2008 and reaffirmed that decision in 2009. The appellate court said that the case could "affect diplomacy, foreign policy and the security of the nation" and that "providing a damages remedy" against government officials would enmesh the courts in assessing the rationale of their policies, "matters that directly affect significant diplomatic and national security concerns."[32]

In a fierce dissent, Judge Barrington D. Parker confronted the majority, saying: "Our role is to defend the Constitution. We do this by affording redress when government officials violate the law, even when national security is invoked as the justification."³³ In June 2010, the Supreme Court refused to hear the case, letting the appeals court decision stand. Fortunately, Arar has had better treatment in Canada, which I describe in chapter 5.

Another case, *El-Masri v. Tenet*, involved Khaled El-Masri, a German citizen of Lebanese heritage who brought a lawsuit in federal district court in Virginia in 2006 against CIA director George Tenet and U.S. officials for his detention and mistreatment.³⁴ In late 2003, while traveling in Macedonia, he was removed from a tourist bus and turned over to CIA agents, who sent him to a prison in Afghanistan, where he was beaten and tortured. When CIA officials realized that they had kidnapped the wrong person, he was flown to Albania and unceremoniously dumped on a roadside in a remote part of the country.³⁵ According to Chancellor Angela Merkel of Germany, Secretary of State Condoleezza Rice privately admitted to her that the United States made a mistake in kidnapping El-Masri, according to a report by the BBC on December 7, 2005.³⁶

In his lawsuit, El-Masri asked for damages and an apology. Claiming that national security information would have to be revealed, the district court dismissed the suit on grounds of state secrets in May 2006. In 2007, the ruling was upheld on appeal and the Supreme Court declined to hear the case. El-Masri was left with no legal remedy in the United States.

El-Masri wrote an essay, "I Am Not a State Secret," published in the *Los Angeles Times* on March 3, 2007, after the Supreme Court ended his quest. He wrote:

> The U.S. government does not deny that I was wrongfully kidnapped. Instead, it has argued in court that my case must be dismissed because any litigation of my claims will expose state secrets and jeopardize American security, even though President Bush has told the world about the CIA's detention program, and even though my allegations have been corroborated by eyewitnesses and other evidence. . . . I did not bring this lawsuit to harm America. I brought the lawsuit because I want to know why America harmed me. I don't understand why the strongest nation on Earth believes that acknowledging a mistake will threaten its security.³⁷

El-Masri has continued to seek recourse in European and international venues, as described in chapter 5.

In the case of *Mohamed v. Jeppesen Dataplan, Inc.*, filed in federal court in Northern California on May 30, 2007, five plaintiffs, all former detainees of the CIA, sought recourse against a subsidiary of Boeing Aircraft that had provided planes and logistical support for the CIA's torture program.[38] The named plaintiff, Binyam Mohamed, an Ethiopian who resided in Britain, was seized by the CIA in 2002 and taken to several countries, including Morocco, where he was tortured with sleep deprivation, shackling, threats, and repeated slashings of his penis with a scalpel.[39] British government officials stated that the detention and interrogations had "a marked effect upon him" and caused "significant mental stress and suffering," according to an article in the *Telegraph* on February 10, 2010.[40] He was able to get monetary relief through the courts in Great Britain, as described in chapter 5, but the claim of Mohamed and the others in the United States was rejected on the grounds of state secrets by the district court in 2008. Upon appeal by the ACLU, a divided Ninth Circuit Court of Appeals upheld the decision on September 10, 2010,[41] and the Supreme Court declined to consider it.[42]

A number of U.S. court cases have also challenged President Bush's authorization of illegal surveillance. In *ACLU v. National Security Agency* in 2006, the ACLU sued the United States on behalf of scholars, journalists, and nonprofit organizations for both illegal wiretapping and data mining, claiming, among other things, that the illegal surveillance violated their First Amendment rights.[43]

The government asserted a state secrets privilege to stop the lawsuit. The trial judge, Anna Diggs Taylor, dismissed the data mining claims on the grounds that the government could not defend them without exposing state secrets. But, as *New York Times* reporters explained in a 2006 article, Judge Taylor did find that the president's warrantless wiretapping program was no longer secret, since it had received extensive publicity and the president himself had admitted its existence in a national broadcast. The judge also rejected the government's claim that it needed to rely on state secrets to defend against this claim and allowed that part of the case to proceed.[44]

Unfortunately, the judge's decision was overruled in July 2007 by the Sixth Circuit Court of Appeals, which found that the plaintiffs did not have standing to sue because they were unable to show how they had been harmed. Of course, the government wouldn't release any information to them, so the plaintiffs couldn't definitively show that they had been wire-tapped. The Supreme Court declined to take the case in 2008. The final result: the lawsuit was ended and the plaintiffs were shut out of court.[45]

In *Al-Haramain Islamic Foundation v. Bush*, filed in 2006[46]—Obama's name was substituted for Bush's later—a foundation and its lawyers said that they were the subjects of illegal surveillance in March and April 2004, and sought damages.[47] The Al-Haramain Foundation was based in Saudi Arabia, and a U.S. branch operated from Ashland, Oregon. The U.S. government inadvertently sent a document to the foundation, indicating that the organization's lawyers had been wiretapped. The lawyers and foundation sued the government in 2006 for penalties under the Foreign Intelligence Surveillance Act (FISA) for conducting wiretapping on them without a warrant. Then things became tricky. Although the plaintiffs had already seen the document showing that they had been wiretapped, it was held to be a state secret and was sealed, and the lawyers were forbidden to mention it. As a consequence, the foundation collected other evidence showing that it had been wiretapped—including a speech referring to the surveillance by an FBI official and posted on the FBI website.

The government refused the opportunity to show the judge information about the legality of the wiretaps in private and explain why the foundation was not entitled to a penalty. Instead, the government simply invoked state secrets to block any inquiry, and sat back. In response, the judge held that the government was in default in a 2010 ruling, and the plaintiffs were granted $26,000 in damages and $2 million in legal fees. In this one case—a rarity—the judge refused to allow the claim of a state secrets privilege to obstruct fairness.[48]

In another case, *Amnesty v. Clapper* (formerly *Amnesty v. McConnell*), the Second Circuit Court of Appeals issued a decision on March 21, 2011, allowing a group of citizens, journalists, and nonprofit organizations to challenge the constitutionality of the Foreign Intelligence Surveillance Amendments Act of 2008, even though they couldn't show definitively that they had been subjected to surveillance.[49] The court said that the plaintiffs, because of their work with persons likely to be the subject of surveillance under the law, had a "reasonable fear" that their communications would be monitored. They suffered actual injury, for example, in being forced to travel outside the United States to meet with clients or others in person in order to assure the privacy of their communications.[50]

The decision allows the case to move forward in the trial court. Since, for the most part, the courts have simply slammed the door to victims of Bush administration lawlessness and misconduct, this decision represents an important breakthrough in the citizen use of civil litigation to challenge a potentially unconstitutional law.

The civil legal process can be a powerful way for people in a democratic society to press legitimate claims and to secure accountability and change. Unfortunately, most of the cases challenging Bush-era illegality have been stopped at the courthouse door.

REFORMING THE STATE SECRETS PRIVILEGE

Use of the state secrets privilege became a tool used with increasing fervor during the Bush administration.

I developed a certain skepticism about government secrecy claims after seeing them used in entirely unnecessary ways. In recent years, I became involved in an effort to declassify U.S. government files relating to Nazi war criminals. I served on a federal panel that oversaw the program, and through it, more than eight million pages of previously secret documents were declassified.[51] In some cases, Nazi documents captured by the United States during the World War II had been classified as U.S. secrets; in other cases, information about the whereabouts of war criminals had been classified. Of the eight million pages, only one page was legitimately withheld for national security purposes; and the rest could have been declassified many years earlier without endangering the United States. The excessive classification and secrecy for all those years didn't serve the best interests of anyone—the government or the public.

The state secrets privilege was first articulated in a 1953 Supreme Court decision in *Reynolds v. United States*, but in recent years, it has been misinterpreted and misapplied well beyond its original scope. In *Reynolds*, widows of personnel killed in the crash of a B-29 bomber sued the U.S. government and asked for the accident report. The government invoked the state secrets privilege and refused to supply the report, claiming it would disclose secret electronic equipment and harm national security. While the *Reynolds* case allowed the state secrets privilege to apply to that document, it did so with caveats. It looked at a balance of needs. In *Reynolds*, the court found that the plaintiff could secure the needed information in other ways—for example, by interviewing survivors of the crash.[52] As a result, the Supreme Court barred the disclosure of the accident report. Years later, when the accident report was finally declassified, it showed that government negligence was a factor in the plane crash. Even though the government may have had legitimate reasons for claiming state secrets, it was also hiding a deeper, darker secret—its own negligence.

Reynolds underscores the fallacy of blindly believing the government's invocation of state secrets. While the case should serve as a hallmark of caution, the courts have regularly ruled in a knee-jerk way in favor of the state secrets privilege. Rather than carefully scrutinize the government request and balance the need for the evidence against the government's claim, the courts have given extreme deference to the government position.

This is not what Congress intended in 1973 when it included a state secrets privilege in the rules of evidence. The legislation—I was a member of Congress at the time and proposed the House bill—required that the state secrets privilege, along with other common-law privileges, such as those for "husband–wife" or "attorney–client" communications, be evaluated on a case-by-case basis, relying upon the court's ability to apply reason and experience. I was prompted to take action on the state secrets provision because President Nixon's Justice Department was attempting to insert an exceptionally strong state secrets privilege in the rules of evidence—a privilege that easily could have been used to hide the misdeeds of an imperial president. Our provision of a case-by-case review by the judge was an alternative to allowing presidents to cover up information unilaterally.

But the courts have simply said yes to executive claims on state secrets and closed down plaintiffs' cases altogether without balancing the plaintiff's needs for evidence with the government's need for secrecy, and without using the test of reason and experience that Congress intended. In addition, the Bush era ushered in "sweeping state secrets assertions" by the government, as Steven D. Schwinn wrote in a 2010 law review article.[53] In failing to investigate the government's claims carefully, the courts have not provided due process to victims. When we considered the legislation in Congress, we did not anticipate that courts would collapse whenever an administration invoked national security: we expected the courts to act as a vital check on power grabs by the executive branch. During the Bush administration, the state secrets privilege became a form of hidden immunity for governmental lawlessness.

Reform of the state secrets privilege is essential. The courts themselves could heighten judicial oversight of claims of state secrets to make sure they are warranted and not a sham. "Judges have the constitutional and legal authority to review and evaluate any evidence," wrote the Constitution Project in Washington, D.C., in a 2007 report on reforming the state secrets privilege. The report calls upon judges to "exercise their independent duty to assess the credibility and necessity of state secrets claims by the executive branch."[54] When the state secrets claim is warranted, measures should be available to allow for the lawsuit to proceed in ways that do not jeopardize national security.

Congress also has the power to revise and regulate the state secrets privilege, and it should do so. Legislation on state secrets should include the following provisions:

1. Courts must examine the actual evidence and reach their own conclusions about whether disclosure will reasonably pose a significant danger to national security. Courts regularly do this on Freedom of Information Act requests and in criminal cases where the government seeks to prosecute, but classified information is involved.

2. The burden of proof should be on the government to show the danger from disclosure.

3. The case should not be dismissed outright until the plaintiffs have had a full opportunity to complete discovery of nonprivileged evidence and to litigate based on that evidence.

4. The court should use experts with security clearance to help scrutinize the claim of privilege.

5. Courts should be empowered to order a nonprivileged substitute for the secret evidence, such as a paraphrased version of a secret document.

The use and seeming overuse of the state secrets privilege has protected governmental lawbreakers from having to answer for their crimes. It leaves people seeking justice out in the cold, and leaves the American public in the dark about the misdeeds of their government. Reining in the expansive use of the state secrets privilege will go a long way toward returning the possibility of accountability to our system.

USING THE POWER OF IMPEACHMENT

Under the Constitution, the president, vice president, judges, and civil officers of the United States may be removed from office for "high crimes and misdemeanors" through impeachment and trial.[55] Impeachment would have been an appropriate way for the nation to respond to the misdeeds of President Bush and Vice President Cheney—and I advocated for it.[56] Since Bush and Cheney are no longer in office, impeachment is no longer available as a practical matter (they do get government benefits—pensions, for example—which leads some people to the theoretical, if unrealistic, suggestion that impeachment is still a possibility).

But another individual inside the Bush administration who participated in a conspiracy to violate the law is currently holding office and may be impeached. That is Jay Bybee, who signed the torture memos while serving as a lawyer in the administration's Office of Legal Counsel.[57] President Bush appointed Bybee to an important judgeship on the federal Ninth Circuit Court of Appeals. Federal judges have lifetime appointments, and there are no time limits for impeachment—proceedings may be brought as long as the judge sits on the bench.

Impeachment proceedings are extremely important tools, not only for removing someone who has abused power, but because the proceedings themselves open up a great deal of information to the public—documents, testimony, witnesses. The House Judiciary Committee, when inquiring into the need for the impeachment of Richard Nixon, was able to use subpoena power, call witnesses, override claims of executive privilege, and secure documents that would otherwise have been hidden. Although Bybee might seem like small potatoes compared to the president and vice president, he holds a critical position in the judiciary, to which he was named while working in the Office of Legal Counsel. There, he helped the highest officials in the land authorize a scheme of torture and cruel and inhuman treatment. Shortly after the torture memos were first made public, the *New York Times* called the documents "a journey into depravity." In an editorial titled "The Torturers' Manifesto," the *Times* said: "These memos make it clear that Mr. Bybee is unfit for a job that requires legal judgment and a respect for the Constitution. Congress should impeach him."[58] The use of impeachment, a vital tool that the nation's founders built into our Constitution, would be an invaluable aid to gaining accountability for Bush administration misdeeds.

OPENING A "TRUTH" (VS. "TRUTH AND RECONCILIATION") COMMISSION

Truth and reconciliation commissions have been used in some countries as vehicles by which people in power can confess to their illegal or immoral human rights abuses. Such a commission was used successfully in South Africa in the years after 1995 when the new national unity government came into power, as described on its official website.[59] Those who testified were offered amnesty, and the information was used to capture the grim history and horror of apartheid.

The idea of a similar truth and reconciliation commission to address abuses of the Bush administration has been circulated from time to time. The idea has drawn support from some human rights advocates and public officials, who believe this process could get out the truth about the torture of detainees. Senate Judiciary Chair Patrick Leahy wrote about the need for an inquiry into Bush administration abuses in 2009.[60] But the situation of South Africa was quite different. During apartheid, South Africa was not a full and free democracy. Blacks and whites were deeply divided and truth and reconciliation was a way of bringing both sides of the country together. The United States is not South Africa. On the issues of torture, the east isn't pitted against the west, blacks against whites, men against women. Instead, we have a wholesale abuse of democracy as the result of the actions of a relatively small handful of people, both civilians and military personnel, who took the law into their own hands and disregarded U.S. constitutional norms, international obligations, statutory law, and all sense of moral decency. In short, reconciliation is not what is needed. The truth is needed. What might be of value is a "truth" commission that is independent and empowered to find the facts, assess responsibility, and seek accountability for the crimes of the Bush administration.

An independent inquiry or truth commission is needed to assess the role of the CIA and officials of our government in the use of torture—those who gave the orders and those who wrote the disgraceful legal opinions, authorizations, and approvals. An independent investigation is necessary to uncover the misdeeds of the Department of Justice, the Pentagon, and the National Security Agency.

During Watergate, a special Senate committee, chaired by Sam Ervin, was charged with ferreting out the truth of the break-in and cover-up, as described by Elizabeth Drew in her 1976 book *Washington Journal*.[61] This led the way for the impeachment inquiry in the House, and ultimately to President Nixon's resignation. The Church Committee, created after Watergate, carefully investigated the government's abuse of power in its use of warrantless surveillance and other spy powers. Its extensive 1976 report,

Intelligence Activities and the Rights of Americans, helped Congress shape new laws balancing national security and civil liberties.[62] The 9/11 Commission built a solid record of the attacks on the World Trade Center and Pentagon for historical review and released a comprehensive report of its findings in 2004.[63]

Truth commissions can be important in lifting the veil on hidden crimes. They must be able to interview witnesses, collect documents, and review the facts. But they also have weaknesses. For example, truth commissions sometimes do not want to assign blame—the 9/11 Commission, for example, was determined to release only the evidence it had gathered about the attacks without affixing fault. Any reviews of Bush administration misconduct cannot shy away from determining responsibility at the highest levels, and must take particular care to avoid grants of immunity, which could jeopardize criminal prosecutions. The strongest possible tool—prosecution—must be available to root out criminal wrongdoing by people acting inside our own government.

Some other nations have begun to establish independent commissions to take account of their role in the Iraq War, as well as torture and other illegal actions. In July 2009, England began the Iraq Inquiry to identify lessons from its involvement in the Iraq War,[64] and, as I describe in chapter 5, the Dutch completed a critical inquiry into the decision making leading up to their country's involvement in the war.[65]

An independent public review of the Bush administration actions related to the war in Iraq, the illegal wiretapping of U.S. citizens, the use of torture and cruelty, destroyed and missing records, and other topics would not, in isolation, offer the type of accountability that criminal prosecutions can offer, and criminal prosecutions would be better. But an independent inquiry would be a valuable additional procedure in securing full disclosure of the facts and beginning a path to accountability.

The country needs to know how powerful individuals took advantage of their offices, manipulated the laws, brought disgrace upon the nation, endangered our troops with an illegal war, caused thousands of deaths, and, at the same time, protected themselves from accountability at every turn. An independent inquiry will at least put the facts on the public record, and not leave the truth to be coated over at will in the glossy memoir genre.

The United States must use all of the possible tools in response to the wayward and illegal behavior of the Bush administration. Seeking accountability and getting the truth out, however possible, is essential. Reforming the law must be a priority. Preventing repetition by another presidential team is a necessity.

Failure to act will suggest that our nation has a dual system of laws—that there is no accountability for those at the top and no recourse for those at the bottom. We need to make sure that President Bush and his team do not leave the legacy that those in high office can break the law and get away with it. And, given the strong response of some other nations described in the next chapter, we need to take our own problems in hand and show our own robust and unflinching commitment to the rule of law.

FIVE

International Justice

Accountability for the Bush Team Abroad

The conservative mayor of London, Boris Johnson, wrote in an opinion piece in the *Telegraph* in mid-November 2010 that former president George W. Bush might think twice before bringing a book tour to London—or anywhere in Europe, for that matter.[1] If Bush did make an appearance, some member of the constabulary "could walk on stage, place some handcuffs on the former leader of the Free World, and take him away to be charged," Johnson wrote. Johnson was responding to admissions of President Bush in his memoir that he had personally approved waterboarding of a U.S. detainee. The mayor called President Bush's position on torture "patently vile and illegal" and agreed that accountability would be a good thing.

The mayor of London was not the first to suggest that President Bush and his team should make international travel plans with care. Bush team members can be held accountable by other nations for war crime violations under international law.

In fact, in February 2011, President Bush canceled a trip to Switzerland, where he was to be the keynote speaker at an annual charity gala in Geneva. "Criminal complaints against Bush alleging torture have been lodged in Geneva, court officials say, and several human rights groups signaled that they were poised to take further legal action," Reuters reported on February 5, 2011.[2]

Actions in other nations to assign responsibility and affix accountability for Bush team misdeeds have seemed promising, but a longer lens reveals that the United States has interfered repeatedly, attempting to throw obstacles in the way of these efforts in order to crush and subvert them. WikiLeaks documents made public in November 2010 and the months that followed paint a picture through leaked U.S. State Department cables of an international cover-up started by the Bush administration. "Not only were reprehensible actions and orders exposed; the cables also provided ample evidence of the doublespeak engaged in by Washington's allies," wrote Javier Moreno, editor of the Spanish newspaper *El País* on December 23, 2010. "Even the least attentive observer cannot fail to be shocked by the maneuvers to shut down three investigations by the High Court [of Spain] that affected the United States," he said.[3]

As *El País* mentions, some of the efforts to obtain international accountability occurred in Spain; others in Germany, Italy, Poland, Lithuania, and in international and regional tribunals. In Paris, human rights lawyers tried to serve former U.S. defense secretary Donald Rumsfeld with legal papers in 2007 for torture, but he swept away after his speaking engagement to avoid service, said Katherine Gallagher in the *Journal of International Criminal Justice*.[4] A prosecuting judge in Spain brought cases against U.S. officials who wrote torture justifications, but he was abruptly removed from the case. Italy did prosecute and convict CIA officers in absentia for plucking a Muslim cleric off its streets and sending him to Egypt to be tortured. The government in Poland began investigating CIA black sites on its soil. A commission in Holland concluded that its leaders acted illegally in cooperating with the United States attack on Iraq. In these places and elsewhere, people were increasingly using the tools of international law to seek accountability for the global transgressions of the Bush administration, as described in an August 2010 article by Shashank Bengali, "Other Countries Probing Bush-Era Torture—Why Aren't We?"[5]

To call the processes slow going is an understatement. Leaked U.S. State Department cables show that almost as soon as investigations in other nations are instituted, the United States begins fierce efforts to stop them and to maintain its cover-up.

President Bush seemed unabashed in claiming that he ordered torture, but people around the world are repulsed. If political leaders and prosecutors in the United States are too paralyzed or unwilling to look at the wrongdoing, proceedings in other nations may act as a counterweight, giving Americans the information—and guts—they need to move forward and demand accountability.

The modern history of international tribunals has grown out of the Nuremberg trials that followed World War II. U.S. Supreme Court justice Robert Jackson, who helped design the procedures, articulated one of its driving principles—that the people at the top who created the policies should be held accountable as much as the people at the bottom. Said Justice Jackson in his opening statement of the Nuremberg trials: "The common sense of mankind . . . demands that the law shall not stop with the punishment of pretty crimes by little people. It must also reach men who possess themselves of great power and make deliberate and concerted use of it."[6]

The Nuremberg trials—officially named the "International Military Tribunal (IMT) at Nuremberg"—of more than two hundred Nazi war criminals provided a modern framework for an international system of accountability and justice for war crimes. The defendants at the dock in these trials included military commanders and top government officials, as well as judges who enforced vicious Nazi policies. The trial of Nazi judicial personnel was made especially vivid in Stanley Kramer's 1961 film *Judgment at Nuremberg* with Spencer Tracy, Burt Lancaster, Marlene Dietrich, and Judy Garland. (Spencer Tracy, playing the head of the tribunal, memorably says, "Before the people of the world . . . this is what we stand for: Justice, truth and the value of a single human being.")[7]

Even before the Nuremberg cases, Japanese war criminals were tried. General Tomoyuki Yamashita was tried by a U.S. military commission in Manila and sentenced to death for the crimes committed by soldiers under his command. In Tokyo trials, judges from multiple nations tried and convicted four Japanese leaders for barbaric cruelties.[8]

Combined, the Nuremberg and Tokyo trials established the concept that government leaders could be held personally accountable for their decisions and actions in unleashing and furthering war crimes and atrocities. Since World War II, international accountability systems have continued to develop and be refined.

Other specialized international courts, such as one on war crimes in the former Yugoslavia, have sprung into being on an ad hoc basis when circumstances demanded a forum for prosecution.[9] On July 1, 2002, a permanent international tribunal, the International Criminal Court (ICC), opened at

The Hague to try individuals for war crimes, crimes against humanity, and genocide. The United States has not ratified the Rome Statute or accepted the jurisdiction of the ICC, although 114 other nations have.[10]

Former heads of state have been charged in these international tribunals. Slobodan Milosevic, president of Serbia, was indicted in 1999 and then put on trial for his role in the genocide of Bosnian Muslims; he died before the trial concluded. Radovan Karadzic, former president of the Bosnian Serb republic, was arrested in July 2008 for war crimes; Omar Hassan al-Bashir, president of Sudan, was indicted for war crimes in Darfur, although he cannot be tried while still in office; Charles Taylor, former president of Liberia, was placed on trial before the ICC for war crimes.

The six types of international tribunals or processes described in this chapter are sometimes able to help secure accountability from those who have perpetrated war crimes or crimes against humanity.

UNIVERSAL JURISDICTION: OTHER NATIONS FILL A GAP

"Universal jurisdiction" does not refer to a specific tribunal or a place, but to a concept in international criminal law that is used to prosecute certain international crimes. It means that a country may prosecute a "compelling crime," no matter where it took place. Ordinarily, a nation has jurisdiction only over crimes occurring on its territory, or to which it has another direct link. Under universal jurisdiction a country can prosecute a crime even though the events have not taken place on its territory and even if the victims and perpetrators do not have a connection with the country, as Human Rights Watch explained in a 2006 publication. Universal jurisdiction is generally limited to crimes of extraordinary gravity. Historically, crimes accorded universal jurisdiction have included piracy and the slave trade. The Nuremberg trials folded into this definition crimes against humanity, such as murder, torture, extermination, mass deportations. Others, such as genocide, were added later.[11]

The rationale for universal jurisdiction is that impunity for horrific crimes threatens the well-being of people everywhere. In essence, the stain of the crimes reaches beyond territorial borders. Without universal jurisdiction, proponents argue, there may be no way to hold top leaders accountable for grave crimes since many of these leaders control the justice systems in their own countries or have populations unwilling or unable to demand a prosecution. Universal jurisdiction becomes a possibility when the nation responsible for the criminal activity fails to act.[12]

The case of Adolf Eichmann, a Nazi tried in Israel, involved the principle of universal jurisdiction. His criminal activity as one of the architects of the "Final Solution" resulted in the murder of millions of Jews. The crimes had taken place in Europe, but thousands of Holocaust survivors in Israel had been victims of his policies.

In the case of the former Chilean dictator Augusto Pinochet, universal jurisdiction had a major role. In 1998, the former dictator was detained in London based on an arrest warrant issued by Baltasar Garzón, a magistrate in Spain. The Spanish judge asked that Pinochet be extradited to Spain to stand trial for genocide, terrorism, and torture as commander and head of state in Chile.

Pinochet's brutal regime in Chile began in 1973 after he led a military coup against the democratically elected president, Salvador Allende. At least 3,100 people were killed or disappeared in the next seventeen years, and thousands more were tortured or exiled. No action had been taken against Pinochet in Chile, and, in fact, his military junta had granted amnesty to him and others for their atrocities. He claimed additional immunity from prosecution as a former head of state.

The Pinochet arrest warrant, notes *Human Rights Brief,* placed the concept of universal jurisdiction front and center. British law lords ruled that Pinochet did not have immunity as a former head of state. But the British foreign minister, Jack Straw, allowed Pinochet to return to Chile on grounds of ill health.[13]

Even though the refusal to extradite Pinochet to Spain disappointed human rights advocates, the matter didn't end there. Pinochet's arrest in London "changed the perception of what was possible," according to legal scholar Naomi Roht-Arriaza.[14] Galvanized by Garzón's bold steps, human rights lawyers and victims initiated proceedings in Chile, filing nearly three hundred cases by the end of 2003. The courts there found Pinochet ineligible for amnesty because some cases of disappearance were still active and the required investigations had not taken place. Pinochet was placed under arrest. Even though he died in Chile without being brought to trial for his crimes, the proceedings against Pinochet suggest that heads of state cannot commit crimes with impunity, and that international processes for accountability can trigger long-overdue actions inside the home country.

Other Chilean officials were brought to justice: hundreds were arrested and dozens were convicted. The Pinochet case emboldened human rights activists in Argentina and created "an unmistakable trend towards greater international justice," wrote Stacie Jonas of the Institute for Policy Studies, "reminding government and military officials that neither amnesty laws nor the mere passage of time could silence the call for justice."[15]

Some cases using the mechanism of universal jurisdiction have been initiated against the Bush administration in other nations, although not with much success. The WikiLeaks release of U.S. State Department cables indicates why: in several instances, the United States strongly pressured other countries to drop cases.

The same Spanish judge who issued the extradition request for Pinochet, Baltasar Garzón, commenced an inquiry into U.S. torture, especially looking at whether lawyers John Yoo, Alberto Gonzales, David Addington, Jay Bybee, William Haynes, and Douglas Feith—sometimes called the "Bush Six"—had facilitated torture, according to the Center for Constitutional Rights.[16] In his original complaint filed on March 17, 2009, Garzón noted that several Spanish citizens were incarcerated in Guantánamo and mistreated there. The case ran into rough seas rather quickly, as described by the Center for Constitutional Rights. The attorney general in Spain raised objections to the case on April 16, 2009, and by April 23 responsibility for inquiring into the matter—which in Spain's system is placed in the hands of an investigating judge—was removed from Garzón and given to Judge Eloy Velasco. Separately, a judicial complaint was filed against Garzón for a completely unrelated matter (allegedly going beyond his authority in launching an investigation into the identity of bodies in mass graves from the fascist Franco era, as described by Carol Rosenberg in the *Miami Herald*).[17] Serious inquiry into the "Bush Six" came to a halt when Velasco decided that he could not proceed without a statement from the U.S. Justice Department that it was *not* investigating the case.

WikiLeaks cables reveal a whole other drama behind the scenes. "Over the last several years, the Embassy of the United States in Madrid wielded powerful resources in an extraordinary effort to impede or terminate pending criminal investigations in Spain which involved American political and military figures assumed to have been involved incidents of torture," wrote the Spanish newspaper *El País* in December 2010.[18] *El País*, which had full access to WikiLeaks documents, said that cables relating to this cover-up extended from 2005 through 2009 under Ambassador Eduardo Aguirre, a Bush appointee, and continued into the Obama administration. In the weeks before the case was taken away from Garzón in mid-April 2009, officials from the United States, including two U.S. senators, met with the chief prosecutor in Spain, as well as the Spanish foreign ministry and the ministry of justice, pressuring them to stop the "Bush Six" inquiry. According to one diplomatic cable, the U.S. officials "underscored that the prosecutions . . . would have an enormous impact on the bilateral relationship" between the United States and Spain, wrote David Corn in *Mother Jones*.[19] After Garzón was pulled off the case, the U.S. embassy officers reported—with approval—that the second judge was "trying shelve the case," according to an embassy cable.[20]

The WikiLeaks releases brought sudden new attention to the "Bush Six"—at least in Spain, where the case was at the top of the news in late November 2010. Faced with Spanish fury and a new petition by human rights lawyers urging the Spanish court to move forward without further delay, Judge Velasco indicated that he must have a response to his inquiry about whether the United States was pursuing the matter of the "Bush Six."[21] Finally, on March 1, 2011, the U.S. Justice Department sent a response, claiming that it intended to investigate and asking that the case be sent to the United States for investigation.[22] Judge Velasco complied, essentially putting the Spanish proceedings on semi-permanent hold. Lawyers from the Center for Constitutional Rights and the European Center for Constitutional and Human Rights appealed Judge Velasco's decision, saying that the United States did not have a serious intent to pursue the matter, wrote Sarah Posner in *Jurist*.[23]

In Belgium, three lawsuits against members of the Bush administration, including President Bush, Defense Secretary Donald Rumsfeld, Deputy Defense Secretary Paul Wolfowitz, General Tommy Franks, and others, were filed by confidential complainants in 2003 for crimes against humanity in Iraq and Afghanistan, reported Reuters.[24] The United States objected and Rumsfeld publicly threatened to halt funding for a new NATO headquarters in Brussels and move it elsewhere, reported the *Guardian*.[25] In response, Belgium repealed its universal jurisdiction law in August 2003, according to Human Rights Watch, and limited the ability to prosecute matters of genocide, war crimes, and crimes against humanity to cases involving Belgian nationals or residents, or to situations in which Belgium had a treaty obligation to prosecute.[26] The cases against U.S. officials were all dismissed.

The Center for Constitutional Rights in New York, working with civil rights attorney Wolfgang Kaleck in Berlin, urged Germany in November 2004 to exercise universal jurisdiction and take criminal action on behalf of four Iraqi citizens against then defense secretary Donald Rumsfeld under Germany's Code of Crimes Against International Law, citing abuse at Abu Ghraib and Guantánamo. The Center for Constitutional Rights explained in "German War Crimes Complaint Against Donald Rumsfeld et al." that the German law "provides for 'universal jurisdiction' for war crimes, crimes of genocide and crimes against humanity. It enables the German Federal Prosecutor to investigate and prosecute crimes . . . irrespective of the location of the defendant or plaintiff, the place where the crime was carried out, or the nationality of the persons involved."[27] Prisoners alleged that they had been beaten, kicked, sexually harassed, stripped naked, bound for long periods, intimidated by the use of dogs, subjected to degrading treatment, and, in one case, raped, according to documents posted by the Center for Constitutional Rights. Rumsfeld was not amused. "The case provoked an angry response from [the] Pentagon, and Rumsfeld himself was reportedly upset," wrote Adam Zagorin in *Time* magazine. "U.S. officials made clear the case could adversely impact U.S.-Germany relations, and Rumsfeld indicated he would not attend a major security conference in Munich, where he was scheduled to be the keynote speaker, unless Germany disposed of the case."[28] The day before the conference, the prosecutor dropped the case, saying the United States was the appropriate venue for these complaints.

After Rumsfeld resigned as secretary of defense, the Center for Constitutional Rights and Kaleck decided to try again, refiling the case in Germany in November 2007, wrote *Time*. The lawyers argued that the United States did not intend to prosecute the case, and filed on behalf of forty-four plaintiffs, including organizations from Argentina, Bahrain, Canada, France, Germany, and elsewhere, and twelve Iraqi citizens with claims of torture. This time, a second German prosecutor dismissed this case, stating that it seemed to be a "symbolic" prosecution and, again, that handling the cases of abuse "remains the task of the justice system of the United States of America."[29]

The attempt to secure prosecution of Rumsfeld in France also fizzled in a case that the Center for Constitutional Rights attempted to bring in 2007. The prosecutors declined, finding that Rumsfeld, although no longer a government official, had immunity since the acts complained of were taken in his official capacity when he was a government official, explained Katherine Gallagher in the *Journal of International Criminal Justice*.[30]

The concept of universal jurisdiction is important in ending impunity and bringing about accountability for heinous crimes when a national government does not have the political will or capacity to act. But President Bush and his team may have calculated correctly that there was a slim likelihood that other nations would dare to take on the prosecution. Where they have dared, the U.S. government has pushed back hard, both privately and publicly, to quash proceedings that might finally expose the crimes and wrongdoings of Bush administration officials.

THE INTERNATIONAL CRIMINAL COURT ADDRESSES
CRIMES AGAINST HUMANITY—MAYBE

On May 6, 2002, President Bush "unsigned" a treaty that had created the International Criminal Court (ICC), the first permanent international court on war crimes and crimes against humanity. President Clinton had signed the treaty on December 31, 2000. But the U.S. commitment didn't last long. John R. Bolton, Bush's undersecretary of state, wrote to the United Nations: "The United States does not intend to become a party to the treaty," according to the *New York Times*.[31]

The ICC was under steady attack by the Bush administration. Defense Secretary Rumsfeld said that the court would be "putting U.S. men and women in uniform at risk of politicized prosecutions." But he actually may have had himself and the suits in the White House in mind. After all, the "unsigning" came only three months after the February signature of President Bush on a memo unleashing brutal treatment in interrogating detainees, precisely the kind of case that might end up in the International Criminal Court. Ironically, the court came into existence on July 1, 2002,[32] at the very same time that Abu Zubaydah was being tortured at the hands of CIA interrogators in a secret prison abroad.

The creation of the court was "the result of a concerted international effort to combat impunity for what are considered to be the most egregious international crimes—crimes that . . . 'deeply shock the conscience of humanity,'" explained Lynn Gentile in a book on international criminal justice. The court has subject-matter jurisdiction limited to "the most serious crimes of concern to the international community as a whole, namely, genocide, crimes against humanity and war crimes," wrote Gentile.[33]

There are three triggers, described in an Amnesty International fact sheet, that can put a case before the ICC, which is physically located in The Hague in the Netherlands.[34] One way is that the court can take jurisdiction of a matter when a country has signed the Rome Treaty establishing the court and asks the ICC to prosecute a case. Second, the UN Security Council can refer matters to the court. This happened in the case of Omar al Bashir, the president of Sudan—particularly significant because it involved a sitting head of state. Al Bashir was indicted for war crimes and crimes against humanity occurring in Darfur: "Not even presidents are guaranteed a free pass for horrific crimes," said Richard Dicker of Human Rights Watch. The United States didn't use its veto to block the Security Council action.[35]

The final way a case comes before the court is when the ICC prosecutor initiates a matter based on events that occurred on the territory of a country that has signed the Rome Treaty. To commence an investigation, the prosecutor needs the approval of a panel of ICC judges, which determines that there is a reasonable basis to proceed with an investigation and that the case falls within the jurisdiction of the court. Before any such prosecution is brought it must be clear that the countries whose nationals are responsible for the crimes are unwilling or unable to investigate or prosecute. According to a report by the Congressional Research Service in July 2010, the court had indicted sixteen people.[36]

Torture is a topic that could potentially be addressed by the ICC—if it has jurisdiction. And jurisdiction might be possible because of the wide-ranging geography of U.S. torture activities. One basis of jurisdiction, as noted above, is when acts occur in countries that are signatories of the Rome Treaty.

CIA agents transported one hundred or more detainees to black sites in other countries, where the prisoners were tortured. Some of those countries—Lithuania, Poland, Romania—are also signatories of the Rome Treaty. Afghanistan, where torture of U.S. detainees is documented, is a signatory of the Rome Treaty, and the CIA air carriers used bases or stopovers in several signatory nations for rendition flights. As a result, the International Criminal Court could take prosecutorial action against those responsible, including U.S. personnel.

A U.S. law professor submitted a complaint to the ICC prosecutor in January 2010, asking for an investigation and arrest warrants for six top U.S. officials—President Bush, Vice President Cheney, Secretary of Defense Rumsfeld, CIA director George Tenet, Condoleezza Rice, and Alberto Gonzales—for the "widespread" and "systemic" policy of rendering individuals to black sites.[37] Even though the United States is not a signatory to the Rome Treaty, the legal complaint asserts that the ICC should open an investigation on its own. Of course, using the ICC poses its own set of difficulties, not the least of which is securing the presence of the U.S. persons before the court.

As in other areas, however, President Bush and his team were taking no chances in protecting themselves. Not only did the president "unsign" the Rome Treaty and withdraw all support for the ICC, the United States began a heavy-handed campaign in August 2002—only a month after the court first opened—to force other countries to sign immunity agreements. These "Bilateral Immunity Agreements," as they are called, prevent other nations from sending claims against U.S. nationals to the ICC for prosecution.[38] The United States threatened to withdraw military aid, and later economic support as well, if immunity agreements were not signed (and virtually all nations, excepting Cuba, Iran, and one or two others, get U.S. aid). Romania—home to a U.S. black site for prisoners—was among the countries that quickly signed the immunity agreement. The Bilateral Immunity Agreements signed by the Bush administration—more than one hundred of them—are still in force, according to the American Non-Governmental Organizations Coalition for the International Criminal Court (AMICC).[39]

In a 2005 column titled "Schoolyard Bully Diplomacy," *New York Times* writer Nicholas Kristof commented that "the Bush administration is delusional in its terror of the [international criminal] court."[40] But perhaps Kristof was wrong, and the Bush administration had everything to fear.

PROSECUTIONS IN OTHER NATIONS BASED ON COUNTRY JURISDICTION

It's a given that every nation has its own justice system, and that each can prosecute crimes that occur on its lands or have another strong connection to the nation. Some countries drawn into the swirl of U.S. torture have started to respond.

Torture at the hands of U.S. personnel or their proxies occurred in many nations—from prisons in Afghanistan to the globally dispersed black sites operated by the CIA. The United States also sent detainees to other nations, knowing that they would be tortured.

In addition, U.S. personnel took part in actions related to torture in other nations, such as Italy and Macedonia, where individuals were kidnapped and forcibly removed to torture sites. Other nations, including Spain and the United Kingdom (for the use of Diego Garcia), were potentially implicated in torture because their airstrips were used for CIA rendition flights. The Legal Affairs Committee of the Council of Europe found that fourteen European countries collaborated with the CIA in a "global spiders' web" of sites.[41]

Any one of these countries could pursue investigations and prosecutions against U.S. persons for violations of criminal laws on the books in their nations—whether murder, assault, kidnapping, or torture. Prosecutions may also be brought for war crimes and other violations of international human rights standards and treaties that have been incorporated into the nation's laws.

If the countries are signatories to the Convention Against Torture or the Geneva Conventions, they are actually obligated to investigate and hold accountable anyone who has violated those treaties.[42] Not only are those who committed the crimes subject to prosecution, but those who planned and ordered heinous crimes such as torture can be charged, as well.[43]

A few countries have prosecuted individuals or taken action because of crimes committed by U.S. nationals on their territory.

One of the most dramatic actions emerged in Italy, where twenty-six Americans were put on trial in absentia, along with four Italian officers. They were accused of seizing Abu Omar, a Muslim cleric, from the streets of Milan in February 2003 and transporting him to Egypt, where he was tortured. Abu Omar was released four years later; no charges were filed against him. In 2009 he told the *Guardian* that his treatment in a Cairo jail had reduced him to a "human wreck."[44]

Following the trial—with the CIA personnel absent—the Italian court released its decision on November 4, 2009, convicting twenty-two CIA operatives and a U.S. Air Force officer, along with two Italian intelligence officials. The judge, in announcing the decision, called it "a significant event," said the *Guardian*, and the case stands as the first—and only—

prosecution for the snatching of suspects by the United States and their rendition to torture sites. The verdict was secured even though much of the prosecution's case was hobbled by Italian state secrecy laws, which caused the exclusion of a great deal of evidence. Each American was sentenced to five years in jail and will be regarded as a fugitive under Italian law. While it is unlikely that the United States will turn over the air force or CIA officers to the Italian government, these individuals might want to curb their travel outside the United States for worry of facing arrest by Interpol.

Other cases of torture by U.S. personnel have emerged in Spain as well, based on concepts of "national" jurisdiction, in which the claimants have a connection to the country or where Spanish facilities were used in their transfer.

In February 2011, one case in Spain was allowed to proceed to a further investigation, a step described as "monumental" and "the first real investigation of the U.S. torture program," by the Center for Constitutional Rights.[45] The Spanish National Court allowed Lahcen Ikassrien to continue pursuing his claim of torture by the United States in the face of an attempt by the Spanish prosecutor to exclude him and reject the claim. Ikassrien, a Moroccan native who had lived in Spain for thirteen years, said that he suffered physical and mental abuse from torture as a detainee in Guantánamo. The issuance of a subpoena for testimony from Major General Geoffrey Miller, the former commanding officer at Guantánamo, was under consideration, an especially important action because "the case will surely move up the chain of command," the Center for Constitutional Rights said to *Jurist.*[46]

Two other cases were pending in Spain. One involved a criminal case against three U.S. soldiers who were accused of killing a Spanish television cameraman during the shelling of a hotel in Baghdad on April 8, 2003. The case went through a lot of hoops, seeming to open and close regularly. According to an article in *El País* in December 2010, U.S. embassy cables released by WikiLeaks bragged of meddling and said that the Spanish government "has been helpful" in getting the case dropped. But the case was revived in court on July 6, 2010, according to *El País*, which said, "After numerous legal maneuvers and pressure, the US Embassy was unable to sweep the prosecution under the rug."[47]

The final Spanish proceeding involved an investigation into the case of Khaled El-Masri of Germany because the U.S. aircraft that transported him to a torture site made a stop in Spanish territory. A Spanish prosecutor sought to issue arrest warrants for the thirteen CIA agents who kidnapped El-Masri in early 2010, according an article by Scott Horton in *Harper's*.[48] WikiLeaks cables showed that the U.S. government again pressured Spain to make the case go away, and little was made public about the forward progress of the case.[49]

Germany also reviewed prosecution of CIA officers for the forced removal of El- Masri.[50] The case went nowhere. Even after a German court issued an arrest warrant for the thirteen CIA agents who had strong-armed and taken El-Masri to a torture site, the German government refused to seek extradition. The leak of U.S. State Department cables by WikiLeaks on November 28, 2010, revealed a familiar backstory: The Bush administration issued not-very-subtle threats to German officials. "American officials exerted sustained pressure on Germany not to enforce arrest warrants against Central Intelligence Agency officers involved in the 2003 kidnapping of a German citizen," wrote Michael Slackman in the *New York Times*.[51] A cable dated February 7, 2007, revealed that the U.S. deputy ambassador, John Koenig, issued "a pointed warning," about a "negative impact" and told Germany to "weigh carefully at every step of the way the implications for relations with the US," according to the *Times*. The warnings worked. "It would be easy to write off the details from the cables as mere trifles if they hadn't been confirmed by reality. In 2007, then–Justice Minister Brigitte Zypries decided not to further pursue the 13 CIA agents," said *Der Spiegel* in December 2010.[52]

Another striking case emerged in Poland, where the CIA ran a secret black-site prison in Stare Kiejkuty. Several U.S. detainees were tortured there and Warsaw prosecutors began investigating possible crimes arising out of detainee abuse at the CIA's site in 2008. Polish government officials could be held accountable in the proceedings, and a great deal of information about the black site could come to light. In October 2009 the U.S. Department of Justice turned down a request from Poland for cooperation in completing a probe, saying that it considered the matter closed, according the article "US Rejects Polish Call for Help in Alleged CIA Prison Probe" by Agence France Presse. In October 2010, a major development occurred in the case when lawyers for detainee Abd Al-Rahim Al-Nashiri announced that the prosecutor had granted him "victim status" in the proceedings. Under the legal system in Poland, this official status gives al-Nashiri's lawyers the right to review evidence and call witnesses. The lawyers said they wanted top CIA officials to testify.[53]

The "victim status" designation also strongly suggests that the prosecutors accord substantial validity to al-Nashiri's claims. The proceedings open the possibility for a fuller disclosure of what happened. In December 2010, Abu Zubaydah, a tortured detainee held in Guantánamo, asked for his case to be folded into the probe as well, reported Agence France Presse. If the Polish prosecutors decide to proceed against U.S. officials, extradition proceedings or arrest warrants would create an international stir. Polish prosecutions might encourage other nations where torture occurred at CIA black sites to take action too, including Lithuania, which has been sluggish, and Romania, which has done nothing.

The Bush administration set a pattern of using threats and whispered recriminations to shut down prosecutions in other nations that are seeking to pursue justice for torture victims or for war crimes. If and when those nations do act, they will add to the global call for the United States to take accountability steps at home.

CIVIL COMPENSATION AND LAWSUITS IN OTHER NATIONS

People detained by the United States without just cause, particularly when tortured, have brought actions in a variety of forums, as described above. Using claims of collaboration with the U.S. torture scheme, some have also sued their own governments for damages. Legitimate civil lawsuits for damages can be powerful tools for digging out the facts and uncovering the source of wrongdoing.

Two major legal settlements have been reached. In November 2010, the British government announced that it would pay a confidential sum, believed to be tens of millions of dollars, to settle lawsuits with sixteen British citizens or legal residents who had been detained and subjected to torture by the United States.[54] Most had been held in Guantánamo prison, but others were held in Afghanistan, Morocco, and Egypt.

The men had alleged that British intelligence agencies colluded in their detention and mistreatment by the United States. They said that they had been subjected to sleep deprivation, extremes of noise, heat and cold, beatings and death threats; one man said that he lost sight in one eye after it was rubbed with a saturated cloth.

The announcement of the settlement in one case came not long after a court ordered the British government to turn over as many as half a million confidential documents. Previously the British had tangled with unrelenting U.S. objections to the release of a seven-paragraph summary of the experiences of detainee Binyam Mohamed, warning that the United States would consider ending security cooperation with Britain, reported the *Jurist* in 2009.[55] One British newspaper, the *Daily Mail*, referred to the settlement with two words: "Hush Money."[56]

Canada also settled with one of its citizens, Maher Arar, who was detained by the United States in 2002 and "rendered" to Syria, where he was tortured. After release, he was exonerated of any wrongdoing. The Canadian government apologized and agreed to pay Arar $9.8 million, although the U.S. courts have refused even to hear his case.[57] In 2003 Arar told *Democracy Now!*: "Since my release I have been suffering from anxiety, constant fear, and depression. . . . But I promise myself one thing—that I will continue my quest for justice."[58]

Civil lawsuits brought in other nations are valuable tools for providing redress to victims of torture, and some have managed to bring out information and details about the U.S. use of torture and the collaboration of other countries. But the extreme resistance of the U.S. government and its willingness to protect CIA and top Bush administration officials make the cases unlikely to result in the justice that Maher Arar and other torture victims seek, or the accountability that Americans deserve.

EUROPEAN COURT OF HUMAN RIGHTS AND INTER-AMERICAN COMMISSION ON HUMAN RIGHTS

When every effort to get justice for Khaled El-Masri in the United States, Germany, and Macedonia came to nothing, he sought help from the European Court of Human Rights and the Inter-American Commission on Human Rights.[59]

Regional international courts may adjudicate complaints that arise in their geographic area. The European Court of Human Rights serves the forty-seven members of the European Union and may act to protect the civil and political rights of citizens.[60] The Inter-American Commission on Human Rights and the Inter-American Court of Human Rights serve the twenty-one members of the Organization of American States in Central, Latin, and South America that have ratified the commission and court. (The United States is not among the ratifying nations.) The commission investigates complaints of human rights violations and appropriate cases may be referred to the court for further action.[61]

In October 2010, the European Court of Human Rights required Macedonia to explain its involvement in the extraordinary rendition of El-Masri in a case brought by the Open Society Justice Initiative, reported Richard Norton-Taylor in the *Guardian*. "The European court of human rights has for the first time told a state it has a case to answer over the CIA's practice of seizing terror suspects and subjecting them to mistreatment in secret jails," wrote Norton-Taylor.[62]

On April 9, 2008, a case was filed before the Inter-American Commission seeking an apology and a declaration that the U.S. rendition program violated El-Masri's rights, according to the ACLU, which is handling the matter.[63]

In 2005, the Inter-American Commission on Human Rights condemned the actions at Guantánamo and called for an end to rendition, according to author Michael Haas. And, in 2008, a detainee in Guantánamo, Djamel Ameziane, filed a complaint with the Inter-American Commission over the conditions of imprisonment, including solitary confinement for six years, torture, and denial of medical care, notes Haas.[64]

Decisions from the European Court or the Inter-American Commission on Human Rights that support accountability could draw attention to disgraceful U.S. torture practices and have a ripple effect on engaging the United States to take steps toward accountability.

INVESTIGATIONS AND INQUIRIES IN OTHER NATIONS

Disturbing events resulting from the actions of the Bush administration have made their way into investigations and inquiries in other nations and by international bodies. While the legal cases have clustered around the torture of detainees, certain commissions and inquiries are also seeking to uncover the truth about how their nations became involved in the Iraq war. Although the commissions have no power to prosecute or punish, their findings can have political ramifications in their own countries, reverberating in the United States as well.

Two countries—Great Britain and the Netherlands—began inquiries into the beginnings of the Iraq War. The Dutch undertook an extensive inquiry into the decision of its government to enter war in Iraq, according to Afua Hirsch in the *Guardian*.[65] In 2009, after years of pressure, the Dutch

prime minister convened a committee chaired by Willibrord Davids, a retired president of the Dutch Supreme Court, to investigate intelligence,
international law, and decision making leading up to the country's war participation. The seven-member special committee of inquiry included two
legal academics and a former member of the Court of European Justice.

In January 2010, the Davids committee issued a report of more than
five hundred pages. In the short seventeen-page English-language version,
the committee uses measured, diplomatic language, but rips into the Dutch
government's actions. Six of its findings condemn the Dutch government's
efforts to justify the legality of the invasion. The committee found that the
invasion had "had no sound basis in international law," and it criticized
the government for viewing the legality of the war as a "subsidiary" issue.

The Dutch group determined that the UN Security Council Resolution from the first Gulf War "cannot reasonably be interpreted as authorizing . . . military force" to invade Iraq in 2003, which was the position
taken by the Dutch government. The committee found that references to
claims about weapons of mass destruction in Iraq were used to distract attention when the real goal was regime change—which would be a prohibited basis for war under international law, and which the government could
reasonably foresee would be the result of the invasion. The committee
said that "the Dutch government lent its political support to a war whose
purpose was not consistent with Dutch government policy . . . ; the Dutch
stance was to some extent disingenuous."

The Davids committee found that full disclosure to parliament had
not been made, nuances in intelligence reports were not communicated
to parliament, and statements made by the minister of defense about the
intelligence reports were not accurate. The Netherlands was included in
the "coalition of the willing" improperly, the committee said. The government's failure to examine the decision making about the Iraq invasion, it
said, was "obstinate" and "it would have been better if an inquiry took place
at an earlier stage."[66]

At first, the Dutch prime minister, Jan Peter Balkenende, criticized the
report and disagreed with its conclusion about the illegality of the war. His
response prompted a huge outcry and, within a day, "brought the government to the brink of crisis," reported the Dutch paper *NRC Handelsblad* on
January 13, 2010. To avoid his government's collapse, Balkenende changed
his position, essentially accepted the report's conclusions, and admitted

that the cabinet should have established a "more adequate legal pretext under international law," said the Dutch paper. The extraordinary findings of the Davids committee—that the Iraq War justifications were inadequate and the war, therefore, illegal—were the first ever from a governmental body and are enormously relevant to U.S. accountability. But the report received scant attention in the States.[67]

Great Britain also began looking into the Iraq War in 2009 "to establish a reliable account of the UK's involvement," according a statement by Sir John Chilcot, chair of the Iraq Inquiry, on July 30, 2010.[68] Generally known as the "Chilcot Inquiry" after the long-standing civil servant and establishment figure, a five-person panel was empowered to take live testimony and to obtain government documents. Several hearings were streamed over the Internet; others have been private. Its proceedings, which are supposed to be independent of the government, are followed regularly in the British press, sometimes on a minute-by-minute basis. Top officials, including former prime minister Tony Blair, have testified to the Chilcot Inquiry.

The actual independence of the group came into question with the WikiLeaks release of U.S. State Department cables in November 2010. One cable revealed that Ellen Tauscher, the U.S. undersecretary for arms control and international security under President Obama, secured a promise from the British defense department in September 2009 that "the UK had 'put measures in place to protect your [the United States'] interests.'" The *Telegraph* recounted on December 1, 2010, that shortly after receipt of the cable, protocols were established in Britain to permit the government to censor the Chilcot Inquiry's report based on commercial and economic interests, including possible damage to international relations. The sequence of events led the Stop the War Coalition in Britain to call the cable "the beginning of the cover-up," according to the *Telegraph*.[69]

Other aspects of the Inquiry have been criticized. No lawyers are on the panel, so some worry that international law will be shortchanged, and the testimony is not under oath.

Despite the criticisms, the Chilcot Inquiry took, in a methodical way, the public testimony of over 125 people by May 2011, uncovering new information about the war-making process and the legality of the war. Eliza Manningham-Buller, former head of MI5, the domestic security branch of the British government, told the panel that the direct threat from Iraq in March 2002 was determined to be "low." She said that there was an overreliance on "fragmentary" intelligence after that—in short, the intelligence did not support the claimed reasons for the attacks. Manningham-Buller also described ramifications for England—the invasion "radicalized hundreds of British Muslims," she said, requiring a substantial budgetary increase to deal with the large threat increase within the country.[70] The attorney general during that time period, Lord Goldsmith, testified that he delivered a memo to Prime Minister Blair on January 30, 2003, stating that UN Resolution 1441 did not authorize the use of military force. But the next day, Prime Minister Blair told President Bush at the White House that he was "solidly" with him.[71] At the same time, Blair told Parliament and the media that a second UN resolution was not legally needed for an invasion, although he had in hand the contrary advice from the attorney general. Curiously, Lord Goldsmith, after arguing for months that the UN resolution did not justify an invasion, abruptly changed his mind days before the invasion following a personal meeting with Blair, the details of which he could not recall. "Honour and duty should have compelled [Goldsmith's] resignation," wrote Stephen Glover in the *Daily Mail* on January 19, 2011. Had he done so, "at the very least, the lawfulness of the invasion would have been much more openly and robustly debated in Parliament and the country," Glover wrote.[72]

The British panel was so disturbed by some testimony that, after calling former prime minister Tony Blair in January 2010, it decided to call him again in 2011. In particular, the panel wanted Blair to address reports that he had given President Bush his word to support an invasion of Iraq no matter what.[73] The panel expressed "grave doubts" about the veracity of statements by Blair in his first appearance; of particular concern was "shattering testimony" by Lord Goldsmith that Blair had misled the country about the legality of the war.[74]

On January 21, 2011, the five Chilcot panel members confronted Blair with contradictory and conflicting versions of events, posting the public testimony on the Iraq Inquiry website.[75] This time, Blair told the Chilcot Inquiry that he disregarded the advice from Lord Goldsmith because it was not based on a formal request and because Blair "was continuing to hold" to another position, specifically, that a second resolution from the UN was not necessary to go to war in Iraq. Blair had difficulty explaining why he failed to keep his cabinet informed of war plans, why he gave the cabinet only the second opinion of the attorney general without mentioning the prior contrary views, what promises he had made to President Bush in the summer of 2002—well before the country had agreed to go to war—and how he could say that Iraq was not cooperating with UN inspectors when the UN inspectors said otherwise. For example, Blair claimed that even though Saddam Hussein was cooperating with weapons inspectors he "had not had 'a genuine change of heart' and still wanted WMD," wrote Chris Ames in the *Guardian*. Ames concluded that the specifics and the evidence made it "clear that he was seeking regime change from an early stage" and that Blair "put his foot in his mouth."[76]

The Chilcot Inquiry has revealed how much of the British war-making decision relied upon deceptions, manipulation of legal opinions, and avoidance of standard checks and balances. Whatever findings are made in the final Chilcot report, the process offers a possible model for inquiry, and one that the United States should seriously consider.

Other investigations across the globe have disclosed critical information as well. Two important reports from the International Committee of the Red Cross provided independent assessments of the U.S. treatment of detainees, as noted earlier. A February 2004 report on Iraqi prisoners held by the United States found mistreatment,[77] and a February 2007 report on fourteen "high value" detainees described "ill-treatment" that "constituted torture."[78]

In July 2010, British prime minister David Cameron, a conservative, announced an independent investigation into Britain's role in mistreatment of detainees "to restore Britain's moral leadership in the world."[79] Cameron told parliamentarians that a judge-led inquiry panel "will have access to all relevant government papers—including those held by the intelligence services." But the inquiry, he said, would not include public hearings, leading a Tory MP, Andrew Tyrie, to call for independence and transparency. "It is in the national interest that we get to the bottom of this, get to the truth and move on," Tyrie said.[80]

Tyrie, also the chair of a separate British parliamentary group on rendition, called the All Party Parliamentary Group on Extraordinary Rendition, complained in January 2011 that the government had refused to release needed information about Britain's complicity in the handling and rendition of detainees.[81]

Canada has reviewed and issued a thousand-page report on the Maher Arar case, and the Royal Canadian Mounted Police was conducting an investigation into wrongdoing by Syrian and American officials, Amy Goodman reported in June 2010.[82]

A 2007 European Parliament report examined and documented more than one thousand CIA rendition flights over Europe, reported Amnesty International in a 2010 publication, *Open Secret: Mounting Evidence of Europe's Complicity in Rendition and Secret Detention*. The European Parliament identified nations that had facilitated flights by the CIA, and those that had likely opened their territories to CIA black sites.[83]

The United Nations has played a role as well. A UN Joint Study on Secret Detention, released in February 2010, decried in the strongest terms the U.S. use of secret detention in the "war on terror," comparing it to the Gulag system in the former Soviet Union and "disappearances" in Latin America, said Amnesty International in its *Open Secret* report in 2010.

In November 2010, the UN Human Rights Council questioned U.S. representative Harold Koh, legal advisor at the State Department, about the mistreatment of detainees in the course of a review of the nation's human rights record. One member of the Council, Germán Mundarain Hernández of Venezuela, urged the United States to close secret detention centers and to "punish those people who torture, disappear and execute detainees arbitrarily and [to] provide compensation to victims."[84] Koh said that the United States was "turning a page" on prior practices and was ensuring humane treatment of all detainees.[85]

Others connected to the UN were not entirely convinced. The outgoing UN Special Rapporteur on torture, Manfred Nowak, an Austrian lawyer, drove home the point that the United States was obligated under the Convention Against Torture to "independently investigate every allegation of torture or suspicion of torture," according to an October 2010 Reuters article.[86] "There are plenty of allegations. Not much has been done," said Nowak. Because of U.S. unwillingness to take these steps on its own, Nowak proposed a probe by a special prosecutor or a panel of international experts. His successor, Juan Ernesto Mendez, a law professor in the United States who suffered torture in Argentina in the 1970s, has agreed, insisting that the United States has a duty to investigate "what happened and by whose orders." Mendez added: "Unfortunately, we haven't seen much in the way of accountability."[87] And in April 2011, the former chief UN nuclear weapons inspector and head of the International Atomic Energy Agency, Mohamed ElBaradei, proposed an international inquiry into the legality of the war in Iraq and a possible war crimes trial, reported Charles J. Hanley in the *Washington Examiner*.[88]

International commissions may bolster and support the efforts of those in the United States who are seeking accountability, but only if they remain independent and free from the type of political manipulation that the WikiLeaks cables show the United States was willing to employ in other investigations. Mounting evidence around the world makes the transgressions of President Bush and Vice President Cheney increasingly difficult to ignore in the United States.

One thing seems clear. The issues are not likely to disappear. German lawyer Wolfgang Kaleck, the general secretary of the European Center for Constitutional and Human Rights, said in 2008 that the international community has become increasingly engaged in seeking accountability for U.S. torture of detainees and human rights abuses. "Many lawyers, many prosecutors, many judges in several European countries took action, and I think there is more to come," he said, "but it will depend very much if there is really something going on in the US. If not, I guess there will be more and more lawsuits here in Europe."[89]

The Bush administration went to great lengths to use its powers while in office to block accountability, and to immunize insiders from prosecution. Even though the United States has forcefully pressured, even threatened, foreign countries into protecting the Bush team from accountability, those nations also have to respond to the political sensibilities of their own people, many of whom are unwilling to wave off or justify crimes against humanity. Members of the Bush administration—and Americans who would follow their example—are on notice that, in a global world, they may face global accountability.

SIX

What to Do

The Time Is Now

What can be done to respond to the misdeeds of President Bush, Vice President Cheney, and their aiders and abettors? And to recover from the damage that they have caused to our democracy?

In the time that has elapsed since they left office, more information has come to light about the destructiveness of their actions. We can see more clearly the lingering effects of impunity and how it works to compound the harm already done to our democracy, our standing in the world, our sense of who we are as a nation, and the real lives of real people injured by war, torture, illegal surveillance, and more. As members of the Bush administration attempt to rewrite history and paint themselves in a positive light, speaking up for truth and accountability becomes more important than ever.

Now is the time to gather new strength in a movement for accountability. Although the task may seem daunting and difficult, positive efforts around the world to secure justice offer a healthy dose of optimism. Success can be measured by the determination of good people who persevere. While it may take many years, the American people will find out why President Bush really invaded Iraq, why he instituted a regime of torture and cruelty previously unknown in American history, and why he put into place a vast program of surveillance of Americans. Ultimately, the appropriate remedies—civil or criminal—will be brought to bear on his conduct.

Recent examples underscore how impunity for grave crimes around the world and in the U.S. has been shattered, sometimes many years later.

On November 26, 2010, sixty years after the fact, the Russian parliament finally acknowledged Josef Stalin's guilt for the massacre of twenty thousand Polish officers in the Katyn Forest.[1] For many years, the charges were deflected; first the Soviet government and then its Russian successor blamed the Nazis. But the truth eventually could not be denied. While Stalin still had his defenders, and though he was not shamed or tried during his lifetime, this determination, fully supported by the historical record, will stain his memory forever.

And after twenty-five years, justice finally began to catch up with Augusto Pinochet, the Chilean dictator, in London, of all places, where he had gone for medical treatment. As the result of an extradition request by the Spanish judge Baltasar Garzón, described in chapter 5, Pinochet was put under house arrest. Chileans took heart from the proceedings abroad and initiated new actions against him for murder and torture.[2] For the last years of his life Pinochet felt the hot breath of accountability on his neck, and the world, including the many he had injured and their families, finally cradled a feeling of real justice.

Even in the United States, sanctuary ended for people who bombed and killed civil rights workers in the South in the 1960s. It took decades, but bold prosecutors were able to bring new cases and win convictions in some of the most horrific instances of segregationist violence—the assassination of Medgar Evers, the bombing that killed four girls at the 16th Street Baptist Church in Birmingham, and the murder of three civil rights workers in Mississippi. People determined to see justice, including family members and crusading journalists, never gave up, and eventually they succeeded.

Time and the truth also caught up with Nazi war criminals who had come to the United States after World War II and were living under false pretenses. Hundreds, possibly thousands, of war criminals who aided the Nazis as concentration camp guards, police officers, and local officials tried to hide their identities. It took more than a quarter of a century for action to be taken. Finally, the law was strengthened, a special Justice Department unit was created, and more than one hundred war criminals left the country, or were deported or extradited. Cases were still being brought more than sixty-five years after the end of World War II.[3]

These examples stand as warning to President Bush and Vice President Cheney and their team that their violations of U.S. law will not be forgotten. By refusing to accept their misdeeds, Americans can send a strong signal that there will be no escape from accountability. Over the long run, it's hard to prevent justice from being done.

At stake in this effort is nothing less than preserving the oxygen that keeps democracy going—and that is the rule of law.

Citizens are the generating power for accountability—and there are many steps that can be taken to achieve it. These efforts range from simple actions to the more complex, and they parallel the strategies of many social change movements. With the information available on the Web from trustworthy sources such as Human Rights Watch, the ACLU, the Center for Constitutional Rights, and others, people concerned about accountability can keep informed of developments as they emerge, and build on them. People have sought resolutions from professional organizations, such as the American Bar Association;[4] others have formed new advocacy groups, such as the National Religious Coalition Against Torture, which published a tool kit and released a video.[5] In Berkeley, California, the local government sponsored "Say No to Torture Week,"[6] while progressive activists in the Midwest secured a meeting with their senator to press for accountability on torture and then posted a video about it on YouTube.[7] Citizen journalism, letters to the editor, blog posts—all can have a cumulative and powerful effect.

What is vital for our democracy is for people to speak out for justice, be informed, expand their reach, and bring others along. Paraphrasing a Talmudic sage, it is not the responsibility of any single person to finish the task, but neither is any person permitted to avoid it.

ACKNOWLEDGMENTS

The authors would like to thank and acknowledge the many people who guided this book along its way. The support and encouragement of Max Palevsky were central to developing this book, and his resolute commitment to fighting for democracy and justice continued to resonate even after his death in 2010. We wish to thank our publisher, Beacon Press, and the terrific people associated with it, in particular, the director and our editor, Helene Atwan, and the assistant to the director, Crystal Paul. Loretta Barrett, our wise and experienced agent and friend, played an invaluable role, as did her colleagues at Loretta Barrett Books, Inc. Especially indispensable and inspiring were the people in our lives who shared their kindness, generosity, and advice, and, for that, we express our deep gratitude to Jennifer Clarke, Jodi Evans, Terry Allen, Angela Bonavoglia, Lory Frankel, Susan Cohen, Michael angel Johnson, and Robert Holtzman.

Introduction

1. "In Bush's Final Days, Are Pardons in the Works?" *All Things Considered*, NPR, November 23, 2008,www.npr.org/.

2. Kenneth Roth, "Will Bush Pardon Himself?" *Daily Beast*, January 18, 2009, www.thedaily beast.com.

3. Brent Budowsky, "Bush Will Issue a Mass Pardon," *Pundits* blog, *Hill*, July 25, 2008, http:// thehill.com/blogs/pundits-blog/.

4. George W. Bush, *Decision Points* (New York: Crown, 2010), p. 170.

5. Dick Cheney, interview with Jonathan Karl, *Good Morning America*, December 15, 2008, http://abcnews.go.com.

6. Elizabeth Holtzman with Cynthia L. Cooper, *The Impeachment of George W. Bush: A Practical Guide for Concerned Citizens* (New York: Nation Books, 2006).

7. "Statement by President George W. Bush, June 26, 2004," PEN America Center website, www.pen.org/.

ONE: Lies That Embroiled Us in War and Occupation in Iraq

1. George W. Bush, 2003 State of the Union Address, January 28, 2003, www.c-spanvideo .org/.

2. "Faces of the Fallen," *Washington Post*, http://projects.washingtonpost.com/fallen/iraq/ (accessed April 5, 2011).

3. Iraq Coalition Casualties Count, *iCasualties*, http://icasualties.org/ (accessed March 27, 2011).

4. Michael E. O'Hanlon and Ian Livingston, *Iraq Index: Tracking Variables of Reconstruction & Security in Post-Saddam Iraq*, Saban Center for Middle East Policy, Brookings Institution, July 28, 2011, www.brookings.edu/iraqindex.

5. Terri Tanielian and Lisa H. Jaycox, eds., *Invisible Wounds of War: Psychological and Cognitive Injuries, Their Consequences, and Services to Assist Recovery*, Rand Corp., Doc. No. MG-720-CCF, 2008, www.rand.org/.

6. Matthew Duss, Peter Juul, and Brian Katulis, "The Iraq War Ledger: A Tabulation of the Human, Financial, and Strategic Costs," Center for American Progress, May 6, 2010, www.americanprogress.org/.

7. Anna Mulrine, "Iraq War: Why Us Military Withdrawal Might Not Happen in 2011," *Christian Science Monitor*, February 17, 2011.

8. Charles Lewis and Mark Reading Smith, "Iraq: The War Card," Center for Public Integrity, January 23, 2008, http://projects.publicintegrity.org/.

9. U.S. Constitution, National Archives, www.archives.gov/.

10. "Fraud Law & Legal Definition," USLegal.com, http://definitions.uslegal.com/ (accessed April 5, 2011).

11. False Statements Accountability Act of 1996 (18 USC § 1001), Legal Information Institute, www.law.cornell.edu/uscode (accessed April 5, 2011).

12. "Roger Clemens Pleads Not Guilty to Six Counts of Lying to Congress," *USA Today*, August 30, 2010.

13. "Roger Clemens Indicted for Perjury," ESPN.com, August 20, 2010, http://sports.espn .go.com/.

14. "Tejada Sentenced to Year's Probation," Associated Press/ESPN, March 26, 2009, http:// sports.espn.go.com/.

15. Criminal Resource Manual, Offices of the United States Attorneys, § 923 1996 Amendments to 18 USC 371, www.justice.gov/.

16. Haas v. Henkel, 216 U.S. 462, 479 (1910).

17. Ibid.; Criminal Resource Manual, § 923, 1996 Amendments to 18 USC 371.

18. "Federal Conspiracy Law: A Brief Overview," Congressional Research Service, April 30, 2010, pp. 8–9, http://www.fas.org/.

19. U.S. v. Haldeman, 559 F.2d 31 (D.C. Cir. 1976), http://openjurist.org/.

20. Ron Suskind, *The Price of Loyalty: George W. Bush, The White House and the Education of Paul O'Neill* (New York: Simon & Schuster, 2004), p. 74.

21. Joseph Cirincione, Jessica T. Mathews, and George Perkovich, with Alexis Orton, "WMD in Iraq: Evidence and Implications," Carnegie Endowment for International Peace, January 2004, p. 16, www.carnegieendowment.org/.

22. Letter to President William J. Clinton, January 26, 1998, www.newamericancentury.org/ iraqclintonletter.htm.

23. "Rebuilding America's Defenses: Strategy, Forces and Resources for a New Century," Project for the New American Century, September 2000, p. 5, www.newamericancentury .org/.

24. Walter Pincus and Dana Milbank, "Al Qaeda-Hussein Link Is Dismissed," *Washington Post*, June 17, 2004.

25. *The 9-11 Commission Report: The Final Report of the National Commission on Terrorist Acts Upon the United States* (Washington, DC: U.S. Government Printing Office, 2004), chapter 8.1, http://govinfo.library.unt.edu/.

26. Richard Clarke, *Against All Enemies* (New York: Free Press, 2004), p. 32.

27. Rebecca Leung, "Clarke's Take on Terror," CBS.com, March 21, 2004, www.cbsnews.com/.

28. Glenn Kessler, "U.S. Decision on Iraq Has Puzzling Past," *Washington Post*, January 12, 2003.

29. Murray Waas, "Key Intelligence Briefing Kept from Hill Panel," *National Journal*, November 22, 2005, Leading to War website, www.leadingtowar.com/.

30. Interviews with Bob Woodward, *Frontline*, PBS, October 12, 2004, www.pbs.org/.

31. William Hamilton, "Bush Began to Plan War Three Months After 9/11," *Washington Post*, April 17, 2004.

32. "Memo from David Manning, March 14, 2002," George Washington University, National Security Archive, www.gwu.edu/~nsarchiv/NSAEBB/ (accessed April 11, 2011).

33. John Prados and Christopher Ames, "The Iraq War–Part II: Was There Even a Decision?" George Washington University, National Security Archive, Electronic Briefing Book No. 328, www.gwu.edu/~nsarchiv/NSAEBB/.

34. "The Secret Downing Street Memo," *Sunday Times* (London), May 1, 2005.

35. Melvin A. Goodman, "The Lies of Karl Rove," *Truthout*, March 17, 2010, www.truthout .org/.

36. Elisabeth Bumiller, "Bush Aides Set Strategy to Sell Policy on Iraq," *New York Times*, September 7, 2002.

37. "Scott McClellan's Confession," from Scott McClellan, *What Happened: Inside the Bush White House and Washington's Culture of Deception* (New York: Public Affairs, 2008), excerpted in *Wall Street Journal*, May 28, 2008.

38. Dan Collins, "Text of Bush Iraq Speech to U.N.," CBS News, September 12, 2002, www .cbsnews.com/.

39. "Bush Presses Iraq Case in Radio Address," CNN, September 14, 2002, http://quiz.cnn .com/.

40. "President Bush, Colombia President Uribe Discuss Terrorism," White House press release, September 25, 2002, http://georgewbush-whitehouse.archives.gov/.

41. "Text of President Bush's Speech in Cincinnati," Associated Press, CBS News, October 7, 2002, www.cbsnews.com/.

42. George W. Bush, radio address, February 8, 2003, http://en.wikisource.org/.

43. "A Transcript of George Bush's War Ultimatum Speech from the Cross Hall in the White House," *Guardian* (UK), March 18, 2003.

44. Vice President Cheney's Speech to the Veterans of Foreign Wars, August 26, 2002, Project for the New American Century website, http://www.newamericancentury.org/ (accessed April 11, 2011).

45. *Meet the Press*, NBC News, September 8, 2002, Professor Vincent Ferraro website, www .mtholyoke.edu/acad/intrel/bush/meet.htm (accessed April 11, 2011).

46. Rice on Iraq, War and Politics," *PBS News Hour with Jim Lehrer*, September 25, 2002, www.pbs.org/.

47. Eric Schmitt, "Rumsfeld Says U.S. Has 'Bulletproof' Evidence of Iraq's Links to Al Qaeda," *New York Times*, September 28, 2002.

48. "A Policy of Evasion and Deception," text of U.S. Secretary of State Colin Powell's speech to the UN on Iraq, *Washington Post*, February 5, 2003.

49. Cirincione, Mathews, and Perkovich, "WMD in Iraq," pp. 16–18.

50. Ibid., p. 55.

51. "IAEA Chief: No Evidence So Far of Revived Iraqi Nuclear Arms Programme," UN News Centre, January 29, 2003, http://www.un.org/; Report from UN Inspectors, International Atomic Energy Agency, January 27, 2003, www.iaea.org/.

52. "Levin Releases Newly Declassified Intelligence Documents on Iraq-al Qaeda Relationship," press release, Office of Carl Levin, April 15, 2005, Federation of American Scientists website, www.fas.org/ (accessed April 11, 2011).

53. Philippe Sands, *Lawless World: Making and Breaking Global Rules* (New York: Penguin, 2006), pp. 272–74.

54. Transcript of ElBaradei's UN presentation, International Atomic Energy Agency, CNN, March 7, 2003, http://articles.cnn.com/.

55. Vice President Dick Cheney, interview, *Meet the Press*, NBC News, transcript, March 16, 2003, www.mtholyoke.edu/acad/intrel/bush/cheneymeetthepress.htm.

56. Lewis and Smith, "Iraq: The War Card."

57. "Bush Sends Letter to Congress on Iraqi Action," CNN, March 21, 2003, http://articles .cnn.com/.

58. Lewis and Smith, "Iraq: The War Card."

59. "Senate Intelligence Committee Unveils Final Phase II Reports on Prewar Iraq Intelligence," press release, Senate Intelligence Committee, June 5, 2008, http://intelligence .senate.gov/.

60. Bush, 2003 State of the Union Address.

61. "The Status of Nuclear Inspections in Iraq by IAEA Director General Dr. Mohamed ElBaradei," statement to the UN Security Council, January 27, 2003, George Washington University, National Security Archive, www.gwu.edu/~nsarchiv/ (accessed March 10, 2011).

62. Joby Warrick, "U.S. Claim on Iraqi Nuclear Program Is Called into Question," *Washington Post*, January 24, 2003.

63. "Iraq's Continuing Programs for Weapons of Mass Destruction," October 2002, Federation of American Scientists website, www.fas.org/ (accessed April 11, 2011).

64. Rebecca Leung, "The Man Who Knew: Ex-Powell Aide Says Saddam-Weapons Threat Was Overstated," *60 Minutes*, CBS News, February 4, 2004, www.cbsnews.com/.

65. Murray Waas, "Insulating Bush," *National Journal*, March 30, 2006.

66. "Timeline: The CIA Leak Case," NPR, July 2, 2007, www.npr.org/.

67. Jason Leopold, "State Department Memo: '16 Words' Were False," *Truthout*, April 17, 2006, www.truth-out.org/.

68. Barton Gellman and Dafna Linzer, "A 'Concerted Effort' to Discredit Bush Critic," *Washington Post*, April 9, 2006.

69. Joseph C. Wilson, "What I Didn't Find in Africa," *New York Times*, July 6, 2003.

70. George Tenet, *At the Center of the Storm: The CIA During America's Time of Crisis* (New York: Harper Collins, 2008), p. 451.

71. "Text of CIA Director George Tenet's statement," July 16, 2003, CNN, http://edition .cnn.com/.

72. "Aide Takes Blame for Uranium Claim," BBC News, July 22, 2003, http://news.bbc .co.uk/.

73. Kungys v. United States, 485 U.S. 759, 770 (1988), http://supreme.justia.com/; also see U.S. v. Gaudin, 515 U.S. 506, 509 (1995), www.law.cornell.edu/.

74. "Obstruction of Congress: A Brief Overview of Federal Law Relating to Interference with Congressional Activities," Congressional Research Service, December 27, 2007, p. 54, on Federation of American Scientists website, www.fas.org/; also see United States v. Gonzales, 435 F.3d 64, 72 (1st Cir. 2006).

75. Government Accountability Act of 1996, HR 535, 104th Cong., 2nd Session, *Congressional Record* (September 25, 1996): H 11138–39, U.S. Government Printing Office, http:// www.gpo.gov/.

76. U.S. Constitution, Article II, § 3.

77. Congressional Joint Resolution to Authorize Use of Force Against Iraq, U.S. Department of Defense, October 11, 2002, https://kb.defense.gov/ (accessed April 11, 2011).

78. "Presidential Letter," March 18, 2003, http://georgewbush-whitehouse.archives.gov/ (accessed April 18, 2011).

79. "Weapons Inspectors Leave Iraq," Associated Press, March 18, 2003, www.cbsnews.com/.

80. Cirincione, Mathews, and Perkovich, "WMD in Iraq," p. 19.

81. David Corn, "George W. Bush: Still Not Telling the Truth about Iraq and WMDs," *Politics Daily*, November 8, 2010, www.politicsdaily.com.

82. Richard Norton-Taylor, "Iraq War Inquiry: Blair Government 'Massaged' Saddam Hussein WMD Threat," *Guardian*, July 12, 2010.

83. Richard Norton-Taylor, "Law unto Themselves," *Guardian*, March 14, 2003.

84. Jim VandeHei and Michael A. Fletcher, "Bush Says Election Ratified Iraq Policy," *Washington Post*, January 26, 2011.

85. 18 USC § 371, "Conspiracy to Defraud the United States," www.law.cornell.edu/uscode/ (accessed April 20, 2011).

86. *Impeachment of Richard M. Nixon, President of the United States: Report of the Committee on the Judiciary, House of Representatives* (Washington, DC: U.S. Government Printing Office, 1974).

87. "Watergate Timeline," "The Watergate Story," *Washington Post*, www.washingtonpost.com/; Watergate documents, FindLaw.com (accessed April 10, 2011).

88. Richard Severo, "H. R. Haldeman, Nixon Aide Who Had Central Role in Watergate, Is Dead at 67," *New York Times*, November 13, 1993.

89. "Summary of October, 1975 Report of Watergate Special Prosecution Force," FindLaw, http://fl1.findlaw.com/news.findlaw.com/hdocs/docs/watergate/watergate_spclpros_rpt .pdf (accessed April 10, 2011).

90. Lawrence E. Walsh, "Final Report of the Independent Counsel for Iran/Contra Matters, Volume I: Investigations and Prosecutions" (DC Cir. August 4, 1993), Part iii, pp. 55–76, Federation of American Scientists website, www.fas.org/ (accessed April 11, 2011).

91. Elizabeth de la Vega, "The White House Criminal Conspiracy," *Nation*, November 14, 2005.

92. "CREW Releases New Report—Without a Trace: The Missing White House Emails & Violations of the PRA," press release, Citizens for Responsibility and Ethics in Washington, April 12, 2007, www.citizensforethics.org/ (accessed April 11, 2011).

93. Wolf Blitzer, "WMDs: Did Iraq Ever Have Them?" CNN, July 14, 2003, http://articles .cnn.com/.

94. George W. Bush, interview with Charlie Gibson, *World News*, ABC, December 1, 2008, http://abcnews.go.com/.

95. Bush, *Decision Points*, pp. 152–53.

96. Walter Pincus, "Bush Memoir Makes Selective Use of Iraq Data," *Washington Post*, November 16, 2010.

97. Michael Kranish and Bryan Bender, "Bush Backs Cheney on Assertion Linking Hussein, Al Qaeda," *Boston Globe*, June 16, 2004.

98. Dick Cheney, remarks, American Enterprise Institute, May 21, 2009, www.aei.org/ (accessed April 11, 2011).

99. Peter Baker, "Rove on Iraq: Without W.M.D. Threat, Bush Wouldn't Have Gone to War," *The Caucus* blog, *New York Times* online, March 2, 2010, http://thecaucus.blogs.nytimes .com/.

100. Bush, interview, *World News*, December 1, 2008.

101. Bush, *Decision Points*, p. 262.

102. Sands, *Lawless World*, pp. 272–74.

103. George W. Bush, "Address to the Nation on War with Iraq," CBS News, March 17, 2003, www.cbsnews.com/.

104. Greg Miller, "Senate War Report Rebukes Cheney, Bush," *Los Angeles Times*, June 6, 2008.

105. Michael Isikoff, "Death in Libya," *Newsweek*, May 12, 2009.

106. Remarks by President Bush on Iraq, Cincinnati Museum Center-Cincinnati Union Terminal, Cincinnati, Ohio, October 7, 2002, http://georgewbush-whitehouse.archives.gov/ (accessed April 20, 2011).

107. Douglas Jehl, "Qaeda-Iraq Link U.S. Cited Is Tied to Coercion Claim," *New York Times*, December 9, 2005.

108. Martin Chulov and Helen Pidd, "Defector Admits to WMD Lies That Triggered Iraq War," *Guardian*, February 15, 2011.

109. Dick Cheney, interview, *Meet the Press*, September 8, 2002, Leading to War website, www.leadingtowar.com/ (accessed April 20, 2011).

110. Michael Isikoff, "The Phantom Link to Iraq," *Newsweek*, April 28, 2002.

111. Cirincione, Mathews, and Perkovich, "WMD in Iraq," pp. 15–18, 47–53.

112. "Senate Intelligence Committee Unveils Final Phase II Reports on Prewar Iraq Intelligence," press release, U.S. Senate Select Committee on Intelligence, June 5, 2008, http:// intelligence.senate.gov/ (accessed April 11, 2011).

113. Bush, "Address to the Nation on War with Iraq."

114. "President Commemorates Veterans Day, Discusses War on Terror," transcript of remarks of President Bush, Tobyhanna, PA, November 11, 2005, http://georgewbush-whitehouse .archives.gov/ (accessed April 11, 2011).

115. "Report on Whether Public Statements Regarding Iraq by U.S. Officials Were Substantiated by Intelligence Information," Select Committee on Intelligence, U.S. Senate, 110th Congress, June 2008, p. 91, http://intelligence.senate.gov/.

116. Ibid., p. 92.

117. "Sen. Kennedy Points to Bush's Iraq Statements," letter to the editor, *Los Angeles Times*, March 15, 2004.

118. "Decoding Mr. Bush's Denials," editorial, *New York Times*, November 15, 2005.

119. Bush, *Decision Points*, pp. 232–38.

120. "Cancer on the Presidency," White House Tapes, Presidential Recordings Program, Miller Center of Public Affairs, University of Virginia, http://whitehousetapes.net/ (accessed April 11, 2011).

121. Mark Thompson, "Shinseki, a Prescient General, Re-Enlists as VA Chief," *Time*, December 8, 2008.

122. David R. Francis, "Are Iraq War Costs Spinning Out of Control?" *Christian Science Monitor*, May 7, 2007.

123. Jane Mayer, *The Dark Side: The Inside Story of How the War on Terror Turned Into a War on American Ideals* (New York: Doubleday, 2008), pp. 135–38.

124. Nancy A. Youssef and Sahar Issa, "Gates: Iraq Outcome 'Will Always Be Clouded by How It Began,'" McClatchy, September 1, 2010, http://www.mcclatchydc.com/.

TWO: Wiretapping Americans

1.   Jules Feiffer, *Little Murders* (New York: Random House, 1968).

2.   Foreign Intelligence Surveillance Act of 1978, 50 USC §§ 1801 et seq.; in general, see

FISA resources listing, Federation of American Scientists, www.fas.org/ (accessed March 26, 2011).

3. James Risen and Eric Lichtblau, "Bush Lets U.S. Spy on Callers Without Courts," *New York Times*, December 16, 2005.

4. George W. Bush, weekly radio address, December 17, 2005, *New York Times* website, www.nytimes.com/.

5. David E. Sanger, "Bush Says He Ordered Domestic Spying," *New York Times*, December 18, 2005.

6. U.S. Constitution, Amendment IV, http://topics.law.cornell.edu/ (accessed April 22, 2011).

7. Seymour M. Hersh, "Kissinger and Nixon in the White House," *Atlantic Monthly*, May 1982.

8. U.S. Senate Select Committee on Intelligence Activities within the United States (Church Committee), *Intelligence Activities and the Rights of Americans: 1976 U.S. Senate Report on Illegal Wiretaps and Domestic Spying by the FBI, CIA and NSA*, Book III: Supplementary Detailed Staff Reports on Intelligence Activities and the Rights of Americans, p. 5, Assassination Archives and Research Center, www.aarclibrary.org/ (accessed July 20, 2011).

9. Major Louis Al. Chiarella and Major Michael A. Newton, "So Judge, How Do I Get That FISA Warrant?" published in *Army Lawyer* (October 1997): 25–36, on Federation of American Scientists website, www.fas.org (accessed March 20, 2011).

10. "American Bar Association Accuses President Bush of Violating Both the Constitution and Federal Law," American Bar Association Task Force Report, February 13, 2006, www.informationclearinghouse.info (accessed April 20, 2011).

11. FISA resources, Federation of American Scientists.

12. "Foreign Intelligence Surveillance Act (FISA)," Center for National Security Studies, www.cnss.org/fisa.htm (accessed July 20, 2011).

13. James McGee and Brian Duffy, *Main Justice: The Men and Women Who Enforce the Nation's Criminal Laws and Guard Its Liberties* (New York: Simon & Schuster, 1996), p. 315.

14. Scott Horton, "Six Questions for Jane Mayer, Author of The Dark Side," *Harper's Magazine*, July 14, 2008, www.harpers.org/.

15. Steve Clemons, "President Bush: On 20 April 2004 States Must Get 'A Court Order' Before Wiretapping Suspected Terrorists," *Washington Note*, January 31, 2006, www.thewashingtonnote.com/.

16. Dan Eggen and Amy Goldstein, "Gonzales's Truthfulness Long Disputed," *Washington Post*, July 30, 2007.

17. Inspectors General of the Department of Defense, Department of Justice, Central Intelligence Agency, National Security Agency, and Offices of the Director of National Intelligence, *Unclassified Report on the President's Surveillance Program* (Report no. 2009–0013-AS), July 10, 2009, p. 5, www.globalsecurity.org/ (accessed April 20, 2011).

18. Dick Cheney to Arlen Specter, June 8, 2006 (response to letter about Terrorist Surveillance Program), About.com, http://civilliberty.about.com/ (accessed March 8, 2011).

19. Ryan Singel, "Whistle-Blower Outs NSA Spy Room," *Wired*, April 7, 2006, http://www.wired.com/magazine/.

20. Leslie Cauley, "NSA Has Massive Database of Americans' Phone Calls," *USA Today*, May 11, 2006.

21. Inspectors General, *Unclassified Report*, pp. 7–9, 30.

22. Jack L. Goldsmith III, "Memorandum for the Attorney General," May 5, 2004, p. 9, American Civil Liberties Union website, www.aclu.org/.

23. Charlie Savage and James Risen, "Federal Judge Finds N.S.A. Wiretaps Were Illegal," *New York Times*, March 31, 2010.

24. Bush, radio address, December 17, 2005.

25. Dan Eggan, "Bush Thwarted Probe into NSA Wiretapping," *Washington Post*, July 19, 2006.

26. Scott Shane, "Cheney Is Linked to Concealment of CIA Project," *New York Times*, July 22, 2009.

27. Cheney to Specter, June 8, 2006.

28. *P.L. 110–55, the Protect America Act of 2007: Modifications to the Foreign Intelligence Surveillance Act*, Congressional Research Service, February 14, 2008, Federation of American Scientists, www.fas.org/ (accessed April 20, 2011).

29. Cynthia L. Cooper, "Terror Talk Crowds Out Thoughtful Discussion: Wiretapping Americans for Foreign Intelligence," *FAIR Extra!*, November/December 2007, www.fair .org (accessed April 20, 2011).

30. Adam Levine, "Bush: Inaction on FISA Endangers U.S.," CNN, February 15, 2008, www .cnn.com (accessed March 20, 2011).

31. "Compromising the Constitution," editorial, *New York Times*, July 8, 2008.

32. FISA Amendments Act of 2008, 50 USC § 1801 et seq. (enacted July 10, 2008), www.law cornell.edu/uscode/ (accessed July 20, 2011).

33. "Beyond FISA," Electronic Frontier Foundation, https://www.eff.org/ (accessed April 20, 2011).

34. Eric Lichtblau and James Risen, "Officials Say U.S. Wiretaps Exceeded Law," *New York Times*, April 15, 2009.

35. Bush, radio address, December 17, 2005.

36. David E. Sanger, "Bush Was Warned bin Laden Wanted to Hijack Planes," *New York Times*, May 16, 2002.

37. Ron Suskind, *The One Percent Doctrine: Deep Inside America's Pursuit of Its Enemies Since 9/11* (New York: Simon & Schuster, 2006), pp. 1–2.

38. *The 9-11 Commission Report*, pp. 254–63, http://govinfo.library.unt.edu.

39. "Ashcroft Tried to Cut Counterterrorism within a Month of Taking Office," Center for American Progress, www.americanprogress.org/ (accessed April 20, 2011).

40. Michael Hirsh, "What Went Wrong," *Newsweek*, May 27, 2002.

41. Bush, radio address, December 17, 2005.

42. *The Authorization for Use of Military Force Against Terrorists*, Pub. L. No. 107-40, 115 Stat. 224 (enacted September 18, 2001), http://news.findlaw.com/ (accessed July 20, 2011).

43. "U.S. Senate Judiciary Committee Holds a Hearing on Wartime Executive Power and the NSA's Surveillance Authority," *Washington Post*, February 6, 2006.

44. Tom Daschle, "Power We Didn't Grant," *Washington Post*, December 23, 2005.

45. Barton Gellman and Jo Becker, "A Different Understanding with the President," *Washington Post*, June 24, 2007.

46. American Civil Liberties Union v. National Security Agency, 493 F. 3d 644 (6th Cir. 2007), pp. 693–790, http://en.wikisource.org/wiki/ACLU_v._NSA/493_F.3d_644/Dissent_ Gilman (accessed July 20, 2011).

47. Douglas Jehl, "Spy Briefings Failed to Meet Legal Test, Lawmakers Say," *New York Times*, December 21, 2005.

48. "Transcript: House Intel Committee Vice-Chairman Harman on 'FNS' on Jan. 8, 2006," *Fox News Sunday*, January 9, 2006, www.foxnews.com/ (accessed March 20, 2011).

49. "Former Intel Chairman Graham: White House Made 'No Reference' to NSA Program in Briefings," *ThinkProgress*, December 18, 2005, http://thinkprogress.org/.

50. Jehl, "Spy Briefings Failed to Meet Legal Test."

51. "Dick Cheney on Fox News Sunday, The Exit Interview," transcript, December 21, 2008, www.clipsandcomment.com/ (accessed March 20, 2011).

52. "Cheney: We Asked If We Needed Approval for Wiretapping, Congress Told Us 'Absolutely Not,'" *ThinkProgress*, December 12, 2008, http://thinkprogress.org.

53. United States v. Shewfelt, 455 F.2d 836, 839 (9th Cir.), cert. denied, 406 U.S. 944 (1972); also see United States v. Martorano, 767 F.2d 63, 66 (3d Cir.), cert. denied, 474 U.S. 949 (1985); United States v. Carr, 740 F.2d 339, 347 (5th Cir. 1984), cert. denied, 471 U.S. 1004 (1985).

54. Inspectors General, *Unclassified Report*, p. 11.

55. Ibid.

56. Ibid., pp. 10, 30.

57. Neil A. Lewis, "Bush Blocked Ethics Inquiry, Gonzales Says," *New York Times*, July 19, 2006.

58. Scott Horton, "Two New OLC Opinions on Warrantless Surveillance," *Harper's*, March 21, 2011.

59. Youngstown Sheet & Tube Co. v. Sawyer, 343 U.S. 579 (1952), www.law.cornell.edu/.

60. Inspectors General, *Unclassified Report*, p. 16.

61. Ibid., fn. 12.

62. Bush, radio address, December 17, 2005.

63. Dick Cheney, interview, *Good Morning America*.

64. Inspectors General, *Unclassified Report*, pp. 31–36.

65. Ibid., p. 36.

66. Goldsmith, "Memorandum for the Attorney General," p. 9.

67. "Illegal, and Pointless," *New York Times*, July 17, 2009.

68. Bush, radio address, December 17, 2005.

69. Youngstown Sheet & Tube Co. v. Sawyer.

70. Adam Liptak and Eric Lichtblau, "Judge Finds Wiretap Actions Violate the Law," *New York Times*, August 18, 2006.

71. American Civil Liberties Union v. National Security Agency, 438 F. Supp.2d 754 (E.D. Mich. 2006), http://fl1.findlaw.com/ (accessed March 20, 2011).

72. Hamdan v. Rumsfeld, 548 U.S. 557, f.n. 23 (2006), http://laws.findlaw.com/ (accessed March 20, 2011).

73. "Sequels: Not Even Earplugs Could Help," *Time*, May 30, 1977 (accessed April 20, 2011).

74. Inspectors General, *Unclassified Report*, p. 13.

75. Elizabeth Bazan and Jennifer Elsea, "Presidential Authority to Conduct Warrantless Electronic Surveillance to Gather Foreign Intelligence Information," Congressional Research Service, January 5, 2006, n. 67, p. 17, www.fas.org/ (accessed March 20, 2011).

76. Dick Cheney, interview, *Good Morning America*.

77. American Civil Liberties Union v. National Security Agency.

78. Dick Cheney, interview, *Good Morning America*.

79. 1 USC § 109, Repeal of Statutes as Affecting Existing Liabilities, www.law.cornell.edu/uscode/ (accessed April 20, 2011).

80. Al-Haramain Islamic Foundation v. Bush, Electronic Frontier Foundation.org (accessed March 20, 2011).
81. Savage and Risen, "Federal Judge Finds N.S.A. Wiretaps."
82. Al-Haramain Islamic Foundation, Inc. v. Obama (N.D.Cal., March 31, 2010, MDL Docket No 06–1791 VRW, Case No. C 07–0109 VRW), Order Re: National Security Agency Telecommunications Records Litigation, pp. 19–20, Electronic Frontier Foundation, www.eff.org/files/filenode/att/alharamainorder33110.pdf; order, December 21, 2010, www.eff.org/files/filenode/att/alharamainorder122110.pdf; judgment, December 22, 2010, www.eff.org/files/filenode/att/alharamainjudgment122210.pdf (all accessed April 11, 2011).
83. "Beyond FISA."
84. Lichtblau and Risen, "Officials Say U.S. Wiretaps."
85. FISA Amendments Act of 2008, Sec. 301(a)(3).
86. Eric Lichtblau and James Risen, "E-Mail Surveillance Renews Concerns in Congress," *New York Times*, June 16, 2009.
87. Ibid.
88. Inspectors General, *Unclassified Report*, p. 31.
89. Jewel v. National Security Agency, Complaint (U.S. N.D., filed September 18, 2008), www.eff.org/files/filenode/jewel/jewel.complaint.pdf.

THREE: Crimes of Torture

1. "Extracts from an Interrogation Log," *Time*, June 12, 2005.
2. Jane Mayer, "Outsourcing Torture," *New Yorker*, February 14, 2005.
3. Tom Lasseter, "U.S. Abuse of Detainees Was Routine at Afghanistan Bases," McClatchy, June 16, 2008, www.mcclatchydc.com.
4. "Poles Urged to Probe CIA 'Black Site,'" CBS World News, September 21, 2010, www.cbsnews.com.
5. Bush, *Decision Points* (New York: Random House, 2010), pp. 169–71.
6. "Rove 'Proud' of US Waterboarding Terror Suspects," BBC, March 12, 2010, http://news.bbc.co.uk.
7. "'This Week' Transcript: Former Vice President Dick Cheney," *This Week*, ABC News, February 14, 2010, http://abcnews.go.com.
8. Jennifer Rosenberg, "Mengele's Children: The Twins of Auschwitz," About.com (accessed April 22, 2011).
9. Eli Rosenbaum, "Prosecuting Nazi War Criminals," Jewish Virtual Library, www.jewishvirtuallibrary.org/ (accessed April 22, 2011).
10. "The Abu Ghraib Files," *Salon*, March 14, 2006.
11. "U.S. Operatives Killed Detainees during Interrogations in Afghanistan and Iraq," press release, American Civil Liberties Union, October 24, 2005, www.aclu.org/; "Autopsy Reports Reveal Homicides of Detainees in U.S. Custody," press release, American Civil Liberties Union, October 24, 2005, http://action.aclu.org/ (accessed April 22, 2011).
12. Abraham Lincoln, "Instructions for the Government of Armies of the United States in the Field" (Lieber Code), April 24, 1863, International Committee of the Red Cross, www.icrc.org/ (accessed April 22, 2011).
13. *Universal Declaration of Human Rights*, December 10, 1948, www.un.org/ (accessed April 22, 2011).
14. *The Geneva Conventions of 1949 and Their Additional Protocols*, International Committee of the Red Cross, www.icrc.org/ (accessed April 22, 2011).

15. *Convention Against Torture and Other Cruel, Inhuman or Degrading Treatment or Punishment*, Human Rights Web, www.hrweb.org/ (accessed April 22, 2011).

16. War Crimes Act of 1996, 18 USC § 2441, http://thomas.loc.gov/ (accessed April 22, 2011).

17. 18 USC §§ 2340–2340A (anti-torture law), Cornell University Law School Legal Information Institute, U.S. Code, www.law.cornell.edu/uscode/ (accessed April 22, 2011).

18. "The Torture Question: Frequently Asked Questions," *Army Field Manual*, on *Frontline*, October 18, 2005, PBS, www.pbs.org/.

19. Mayer, *Dark Side*, pp. 93–94.

20. Mayer, "Outsourcing Torture."

21. U.S. Senate Committee on Armed Services, *Inquiry into the Treatment of Detainees in U.S. Custody*, November 20, 2008, pp. xii-xxvii, 1–15, http://armed-services.senate.gov/ (accessed April 22, 2011).

22. Ibid.

23. Joseph Margulies, "The More Subtle Kind of Torment," *Washington Post*, October 2, 2006.

24. Barton Gellman and Jo Becker, "Pushing the Envelope on Presidential Power," *Washington Post*, June 25, 2007.

25. Colin Powell, "Draft Decision Memorandum for the President on the Applicability of the Geneva Conventions to the Conflict in Afghanistan," George Washington University, National Security Archive, http://www.gwu.edu/~nsarchiv/ (accessed April 11, 2011).

26. George W. Bush, "Humane Treatment of al Qaeda and Taliban Detainees," memorandum to the vice president, secretary of state, et al., February 7, 2002, http://www.torturing democracy.org/documents/ (accessed April 22, 2011).

27. U.S. Senate Committee on Armed Services, *Inquiry into the Treatment of Detainees*, p. xxvi.

28. Albert D. Biderman, "Communist Attempts to Elicit False Confessions from Air Force Prisoners of War," *Bulletin of the New York Academy of Medicine* 33, no. 9 (September 1957): 616; www.torturingdemocracy.org/documents/19570900.pdf (accessed April 22, 2011).

29. Scott Shane, "China Inspired Interrogations at Guantánamo," *New York Times*, July 2, 2008.

30. U.S. Senate Committee on Armed Services, *Inquiry into the Treatment of Detainees*, p. xxxi.

31. Ibid., p. 15.

32. Bush, *Decision Points*, p. 169.

33. Central Intelligence Agency, Inspector General, "Special Review, Counterterrorism, Detention and Interrogation Activities (September 2001–October 2003)," May 7, 2004, pp. 12–14, 35, 84–85, 90, George Washington University, National Security Archive, *Torturing Democracy* website, http://www.gwu.edu/~nsarchiv/torturingdemocracy/ (accessed April 22, 2011),

34. Jan Crawford Greenburg, Howard L. Rosenberg, and Ariane de Vogue, "Top Bush Advisors Approved 'Enhanced Interrogation,'" ABC News, April 9, 2008, http://abcnews .go.com/.

35. U.S. Department of Justice, Office of Professional Responsibility, *Investigation into the Office of Legal Counsel's Memoranda Concerning Issues Relating to the Central Intelligence Agency's Use of "Enhanced Interrogation Techniques" on Suspected Terrorists*, July 29, 2009, p. 16, http://judiciary.house.gov/ (accessed June 20, 2011).

36. Jack Goldsmith, *The Terror Presidency: Law and Judgment Inside the Bush Administration* (New York: Norton, 2007), pp. 149–50.

37. John Bybee to Alberto Gonzales, "Re: Standards of Conduct for Interrogation under 18 U.S.C. §§ 2340–2340A," memorandum, August 1, 2002, George Washington University,

National Security Archive, Electronic Briefing Books, www.gwu.edu/~nsarchiv/
NSAEBB/.

38. John Yoo to Alberto Gonzales, memorandum, August 1, 2002, FindLaw.com.

39. Jay Bybee to John Rizzo, "Interrogation of al Qaeda Operative," memorandum, August
1, 2002, Washington Research Library Consortium, Digital Object Catalog, http://dspace
.wrlc.org/doc/.

40. Office of Professional Responsibility, *Investigation into the Office of Legal Counsel's Memoranda*, p. 58.

41. CIA, "Special Review, Counterterrorism Detention" p. 38.

42. Office of Professional Responsibility, *Investigation into the Office*, p. 124.

43. CIA, "Special Review, Counterterrorism Detention," p. 7.

44. Ibid., pp. 37, 47.

45. Sherry Jones, *Torturing Democracy* website, annotated transcript, www.torturingdemocracy
.org/ (accessed April 22, 2011).

46. Eric Weiner, "Waterboarding: A Tortured History," National Public Radio, November
3, 2007, www.npr.org/ (accessed April 22, 2011).

47. Jason Leopold, "Comey Emails Illustrate Concerns over Torture Policies," *Truthout*,
June 8, 2009, http://archive.truthout.org/; for Comey e-mails, see "Justice Department
Communication on Interrogation Opinions," http://documents.nytimes.com/justice
-department-communication-on-interrogation-opinions#p=1.

48. Philippe Sands, *Torture Team: Rumsfeld's Memo and the Betrayal of American Values* (New
York: Palgrave Macmillan, 2008), pp. 1–4.

49. Ryan Pollyea, "Mancow Waterboarded, Admits It's Torture," NBC Chicago, May 22,
2009, www.nbcchicago.com/.

50. Dan Eggen, "Cheney Defends 'Dunk in the Water' Remark," *Washington Post*, October
28, 2006.

51. Ted Roelofs, " 'I'd Do It Again' Former President Bush Tells Grand Rapids Crowd about
Waterboarding Terrorists," *Grand Rapids (MI) Press*, June 2, 2010, www.mlive.com/

52. U.S. Senate Committee on Armed Services, *Inquiry into the Treatment of Detainees*, p. xviii.

53. Justine Sharrock, *Tortured: When Good Soldiers Do Bad Things* (Hoboken, NJ: John Wiley
& Sons, 2010), p. 4.

54. Bob Woodward, "Detainee Tortured, Says U.S. Official," *Washington Post*, January 14,
2009.

55. U.S. Senate Committee on Armed Services, *Inquiry into the Treatment of Detainees*, p. xxi.

56. *Article 15-6, Investigation of the 800th Military Police Brigade* (Taguba Report on Treatment
of Abu Ghraib Prisoners in Iraq), FindLaw.com (accessed July 20, 2011).

57. Rebecca Leung, "Abuse of Iraqi POWs by GIs Probed," CBS News, April 28, 2004, www
.cbsnews.com/.

58. Lawrence J. Korb and John Halpin, "Cover-Up of Abu Ghraib Torture Puts Troops at
Risk," Center for American Progress, May 11, 2004, www.americanprogress.org/ (accessed
April 22, 2011).

59. Robert Siegel, "Abu Ghraib Report Faults Top Leadership," *All Things Considered*, NPR,
August 24, 2004, www.npr.org/.

60. Jonathan Karl, " 'High-Value' Detainees Transferred to Guantanamo," ABC News, September 6, 2006, http://abcnews.go.com.

61. "President Bush's Speech on Terrorism," transcript, *New York Times*, September 6,
2006.

62. John Cochran, "Showdown over Destroyed CIA Tapes This Week," ABC News, January 13, 2007, http://abcnews.go.com.

63. Dick Cheney, interview (transcript), *Face the Nation*, CBS News, May 10, 2009, www.cbsnews.com/.

64. *ICRC Report on the Treatment of Fourteen "High Value Detainees" in CIA Custody*, International Committee of the Red Cross, February 2007, www.nybooks.com/.

65. Central Intelligence Agency, "Special Review, Counterterrorism Detention," p. 91.

66. George W. Bush, Executive Order 13440 of July 20, 2007, "Interpretation of the Geneva Conventions Common Article 3 as Applied to a Program of Detention and Interrogation Operated by the Central Intelligence Agency," Federation of American Scientists, www.fas.org/ (accessed May 6, 2011).

67. Major General Antonio Taguba, preface, *Broken Laws, Broken Lives: Medical Evidence of Torture by US Personnel and Its Impact*, Physicians for Human Rights, June 2008, http://physiciansforhumanrights.org/.

68. *Geneva Conventions of 1949*.

69. Dwight D. Eisenhower to E. Roland Harriman, August 1, 1955. In *The Papers of Dwight David Eisenhower*, eds. L. Galambos and D. van Ee, doc. 1536, http://www.eisenhowermemorial.org.

70. "The Torture Question: Frequently Asked Questions."

71. "Amending the Amendments: War Crimes Act of 1996," *Intlawgrrls*, http://intlawgrrls.blogspot.com (accessed April 22, 2011).

72. John Barry, Michael Isikoff, and Michael Hirsh, "The Roots of Torture," *Newsweek*, May 24, 2004.

73. Alberto R. Gonzales, "Decision re Application of the Geneva Convention on Prisoners of War to the Conflict with Al Qaeda and the Taliban," memorandum, January 25, 2002, *Torturing Democracy* website, www.torturingdemocracy.org (accessed April 22, 2011).

74. Colin Powell, "Draft Decision Memorandum."

75. William H. Taft IV, memorandum, February 2, 2002, *Torturing Democracy* website, http://www.gwu.edu/~nsarchiv/torturingdemocracy/ (accessed April 11, 2011).

76. Bush, "Humane Treatment of al Qaeda."

77. Central Intelligence Agency, "Special Review, Counterterrorism Detention."

78. Mark Mazzetti and Scott Shane, "Interrogation Debate Sharply Divided Bush White House," *New York Times*, May 4, 2009.

79. "GOP Senators Urge Bush to Back Torture Ban Bill," Associated Press, November 6, 2005, www.foxnews.com/.

80. Josh White, "President Relents, Backs Torture Ban," *Washington Post*, December 16, 2005.

81. Ibid.

82. Office of Professional Responsibility, *Investigation into the Office*, p. 152.

83. Detainee Treatment Act of 2005, 42 USC § 2000dd, http://jurist.law.pitt.edu/.

84. Detainee Treatment Act, signing statement, http://georgewbush-whitehouse.archives.gov/.

85. Charlie Savage, "Bush Could Bypass New Torture Ban," *Boston Globe*, January 4, 2006, www.boston.com/.

86. Hamdan v. Rumsfeld, 548 U.S. 557 (2006), www.oyez.org/cases/2000–2009/2005/2005_05_184.

87. Office of Professional Responsibility, *Investigation into the Office*, p. 153.

88. "President Discusses Creation of Military Commissions to Try Suspected Terrorists," press release, September 6, 2006, http://georgewbush-whitehouse.archives.gov/.

89. R. Jeffrey Smith, "War Crimes Act Changes Would Reduce Threat of Prosecution," *Washington Post*, August 9, 2006.

90. Military Commissions Act of 2006, 10 USC §§ 948–949, http://frwebgate.access.gpo.gov/.

91. Statement of Alberto J. Mora, Senate Committee on Armed Services Hearing on the Treatment of Detainees in U.S. Custody, June 17, 2008, Federation of American Scientists website, www.fas.org/.

92. 18 USC §§ 2340–2340A (anti-torture law).

93. Ronald Reagan, "Message to the Senate Transmitting the Convention Against Torture and Inhuman Treatment or Punishment," May 20, 1988, www.reagan.utexas.edu/archives/.

94. George Bush, interview with Martha Raddatz, ABC News, April 11, 2008, http://abcnews.go.com/.

95. U.S. Department of Justice, "A Review of the FBI's Involvement in and Observations of Detainee Interrogations in Guantanamo Bay, Afghanistan, and Iraq," May 2008, http://graphics8.nytimes.com/packages/pdf/washington/20080521_DETAIN_report.pdf, pp. 67–69.

96. Colonel Lawrence B. Wilkerson, "The Truth about Richard Bruce Cheney," *Washington Note*, May 13, 2009, www.thewashingtonnote.com/.

97. U.S. Department of Justice, "Detainee Interrogations," pp. 181, 183, 204.

98. "U.S. Operatives Killed Detainees During Interrogations in Afghanistan and Iraq," press release, American Civil Liberties Union, October 24, 2005, www.aclu.org/.

99. Deborah Colson and Avi Cover, "Tortured Justice: Using Coerced Evidence to Prosecute Terrorist Suspects," Human Rights First, April 2008, www.humanrightsfirst.org/.

100. Joseph Margulies, "Abu Zubaydah's Suffering," *Los Angeles Times*, April 30, 2009.

101. U.S. Senate Committee on Armed Services, *Inquiry into the Treatment of Detainees*, pp. 140–41.

102. Evan Wallach, "Drop by Drop: Forgetting the History of Water Torture in the U.S. Courts," *Columbia Journal of Transnational Law* 45 (2007): 468, 504.

103. Mazzetti and Shane, "Interrogation Debate Sharply Divided Bush White House."

104. Bush, *Decision Points*, p. 171.

105. George W. Bush, interview with Matt Lauer, NBC News Special, *Decision Points*, November 8, 2010, www.msnbc.msn.com/.

106. Goldsmith, *Terror Presidency*, pp. 130–31.

107. Office of Professional Responsibility, *Investigation into the Office*, pp. 11, 252–54.

108. "OPR Report on the Torture Memos," Alliance for Justice, www.afj.org/.

109. United States of America v. Alstötter et al. ("The Justice Case"), 1948, www.law.umkc.edu/faculty/projects/ftrials/nuremberg/Alstoetter.htm.

110. Karl, " 'High-Value' Detainees Transferred."

111. Cheney, remarks, American Enterprise Institute.

112. Jones, *Torturing Democracy*.

113. George W. Bush, interview with Matt Lauer, November 8, 2010.

114. U.S. Senate Committee on Armed Services, *Inquiry into the Treatment of Detainees*, p. xxv.

115. Cheney, remarks, American Enterprise Institute.

116. Carrie Johnson and Josh White, "Audit Finds FBI Reports of Detainee Abuse Ignored," *Washington Post*, May 21, 2008.

117. Watts v. Indiana, 338 U.S. 49 (1949), http://supreme.justia.com/us/338/49/.

118. Cheney, remarks, American Enterprise Institute.

119. "President Bush's Speech on Terrorism."

120. Ali Soufan, "My Tortured Decision," *New York Times*, April 22, 2009.

121. Tom Lasseter, "Day 1: America's Prison for Terrorists Often Held the Wrong Men," McClatchy, June 15, 2008, www.mcclatchydc.com/.

122. David Rose, "Tortured Reasoning," *Vanity Fair*, December 16, 2008.

123. Dan Froomkin, "The Two Most Essential, Abhorrent, Intolerable Lies of George W. Bush's Memoir," *Huffington Post*, November 22, 2010, www.huffingtonpost.com/.

124. Scott Shane and Charlie Savage, "Bin Laden Raid Revives Debate on Value of Torture," *New York Times*, May 3, 2011.

125. Adam Goldman and Matt Apuzzo, "One Unwary Phone Call Led US to Bin Laden Doorstep," Associated Press, May 2, 2011, http://news.yahoo.com/.

126. Greg Sargent, "Exclusive: Private Letter from CIA Chief Undercuts Claim Torture Was Key to Killing Bin Laden," *The Plum Line*, *Washington Post* blog, May 16, 2011, www .washingtonpost.com/.

127. "McCain: U.S. Torture Did Not Lead to Bin Laden," CBS News, May 12, 2011, www .cbsnews.com/.

128. Jehl, "Qaeda-Iraq Link U.S. Cited."

129. "Obama Pledges 'Full Support' to CIA, Defends Release of Interrogation Memos," Fox News, April 20, 2009, www.foxnews.com/.

130. Karen DeYoung and Peter Baker, "Bush Detainee Plan Adds to World Doubts of U.S., Powell Says," *Washington Post*, September 19, 2006.

131. Central Intelligence Agency, "Special Review, Counterterrorism Detention," p. 91.

132. "Brains not Brutality," *Today*, BBC Channel 4, November 9, 2010, http://news.bbc.co.uk/.

133. Haroon Siddique and Chris McGreal, "Waterboarding Is Torture, Downing Street Confirms," *Guardian*, November 9, 2010, www.guardian.co.uk/.

134. Andrew Porter, "David Cameron: Waterboarding Does Not Save Lives," *Telegraph*, November 11, 2010, www.telegraph.co.uk/.

135. "CIA Treatment of Suspected Terrorist to Be Investigated," *Warsaw (Poland) Business Journal*, September 22, 2010, www.wbj.pl.

136. *Broken Laws, Broken Lives*, Physicians for Human Rights, June 2008, http://brokenlives .info/?page_id=23.

137. "Experiments in Torture: Medical Group Accuses CIA of Carrying Out Illegal Human Experimentation," *Democracy Now!*, June 8, 2010, www.democracynow.org/2010/6/8/ experiments_in_torture_medical_group_accuses.

138. "Guidelines on Medical and Psychological Support to Detainee Rendition, Interrogation and Detention," American Civil Liberties Union, Office of Medical Services, May 17, 2004, www.aclu.org/.

139. Steven Bradbury to John A. Rizzo, "Re: Application of 18 USC §§ 2340–2340A to Certain Techniques That May Be Used in the Interrogation of a High Value al Qaeda Detainee," memorandum, May 10, 2005, http://luxmedia.com.edgesuite.net/aclu/ olc_05102005_bradbury46pg.pdf.

140. Josh White, "Documents Tell of Brutal Improvisation by GIs," *Washington Post*, August 3, 2005.

141. Hina Shamsi, *Command's Responsibility: Detainee Deaths in U.S. Custody in Iraq and Afghanistan*, ed. Deborah Pearlstein, *Human Rights First*, February 2006, www.humanrights first.org/.

FOUR: Accountability at Home

1.   George W. Bush, remarks on signing the No Child Left Behind Act, quoted at www2
     .ed.gov/admins/lead/account/stateacct/edlite-slide002.html.
2.   David Morgan, "Bush: I've Made No Mistakes Since 9/11," Reuters, April 14, 2004, www
     .commondreams.org/.
3.   "Bush Admits Mistakes, Defends Decisions," MSNBC video excerpt, November 9, 2010,
     http://today.msnbc.msn.com/.
4.   *Watergate Special Prosecution Force Report* (Washington, DC: U.S. Government Printing
     Office, October 1975).
5.   Ethics in Government Act of 1978, 28 USC 591–599.
6.   Bruce Shapiro, "Men in Black (Robes)," *Salon*, February 4, 1998, www.salon.com/.
7.   "Key Players in the CIA Leak Investigation," *Washington Post* online, July 3, 2007, www
     .washingtonpost.com/.
8.   "Attorney General Declines to Investigate Bush Advisers," CNN, February 29, 2008,
     http://articles.cnn.com/.
9.   "Mukasey's Contrast," *New York Sun*, January 3, 2008, www.nysun.com/.
10. "A Case for Accountability," *New York Times*, January 25, 2011.
11. Jack Maskell, "Independent Counsel Provisions: An Overview of the Operation of
     the Law," Congressional Research Service, March 20, 1998, p.11, www.policyarchive
     .org/.
12. Carrie Johnson, "Prosecutor to Probe CIA Interrogations," *Washington Post*, August 25,
     2009.
13. "Attorney General Eric Holder Regarding a Preliminary Review into the Interrogation
     of Certain Detainees, U.S. Department of Justice," news release, U.S. Department of
     Justice, August 24, 2009.
14. "Statement of the Attorney General Regarding Investigation into the Interrogation of
     Certain Detainees," U.S. Department of Justice, June 20, 2011, www.justice.gov/.
15. "How 'Grave Breaches' Are Defined in the Geneva Conventions and Additional Protocols:
     FAQ," April 6, 2004, International Committee of the Red Cross Resource Centre, www
     .icrc.org/.
16. FISA Amendments Act of 2008, 50 USC § 1801 et seq., www.govtrack.us/.
17. Spencer S. Hsu, "Government Reports Violations of Limits on Spying Aimed at U.S.
     Citizens," *Washington Post*, December 3, 2010.
18. "Summary of FISA Amendments Act FOIA Documents Released on November 29, 2010,"
     American Civil Liberties Union, www.aclu.org.
19. Eric Lichtblau and James Risen, "Officials Say U.S. Wiretaps Exceeded Law," *New York
     Times*, April 15, 2009.
20. Senator Russ Feingold, "The Problems with the FISA Bill," Counterpunch, July 9, 2008,
     www.counterpunch.org.
21. "Court Reinstates ACLU Lawsuit Challenging Unconstitutional Spying Law," news re-
     lease, American Civil Liberties Union, March 21, 2011, www.aclu.org.
22. 18 USC § 2071, Justia.com, ttp://law.justia.com/ (accessed April 11, 2011).
23. "C.I.A. Interrogation Tapes," Times Topics, *New York Times*, November 9, 2010.
24. "A Case for Accountability," *New York Times*.
25. Michael Isikoff, "CIA Faces Second Probe over Videotape Destruction," NBC News,
     November 10, 2010, www.msnbc.msn.com.
26. Federal Records Act of 1950, 44 USC § 3301, National Archives, http://www.archives
     .gov/ (accessed April 11, 2011).

27. *The Untold Story of the Bush White House Emails*, report, Citizens for Responsibility and Ethics in Washington, August 30, 2010, www.scribd.com/doc/48889149/Untold-Story -of-the-Bush-White-House-Emails.

28. Office of Professional Responsibility, *Investigation into the Office*, fn. 3.

29. Anne Weismann, "The Case of the Missing John Yoo Emails Is Solved—Or Is It?" Citizens for Responsibility and Ethics in Washington, February 25, 2011, www.citizensforethics .org/ (accessed April 11, 2011).

30. Arar v. Ashcroft, 414 F. Supp.2d 250, 255 (E.D.N.Y. 2006).

31. Arar v. Ashcroft, 585 F. 3d 559 (2d Cir. 2009), opinion of Judge Robert Sack, p. 14, Center for Constitutional Rights, http://ccrjustice.org/.

32. Ibid., majority opinion, pp. 37–41.

33. Ibid., Opinion of Judge Barrington D. Parker, p. 2, Center for Constitutional Rights, http://ccrjustice.org/.

34. El-Masri v. Tenet, 437 F. Supp.2d 530 (E.D.Va. 2006), www.aclu.org/files/pdfs/safefree/ elmasri_order_granting_motion_dismiss_051206.pdf; 479 F.3d 296 (4th Cir. 2007), http:// law.justia.com/cases/federal/appellate-courts/F3/479/296/589216/, cert. denied 552 U.S. 947 (2007).

35. "El Masri v. Tenet," American Civil Liberties Union, www.aclu.org.

36. "Man Sues CIA over Torture Claims," BBC, December 7, 2005, http://news.bbc .co.uk.

37. Khaled El-Masri, "I Am Not a State Secret," *Los Angeles Times*, March 3, 2007.

38. "ACLU Sues Jeppesen Dataplan in San Jose for Participation in Seventy CIA Kidnapping and Torture Flights," news release, American Civil Liberties Union of Northern California, May 30, 2007, www.aclunc.org/.

39. "Profile: Binyam Mohamed," BBC News, February 12, 2010, http://news.bbc.co.uk/2/ hi/uk_news/7906381.stm.

40. "Binyam Mohamed: The Secret Torture File," *Telegraph*, February 10, 2010.

41. Binyam Mohamed v. Jeppesen Dataplan, Inc. (9th Cir. No. 08–15693, September 8, 2010), www.ca9.uscourts.gov/datastore/opinions/2010/09/07/08-15693.pdf.

42. "Supreme Court Denies Cert Mohamed v. Jeppesen in a Blow to Torture Accountability," Alliance for Justice, May 16, 2011, http://afjjusticewatch.blogspot.com/ (accessed June 2, 2011).

43. American Civil Liberties Union v. National Security Agency, Case No. 06-CV-10204 (E.D. Mich. August 17, 2006), FindLaw, http://fl1.findlaw.com/news.findlaw.com/ nytimes/docs/nsa/aclunsa817060pn.pdf.

44. Adam Liptak and Eric Lichtblau, "Judge Finds Wiretap Actions Violate the Law," *New York Times*, August 18, 2006.

45. "ACLU v. NSA: The Challenge to Illegal Spying," American Civil Liberties Union, www .aclu.org/national-security/aclu-v-nsa-challenge-illegal-spying.

46. Al-Haramain Islamic Foundation v. Bush, Electronic Frontier Foundation, www.eff.org/ cases/al-haramain.

47. Al-Haramain Islamic Foundation v. Obama, order, December 21, 2010, Electronic Frontier Foundation, www.eff.org/files/filenode/att/alharamainorder122110.pdf.

48. Savage and Risen, "Federal Judge Finds N.S.A. Wiretaps."

49. Amnesty v. Clapper, Docket No. 09–4112-cv (2nd Cir. March 21, 2011), American Civil Liberties Union, www.aclu.org/ (accessed April 18, 2011).

50. "Court Reinstates ACLU Lawsuit Challenging Unconstitutional Spying Law," press release, American Civil Liberties Union, March 21, 2011, www.aclu.org/.

51. "National Archives Issues New Report on Nazi War Crimes," press release, National Archives, December 10, 2010, http://www.archives.gov/.

52. Reynolds v. United States, 345 U.S. 1 (1953).

53. Steven D. Schwinn, "The State Secrets Privilege in the Post-9/11 Era," *Pace Law Review* 30, no. 2 (2010): 778, 831.

54. "Reforming the State Secrets Privilege," Constitution Project, May 31, 2007, ii, www .constitutionproject.org/ (accessed April 22, 2011).

55. U.S. Constitution, Article II, § 4, Cornell University Law School, Legal Information Institute, http://topics.law.cornell.edu/.

56. Holtzman and Cooper, *Impeachment of George W. Bush*.

57. "The Bush Admin's Secret OLC Memos," American Civil Liberties Union, www.aclu .org/ (accessed April 18, 2011).

58. "The Torturers' Manifesto," *New York Times*, April 19, 2009.

59. South African Truth and Reconciliation Commission, official website, www.justice.gov .za/trc/.

60. Patrick Leahy, "A Truth Commission to Investigate Bush-Cheney Administration Abuses," *Huffington Post*, February 12, 2009.

61. Elizabeth Drew, *Washington Journal: The Events of 1973–1974* (New York: Vintage, 1976), pp. 16–17.

62. U.S. Senate Select Committee, *Intelligence Activities*.

63. *The 9/11 Commission Report*.

64. "Statement by Sir John Chilcot about the First Set of Public Hearings," Iraq Inquiry, www.iraqinquiry.org.uk/ (accessed April 11, 2011).

65. Afua Hirsch, "Iraq Invasion Violated International Law, Dutch Inquiry Finds," *Guardian*, January 12, 2010.

FIVE: International Justice

1. Boris Johnson, "George W. Bush Can't Fight for Freedom and Authorise Torture," *Telegraph*, November 15, 2010.

2. "Bush's Swiss Visit Off after Complaints on Torture," Reuters, February 5, 2011, www .reuters.com.

3. Javier Moreno, "Why El País Chose to Publish the Leaks," *El País in English*, December 12, 2010.

4. Katherine Gallagher, "Efforts to Hold Donald Rumsfeld and Other High-level United States Officials Accountable for Torture," *Journal of International Criminal Justice* 7, no. 5 (2009): 1087–1116.

5. Shashank Bengali, "Other Countries Probing Bush-Era Torture—Why Aren't We?" McClatchy, August 18, 2010, www.mcclatchydc.com/.

6. Robert H. Jackson, opening statement, Nuremberg Trials, 1945, *The Supreme Court: Supreme Court History*, "Primary Sources," PBS, www.pbs.org/ (accessed April 22, 2011).

7. "Judge Dan Haywood Delivers Decision of the Court," *American Rhetoric: Movie Speeches*, www.americanrhetoric.com (accessed April 22, 2011).

8. "Japanese War Criminals Hanged in Tokyo," History.com, www.history.com/.

9. Michael Haas, *George W. Bush, War Criminal? The Bush Administration's Liability for 269 War Crimes* (Westport, CT: Praeger Publishers, 2008), pp. 221–37.

10. International Criminal Court, www.icc-cpi.int/ (accessed April 22, 2011).

11. "Universal Jurisdiction in Europe," Human Rights Watch, June 27, 2006, www.hrw.org/ en/node/11297/section/2.

12. "Universal Jurisdiction: Questions and Answers Concerning Universal Jurisdiction," Amnesty International, www.amnestyusa.org/ (accessed July 20, 2011); "Universal Jurisdiction: The Duty of States to Enact and Implement Legislation," Amnesty International, August 31, 2001, www.amnesty.org/ (accessed July 20, 2011).

13. Stacie Jonas, "The Ripple Effect of the Pinochet Case," *Human Rights Brief* 11, no. 3 (May 24, 2004): 36–38, Global Policy Forum, www.globalpolicy.org/ (accessed April 22, 2011).

14. Naomi Roht-Arriaza, *The Pinochet Effect: Transnational Justice in the Age of Human Rights* (Philadelphia: University of Pennsylvania Press, 2004).

15. Jonas, "Ripple Effect of the Pinochet Case."

16. "The Spanish Investigation into U.S. Torture," Center for Constitutional Rights, http://ccrjustice.org/ (accessed April 22, 2011).

17. Carol Rosenberg, "WikiLeaks: How U.S. Tried to Stop Spain's Torture Probe," *Miami Herald*, December 25, 2010.

18. Scott Horton, "The Madrid Cables," *Harper's*, December 1, 2009.

19. David Corn, "Obama and GOPers Worked Together to Kill Bush Torture Probe," *Mother Jones*, December 1, 2010.

20. "US Embassy Cables: Second Investigation Opened into Alleged US Torture of Terrorism Detainees," *Guardian*, December 1, 2010.

21. "US Refuses to Investigate Bush Lawyers' Role in Torture," European Center for Constitutional and Human Rights, www.ecchr.de/ (accessed April 30, 2011).

22. Mary Ellen Warlow to Paula Monge Royo, letter, March 1, 2011, Center for Constitutional Rights, http://ccrjustice.org/ (accessed April 30, 2011).

23. Sarah Posner, "Spain Court Turns Over Guantanamo Torture Investigation to US," *Jurist*, April 13, 2011, http://jurist.org.

24. "Belgium Gets War Crimes Cases Against Bush/Blair," Reuters, June 19, 2003, www.commondreams.org/.

25. Ian Black, "Belgium Gives in to US on War Crimes," *Guardian*, June 24, 2003.

26. "Universal Jurisdiction in Europe," Human Rights Watch.

27. "German War Crimes Complaint Against Donald Rumsfeld et al.," Center for Constitutional Rights, http://ccrjustice.org/ (accessed April 22, 2011).

28. Adam Zagorin, "Exclusive: Charges Sought against Rumsfeld over Prison Abuse," *Time*, November 10, 2006.

29. "Re: Criminal Complaint against Donald Rumsfeld et al.," notarized document by German federal prosecutor, Karlsruhe, Germany, April 5, 2007, Center for Constitutional Rights,http://ccrjustice.org/ (accessed April 22, 2011).

30. Gallagher, "Efforts to Hold Donald Rumsfeld."

31. Neil A. Lewis, "U.S. Rejects All Support for New Court on Atrocities," *New York Times*, May 7, 2002.

32. Rome Statute of the International Criminal Court, United Nations Treaties Collection, http://untreaty.un.org/ (accessed April 22, 2011).

33. Lynn Gentile, "Understanding the International Criminal Court," in *African Guide to International Criminal Justice* (Institute for Security Studies, 2008), p. 99, www.issafrica.org/ (accessed April 22, 2011).

34. "The International Criminal Court," fact sheet, Amnesty International, www.amnestyusa.org/international_justice/pdf/IJA_Factsheet_1_International_Criminal_Court.pdf.

35. "Bashir Warrant Is Warning to Abusive Leaders," Human Rights Watch, February 3, 2010, www.hrw.org (accessed April 22, 2011).

36. "International Criminal Court Cases in Africa: Status and Policy Issues," Congressional Research Service, July 14, 2010, www.policyarchive.org/ (accessed April 22, 2011).

37. "International Arrest Warrants Requested," Bush to The Hague, January 19, 2010, www.bushtothehague.org/.

38. Elizabeth Becker, "U.S. Ties Military Aid to Peacekeepers' Immunity," *New York Times*, August 10, 2002.

39. "Bilateral Immunity Agreements," American Non-Governmental Organizations Coalition for the International Criminal Court (AMICC), www.amicc.org/ (accessed April 22, 2011).

40. Nicholas D. Kristof, "Schoolyard Bully Diplomacy," *New York Times*, October 16, 2005.

41. Jamie Jansen, "Europe Rights Watchdog Says CIA Prisons, Rendition Flights Involve 'Web' of Nations," *Jurist*, June 7, 2006, http://jurist.org/.

42. *The Convention Against Torture*, Human Rights Web, www.hrweb.org/legal/cat.html; *Geneva Conventions*, International Committee of the Red Cross, www.icrc.org/.

43. *Convention Against Torture*, Articles 13–14; *Geneva Conventions*, Article 146.

44. John Hooper, "Italian Court Finds CIA Agents Guilty of Kidnapping Terrorism Suspect," *Guardian*, November 4, 2009.

45. "Spanish Investigation into U.S. Torture."

46. Maureen Cosgrove, "Spain Court Allows Guantanamo Torture Investigation to Continue," *Jurist*, February 26, 2011, http://jurist.org/.

47. Mónica Ceberio Belaza, "How US Worked to Get Three Soldiers Off the Hook for Cameraman's Death," *El País*, December 1, 2010.

48. Scott Horton, "Arrest of 13 CIA Agents Sought in Spain," *Harper's*, May 12, 2010.

49. "The El Masri Case," European Center for Constitutional and Human Rights, www.ecchr.eu/ (accessed April 30, 2011).

50. "Man Sues CIA over Torture Claims," BBC, December 7, 2005, http://news.bbc.co.uk/.

51. Michael Slackman, "Officials Pressed Germans on Kidnapping by C.I.A.," *New York Times*, December 8, 2010.

52. Matthias Gebauer and John Goetz, "Cables Show Germany Caved to Pressure from Washington," *Der Spiegel*, December 9, 2010.

53. "US Rejected Polish Call for Help in Alleged CIA Prison Probe," Agence France Presse, December 28, 2010, www.alternet.org/.

54. "Accountability for Torture (in Britain)," *New York Times*, November 16, 2010.

55. Andrew Gilmore, "UK Judges Reveal US Threatened to Withhold Intelligence if Guantanamo Torture Disclosed," *Jurist*, February 4, 2009, http://jurist.law.pitt.edu/.

56. Tim Shipman, "Hush Money: Multi-million Pound Payouts to Silence British Terror Suspects Held in Guantanamo," *Daily Mail*, November 16, 2010.

57. Dahlia Lithwick, "Nowhere to Hide," *Slate*, June 16, 2010.

58. "Canadian Man Deported by U.S. Details Torture in Syria," *Democracy Now!*, November 7, 2003, www.democracynow.org/.

59. "El Masri Case," European Center for Constitutional and Human Rights.

60. European Court of Human Rights, www.echr.coe.int/.

61. Inter-American Commission on Human Rights, Organization of American States, www.cidh.oas.org (accessed April 30, 2011).

62. Richard Norton-Taylor, "Macedonia Called to Account over Extraordinary Rendition Case," *Guardian*, October 14, 2010.

63. "El-Masri v. Tenet," American Civil Liberties Union, November 29, 2010, www.aclu.org/.

64. Haas, *George W. Bush, War Criminal?*, p. 230.

65. Afua Hirsch, "Iraq Invasion Violated International Law, Dutch Inquiry Finds," *Guardian*, January 12, 2010.

66. *Commission Report on Investigation of Decision Making on Iraq* (Davids committee report), 2010, http://weblogs.nrc.nl/discussie/files/2010/01/rapport_commissie_irak.pdf, pp. 517–33; Dorian De Wing, "Dutch Davids Commission Releases Report on Dutch Government Support for Iraq Invasion," *The Moderate Voice*, January 12, 2010, http://the moderatevoice.com/.

67. "Dutch Cabinet Admits Fault, Averts Crisis," *NRC Handelsblad*, January 13, 2010, http:// vorige.nrc.nl/international/article2458168.ece.

68. "Sir John Chilcot's Closing Statement, 30 July 2010," Iraq Inquiry, www.iraqinquiry.org .uk/ (accessed April 30, 2011).

69. Christopher Hope, "WikiLeaks: British Government Promised to 'Protect US Interests' at Chilcot Inquiry," *Telegraph*, December 1, 2010.

70. Andrew Sparrow, "Eliza Manningham-Buller at the Iraq Inquiry—20 July," *Guardian*, July 20, 2010.

71. Tim Shipman and Ian Drury, "Blair 'Misled MPs on Legality of War' Law Chief Who Advised ex-PM Tells Iraq Inquiry," *Daily Mail*, January 18, 2011.

72. Stephen Glover, "At Last, the Damning Evidence That Should Bury Blair for His Lies over Iraq," *Mail Online, Daily Mail*, January 19, 2011, www.dailymail.co.uk/.

73. Nigel Morris, "Blair Recalled to Face Further Questions on Build-Up to Iraq War," *Independent*, December 9, 2010.

74. Brian Brady, "Chilcot to Grill Blair on How He 'Misled' Iraq War Inquiry," *Independent*, January 16, 2011.

75. "Evidence of the Rt. Honorable Tony Blair," Iraq Inquiry, January 21, 2011, www.iraq inquiry.org.uk/.

76. Chris Ames, "Blair Dug His Own Hole at the Chilcot Inquiry," *Guardian*, January 21, 2011.

77. *Report of the International Committee of the Red Cross (ICRC) On the Treatment by the Coalition Forces of Prisoners of War and Other Protected Persons by the Geneva Conventions in Iraq During Arrest, Internment and Interrogation*, International Committee of the Red Cross, February 2004, http://msnbcmedia.msn.com/.

78. "ICRC Report on the Treatment of Fourteen 'High Value Detainees' in CIA Custody," International Committee of the Red Cross, February 2007, p. 26, www.nybooks .com/.

79. "David Cameron Announces Torture Inquiry," *Telegraph*, July 6, 2010.

80. Patrick Wintour and Ian Cobain, "David Cameron Agrees Terms of UK Torture Inquiry," *Guardian*, June 29, 2010.

81. Emily Dugan, "MPs Refused the Facts on UK's Part in Rendition Cases," *Independent*, January 2, 2011.

82. Amy Goodman, "Mounties Probe U.S. Role in Kidnapping and Torture of Canadian Citizen," AlterNet, June 17, 2010, www.alternet.org/.

83. *Open Secret: Mounting Evidence of Europe's Complicity in Rendition and Secret Detention*, Amnesty International, November 2010, pp. 10–11, www.amnesty.org/.

84. Mark Tran, "UN Human Rights Council Urges US to End Death Penalty," *Guardian*, November 5, 2010.

85. Harold Hongju Koh, "Response of the United States of America to Recommendations of the United Nations Human Rights Council," press release, November 9, 2010, www .state.gov/.

86. Louis Charbonneau, "UN Investigator Urges Probe of Alleged US Torture," Reuters, October 27, 2010, www.commondreams.org/.

87. Stephanie Nebehay, "UN Expert Urges Full US Torture Investigation," Reuters, November 16, 2010, www.commondreams.org/.

88. Charles J. Hanley, "ElBaradei Suggests War Crimes Probe of Bush Team," *Washington Examiner*, April 22, 2011.

89. "Senate Report Finds Rumsfeld Directly Responsible for US Torture of Prisoners," *Democracy Now!*, December 12, 2008, www.democracynow.org (accessed April 22, 2011).

SIX: What to Do

1. Tom Parfitt, "Russian Parliament Admits Guilt over Polish Massacre," *Guardian*, November 25, 2010.

2. "Timeline: The Pinochet Legal Saga," BBC, December 11, 2006, http://news.bbc.co.uk/.

3. Alex Holt, "Investigators Race the Clock to Bring Hiding Nazi War Criminals to Justice," *St. Petersburg (FL) Times*, June 7, 2010.

4. "Michael Posner on the ABA's Strong Stand Against Torture and Official Cruelty," *Daily Journal*, reprinted, *Human Rights First*, August 17, 2007, http://www.humanrightsfirst.org (accessed April 22, 2011).

5. National Religious Campaign Against Torture, http://www.nrcat.org/ (accessed April 22, 2011).

6. Rachel Banning-Lover, "Berkeley Demonstrates Against Torture," *Daily Californian*, October 13, 2010, http://blog.dailycal.org.

7. "Stop Torture at the Top," UpTakeVideo, November 26, 2010, http://www.youtube.com/ (accessed April 22, 2011).